The Politics
of Joint University
and Community
Housing Development

The Politics of Joint University and Community Housing Development

Cambridge, Boston, and Beyond

Richard Sobel

Forewords by Brett Donham
and Antony Herrey

LEXINGTON BOOKS
Lanham • *Boulder* • *New York* • *Toronto* • *Plymouth, UK*

Published by Lexington Books
An imprint of The Rowman & Littlefield Publishing Group, Inc.
4501 Forbes Boulevard, Suite 200, Lanham, Maryland 20706
www.rowman.com

16 Carlisle Street, London W1D 3BT, United Kingdom

British Library Cataloguing in Publication Information Available

Library of Congress Cataloging-in-Publication Data

Sobel, Richard, 1949-
  The politics of joint university and community housing development : Cambridge, Boston, and beyond / Richard Sobel ; foreword by Brett Donham and Antony Herrey.
    pages cm.
  Includes bibliographical references and index.
  ISBN 978-0-7391-9187-3 (cloth : alk. paper) — ISBN 978-0-7391-9188-0 (electronic)
1. Housing development—Massachusetts—Boston. 2. Community and college—Massachusetts—Boston. 3. Housing development—Massachusetts—Cambridge. 4. Community and college—Massachusetts—Cambridge. 5. Massachusetts Institute of Technology—Student housing. 6. Harvard University—Student housing. I. Title.
  HD7303.M4S63 2014
  307.3'3609744—dc23
                                                                    2014011361

Printed in the United States of America

For

People Seeking and Saving Housing

&

Walter H. Sobel, FAIA Home and Studio

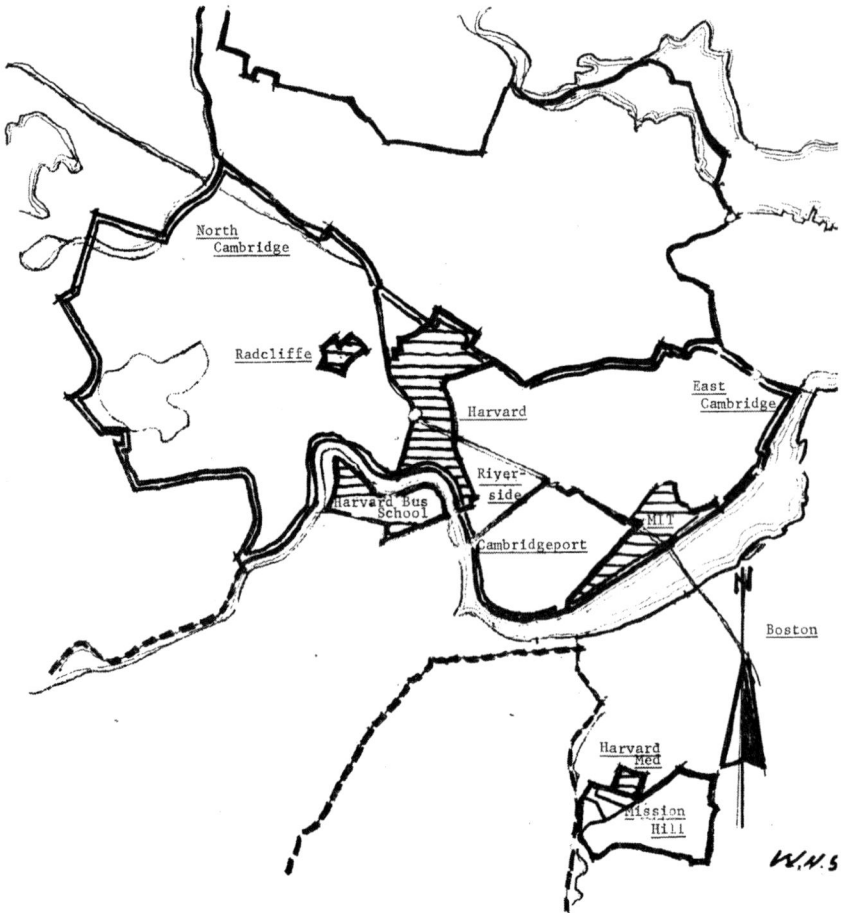

Map 1. The Communities and Universities
Credit: Walter H. Sobel, FAIA

Contents

Maps, Tables, and Pictures

MAPS

TABLES

PICTURES

Preface to
the 2014 Edition

While housing created through cooperation, and conflict between university and community may seem an unusual idea, it has long been a reality. Little known community/university housing projects exist in several cities and have been planned in others. This book informs and encourages the understanding and development of community/university housing. The story reveals the political and technical dynamics of joint development of housing involving both communities and universities.

Since Cambridge, home of Harvard University and Massachusetts Institute of Technology, contains the outstanding examples of community/university housing, *The Politics of Joint University and Community Housing Development* focuses on the dozen projects begun there by the late 1960s and early 1970s. Following the Cambridge cases, it discusses a major project in Mission Hill near Harvard Medical School in Boston. Then it briefly presents projects in other parts of the country. The book provides a range within the definitions of community/university housing—from housing developed and provided by university for community, to housing fully jointly developed and shared by community and university members.

THE CAMBRIDGE STUDY

Concentrating on Cambridge reflects the notability of the schools and projects as well as the spirit to this city. As novelist Alan Lelchuk aptly phrased it, "One had the sense that if answers to man's problems were to be found, they were to be found here or nowhere. Intellectual leaders were to Cambridge as prizefighters and baseball heroes were to the rest of America." This explains why Cambridge residents both asked the universities for help in solving city housing problems and expected the schools to respond by building housing. Yet these prestigious schools made many mistakes in the very human process of building community housing. Other schools have also sponsored joint housing.

The Cambridge and Boston cases explore the historical, political, and economic reasons for developing community housing. Discussing only the physical and economic features of building housing, or passing quickly over the history of the projects, would miss the human context and background on why and how the physical structures came into being. It would neglect the important ingredient of what part the community—which ultimately benefits from community housing or suffers from the lack of it—had in the creation and development of the projects. Since community housing involved a process as well as a result, the book describes actions and forces in detail in the sections on community participation.

THE USEFULNESS OF THE STUDY

A number of features contribute to the usefulness to readers. First, two people well acquainted with community/university housing and politics—one from an institution, the other from the community—introduce and provide perspective from 1975 and beyond on the cases. Former Director of MIT's Real Estate Office and head of the Institute's community housing efforts, Antony Herrey, later Director of Real Estate and Negotiated Investments at The Ford Foundation, explained the involvement of universities in problems like housing as the result of social cross-pressures (Herrey, 1969). An alumnus of both Harvard and MIT, Herrey describes the differences between the two schools' approaches to dealing with housing and politics problems, contrasting the humanistic ivory tower outlook of Harvard to the technological, pragmatic approach of MIT. His stress on the importance of imaginative and forceful institutional leadership, with high-level support for solving problems, adds important insights here. In dealing with outside community problems, leadership becomes a "key element" in positive university involvement in the city (Nash, 1973; Coleman, 1974, 17).

Long involved in community/university relations in Cambridge and Boston, architect Brett Donham points out important lessons and realities for community members about joint housing participation (Donham, 1972). He explains clearly why universities become involved in community housing, and also reveals the possible uses and limitations of research for community. Harvard alumnus Donham's acumen in these community/university areas was underscored by his choice as the community architect for an important community/university housing project in Cambridge (Donham, 1972).

While this study concentrates on unusually sophisticated universities and one metropolitan area, the Cambridge and Boston experiences are useful to other community/university contexts. Besides discussing housing programs of national concern, the report examines levels of community participation—from community control to consultation—and reveals conflicts between institutional and community development needs. It explores university responsibility, rhetoric versus reality, and the educational values of community housing participation. The lessons and suggestions drawn from the experiences reported here both point in positive directions and warn of problems to avoid. On a simple level, the book provides ideas, methods, models and assurances that new things can be done, because they already have been.

This study may be particularly helpful for other university/communities encountering problems like those in Cambridge and Boston. Many other university communities—Berkeley, Stanford, and Santa Barbara in California; Austin in Texas; Amherst and Boston in Massachusetts; Princeton and New Brunswick in New Jersey—experience transformational housing pressures and crises. An increase in nontraditional students who seek off-campus living, relaxed residency requirements, and major enrollment increases at public institutions can create housing problems that community/university housing can help solve. This book and community/university housing may become increasingly relevant if enduring headlines like "Author Predicts Regeneration of Inner Cities by Energy Crisis" turn out to be true. As more people move into attractive areas of cities near universities, housing pressures there will increase.

In gathering together varied experiences, *The Politics of Joint University and Community Housing Development* discusses the success and failings of the university participation, particularly in terms of university-stated goals and rhetoric. Its lessons can inform the development of new community housing elsewhere. Finally, because housing is an issue for the political and institutional bodies and community groups of all cities, the general features and information of this book may interest a wide range of community, university, and other urban groups. The book is also especially pertinent to institutions like hospitals that also have community and housing problems, and to civic groups that can help solve a range of housing problems. To provide a context on how this book came to publication, the epilogue reflects on its construction.

IN SUM

Though the violent conflicts at Columbia and in Newark in the 1960s receded and university/community affairs are less often in the headlines, the "urban crisis" is not over. The need to pursue better community/university relations continues. In encouraging cooperation between communities and universities, this study reveals the social opportunities and political challenges that make encouraging more joint development of housing a fundamentally inspiring story.

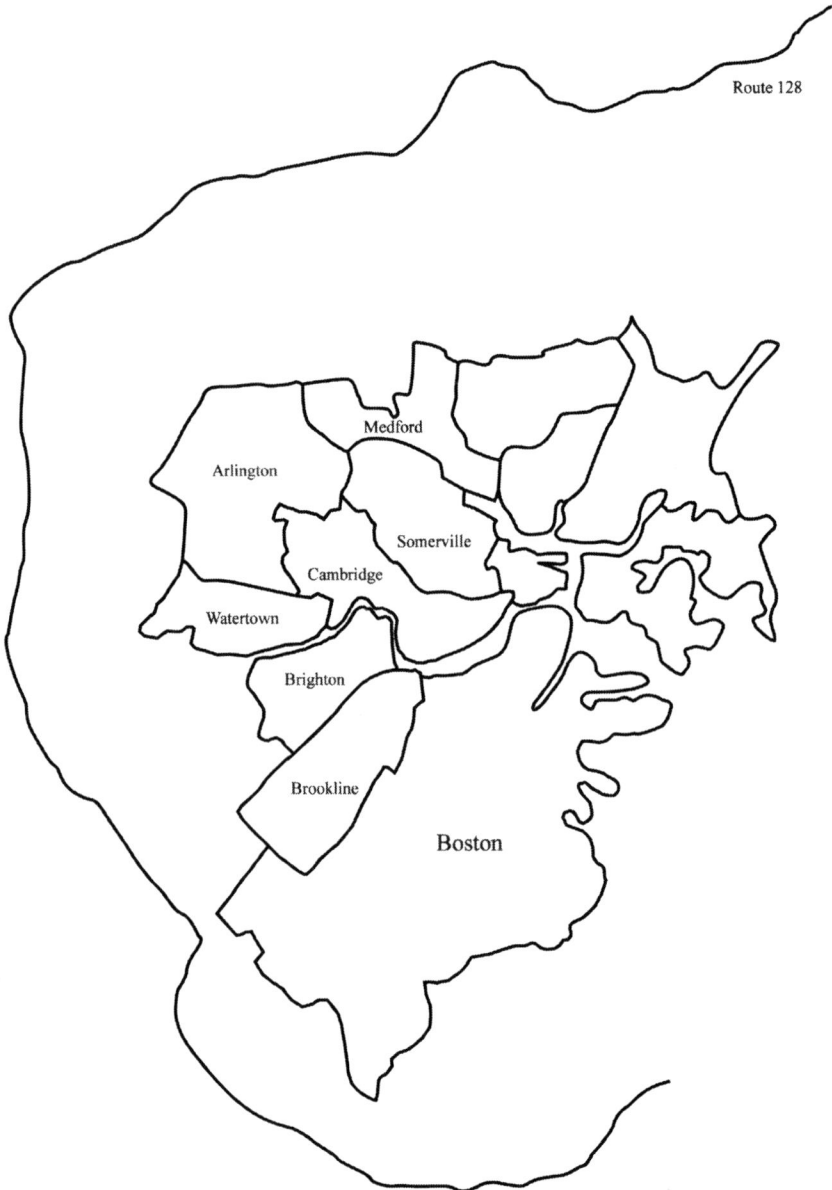

Route 128

Medford

Arlington

Somerville

Cambridge

Watertown

Brighton

Brookline

Boston

Map 2.   Greater Boston
Credit: Han Gyeol Kim

University Foreword

The modern university often seems schizophrenic in confronting public issues. At times it appears to seek an important role amid the issues of the day. At others, it flees from worldly pressures and withdraws into its ivory tower.

Between exhortations from powerful constituencies for social justice, "relevance," and moral leadership, on the one hand, and for "pursuit of excellence," superior academic standards, and political neutrality, on the other, most academic institutions have simply responded to the stronger pressures of the moment while resisting the weaker. If, as a result, the universities have seemed ambivalent about their responsibilities—mounting persuasive arguments for activism on one occasion and for passivity on another—the explanation is to be found in their failure to establish a satisfactory policy to deal with controversial public issues.

The university, to be sure, is being asked to do too much. It is not surprising in a technocratic society that the public demands solutions to most problems from its universities. Moreover, in an age when moral values are believed to be in decline, society increasingly looks to its centers of learning for guidance on moral issues—a naïve act of faith, perhaps based on the ancient respect for the wise man and his renunciation of worldly ambitions. These demands on the universities exceed their capabilities, and the universities in consequence appear to oscillate from one position to another without any policy to guide them.

That is the context, as I see it, for the chronicle that follows of how two distinguished educational institutions in Cambridge, Massachusetts, responded to serious housing problems in their community during the late 1960s and early 1970s. In an era consumed by the passions of war in Southeast Asia and the battle for black equality in America, the universities were ill-prepared for the pressures and complexities of housing politics in Cambridge. The unfolding story, ably told here by Richard Sobel, illustrates two sharply different responses to unprecedented pressures applied to two educational institutions, neither of which was initially prepared for such pressures or possessed a policy to cope with them.

The case of Harvard exemplifies the institution in search of a policy. A humanistic university with a well-founded reputation in the liberal arts but with disdain for vocational studies, Harvard had traditionally neglected and often ignored the Cambridge community and city government. Harvard was considered by its Cambridge neighbors to be too concerned with world problems to recognize the parochial problems at its doorstep. Beginning with the conviction that Harvard, as an educational institution had no business becoming involved in housing ventures with the local community, the administration ultimately found itself forced by pressure groups to reverse itself and engage in the very activities it earlier had resisted. Harvard never could shed the image of "too little and too late," always appearing to respond to demands grudgingly and inadequately. In the end Harvard did much of what it originally declared it would not do but received little credit for doing so.

Massachusetts Institute of Technology, on the other hand, a technological institution-preeminent in engineering, had traditionally maintained reasonably good relations with the Cambridge community and excellent relations with the city government. With a pragmatic outlook and an intellectual orientation toward "problem solving," MIT was an institution that responded readily to practical challenges. While it is true that external pressures originally prodded MIT into action so far as Cambridge housing problems were concerned, it is also true that MIT began to act very early. MIT was usually in the lead, actually anticipating demands rather than responding to them, and from its participation in community housing emerged with a stronger reputation in the city.

What, aside from differences in the nature of the two institutions, was responsible for the difference in results? The answer, very simply, is leadership. MIT provided forceful and enlightened leadership, developing new policy in the face of unfamiliar problems and pressures.

At an early stage my staff and I at MIT analyzed the housing situation and proposed an ambitious program. Legal counsel was pressed to answer serious legal questions raised by MIT's unprecedented program to house non-MIT personnel. At a critical point Dr. James R. Killian Jr., MIT's Chairman, persuaded the MIT Corporation to commit its full support and the substantial funds necessary to launch the program. Thereafter I was given all necessary backing within the institution to carry out our program.

It was our unequivocal conclusion that MIT could not shirk significant responsibilities to the Cambridge community in the housing sector, and we emphatically committed MIT to this position in various public statements. Having assumed this responsibility, we emphasized that MIT would stand behind its commitment to supply substantial housing resources for low-income groups.

The leadership issue emerges again and again, in Richard Sobel's account, as the crucial difference in the response of these two Cambridge universities and explains why MIT proved far more successful in its actual accomplishments as well as in its "image." If the report accomplishes nothing further than to emphasize the need by educational institutions for imaginative and forceful leadership to cope with community problems then it will deserve generous praise from all those who have labored in this area. Firm support from the top is the essential ingredient for success in University/Community relations. In steering objectively through the tangled history of many of Cambridge's community conflicts of the last decade, Richard Sobel has produced an accurate and impartial history. It should prove invaluable to administrators at urban institutions, providing effective object lessons in how to—and especially how not to—operate in the community relations arena. I commend it for serious study to anyone planning an institutional role in community affairs.

Antony Herrey
New York City

Community Foreword

Several very important lessons for community groups are contained in this study. First, universities will not act out of pure altruism in assisting with community housing but rather, out of a desire to satisfy their own needs. Therefore, community groups must recognize and then harness these needs to their own purposes. Second, universities are not good at everything and should not be asked to do everything. Universities, whose mission is educational and research, are not equipped to manage the development function and will put their own goals and credibility foremost.

Third, this study reinforces the natural instinct of community groups that political pressure, as often as good intentions and kind words, produces the action they desire. Finally, I find it useful to learn what a pioneering effort the Cambridge attempts at Community/University housing was. One's expectations, if not one's hopes, come into perspective. The techniques are new, and patience, trust, and sincere effort by all parties are required.

However, any study of this kind is doomed to have little direct and immediate impact on community groups and the way they behave. Most activists in community groups are political people, in the best sense of the word, and they tend not to add to their body of relevant information and experience by reading about it. They talk, they listen, they go to meetings; they do.

Indirectly, over a period of time, by means of the professional and technical people associated with community groups, this study will be of great help. Professionals are conservative people; they want to know, "will it work, has it been done before, what can we learn from similar situations?"

This study provides great support for their concerns and, to the extent that professionals continue to have influence with community groups, this study is useful reading.

Brett Donham
Boston

Part I

THE CAMBRIDGE STUDY

Chapter One

Cambridge and Responses
to the Housing Crisis

Across the Charles River from Boston, Cambridge fascinates people as a city. A community in flux, it is diverse, polyglot, industrial, and pedagogical. Large blue-collar, professional, student, and otherwise academic populations reside in its varied neighborhoods. A "city of renters," its housing units run from two-flats to mansions. Still characteristic of the town are its 20,000 families, ranging from millionaires to the homeless poor. Many of its 100,000 residents populate the Irish, Italian, Black, and WASP communities. People there speak so many tongues that an early community housing survey had to be translated into Spanish, Portuguese, Italian, Greek, and Polish.

Perhaps best known as the home of Harvard and MIT, Cambridge would be more like its more industrial, blue-collar neighbor, Somerville, but for the two elite schools. In fact, though Harvard's founding in 1636 renamed "Newtowne" after the home of the famous British University, only since World War II have universities loomed so large in the formerly "workingman's" Massachusetts town. A product of the industrial revolution, MIT moved from Boston (home of Harvard Medical School) at the end of World War I. Today, Cambridge is "dominated by our two giants of wisdom, one speaking for the past, the other for the future" (Lelchuk, 1974). Thereby, Cambridge has lost some of the diversity the academic community often acclaims.

This trend and the university influences are not universally appreciated. Echoing Cantabrigian e.e. cummings' "Cambridge Ladies," *The Best and the Brightest* found the town's academic nature "very traditional and somewhat stuffy" (Halberstam, 1972, 157). Many local residents—including cabdrivers preferring Harvard become the city college—dislike the universities' impact. The presence of the two academic centers attracts the scholarly, the affluent, the ambitious, and the avant-garde to their environs, and brings clashes and notoriety to the city.

BACKGROUND ON THE HOUSING CRISIS

Cambridge has undergone significant changes. Like many older American cities, its population dropped from 120,000 in 1950 to 100,000 in 1960. Fifty years ago there were several thousand more families and far fewer non-family households. The industrial base has shrunk considerably, a phenomenon reflected in fewer blue-collar jobs, increased industrial unemployment, and expanding professional and technical sectors. The housing situation in Cambridge closely reflects these changes.

Like numerous U.S. cities, Cambridge, probably more than the others shown in the Boston area in map 1.1, has experienced housing problems over

Map 1.1.   Cambridge and Vicinity
Credit: H. Kim

the years. Postwar rent controls until the mid-1950s represented their tenacity; yet the 1960s saw worse. During this time, there was a widely recognized housing crisis in the city.

The problem has essentially been a pervasive lack of housing at prices most people can afford. A minimal vacancy rate has accompanied steadily rising rents. As a result, both finding and paying for an apartment has been a trial. Keeping a home has not been easy either. Many long-established residents have been driven out of town by rising rents and increasing property taxes. This trend began in the early 1950s (Duehey, 1970a, 26). Grown children of long-time residents have often had to move elsewhere for lack of an affordable place in their native city. Low-income groups, particularly minorities and the elderly, but also students, have been under severe pressure. In the words of the City Manager, "low-income people constantly face the specter of having to leave Cambridge, or to tolerate poor housing conditions at continually increasing rents, because they have no other choice" (Duehey, 1970a, 18).

Startling rent increases in a town of 80 percent renters have been the most obvious symptom of the crisis. Accompanying price increases in all other items, the rent rises have been a greater burden.

> The median household rent has increased almost ninety percent since 1960. In 1950, the median contract rent for all housing units was $35.90; in 1960, $63.00; by 1970 it is $119.00. This is more than three times the median rent increase for the Boston metropolitan area, and substantially greater than the consumer price index increase of 24 percent for U.S. cities (Cambridge Community Development Program, 1972b, 26).

Headlines in *The Cambridge Chronicle* said it all: "High Rents Seen Forcing Residents to Leave the City. Study Shows Poor and Elderly Hardest Hit by Squeeze." Rent control after September 1970 moderated the situation somewhat, but rents were still high. Controls were under constant attack from landlords and in late 1974 vacancy decontrol began and an across-the-board rent increase, fought by tenants group, was granted. A city report in 1973 said that without significant public action, "spiraling rents throughout the city will resume as rent control is phased out" (Cambridge Department of Planning and Development, 1973, 47).

The results of a summer 1968 survey of elderly housing by the Cambridge Economic Opportunities Committee showed how severe conditions had become in human terms. The elderly were "not poor [but], destitute." Of the 1,500 elderly willing to state an income, almost two-thirds received under $1,500 per year (93 percent less than $3,000), and more than 55 percent were paying over half of their income for rent![1] The Cambridge Community Development Program found in 1969 that 60 percent of all Cambridge elderly were living on less than $4,000 a year and fully three-quarters on less than $6,000. Of those in the lowest group, 95 percent were paying over 35 percent of their limited incomes for shelter (Cambridge Community Development Program, 1969).

These troubled conditions appeared in an exodus of 8,000 families from 1950 to 1970, many involuntarily.[2] This was not just the middle-class flight to the suburbs, because attractive Cambridge lost a full 50 percent more families from 1960 to 1970 than its same-sized neighbor, Somerville (Cambridge Community Development Program, 1972a). "Property values and rents have soared. . . . Rents have risen so high it has become impossible for many low-income families to remain in their apartments or to find suitable units in Cambridge which they can afford" (Cambridge Community Development Program, 1972b, 18). And economic and development pressures on the remaining families provided insight into what pushed their brethren out: twice as many low-income families lived in overcrowded units as the overall population (Cambridge Community Development Program, 1972b, 23). In 1969 alone, half of all Cambridge families experienced rent increases. And, among the low-income people who could still move *within* Cambridge, where rental vacancy rates have been about 1 percent, one in six did so because of high rents (Cambridge Community Development Program, 1972b, 30). A series of city reports, "Housing Needs in Cambridge," summed up the crisis, and a possible solution, in 1972, 3,600 of 3,850 low-income elderly and 4,900 of 8,550 lower-income families were paying more than 25 percent of their incomes for housing (Ad Hoc Housing Development Task Force, 1969; Community Development Program, 1971, 8). The reports concluded that at least 2,750 low-income units were needed for the elderly and 4,450 low and moderate units needed for families (Cambridge Community Development Program, 1971, 3; 1972b, 36, 8).

Even with the progress in the years reflected in this book, a Massachusetts Department of Community Affairs survey found a need for 3,500 elderly and 5,000 family units in Cambridge (*Cambridge Chronicle*, April 18, 1974). A 1969 Cambridge Planning Board Report found that Cambridge could accommodate 5,000 to 15,000 new housing units of all types.

THE HOUSING CRISIS AND THE TRANSFORMATION OF CAMBRIDGE

The housing crisis in Cambridge has complex origins. Prominently among the factors are university-related expansion, an influx of research and development firms, and major increases in the number of young people, particularly students and R&D related professionals, seeking to live nearby. All the factors add up to a "Transformation of Cambridge." The city has changed from a predominantly blue-collar, industrial center and family town, to a technology-oriented "Universe-City" of professionals and college-related, young and single individuals.

The results of the transformation have serious implications for Cambridge's future.

> If Harvard and MIT expand, the housing stock available for longtime residents must contract; if a new research and development [firms] locates [near a University] in the city, a meat-packing firm will be displaced; if new high-rise luxury apartments will be built to accommodate the middle-class professional who flocks to the universities, then the working class will be forced to leave their homes. Two different socio-economic groups within the city are competing, consciously and unconsciously, for control of [a constant amount of] land. If one group wins, must the other lose? Behind any talk of a housing crisis in the city lies a question: Who will inherit the Cambridge of the future? (Duehey, 1970a, 1).

THE ROLES OF THE UNIVERSITIES: HARVARD AND MIT[3]

"Harvard and MIT, by their presence as much as by their actions, constitute the most important force shaping the physical and socioeconomic character of Cambridge" (McNally, 1970, 49). "The University of Cambridge"—as the schools together are sometimes called—are prime factors, both directly and indirectly, in the transformation and housing crisis that have affected the city. Over fifteen years Harvard and MIT obtained about 1,300 city housing units. Harvard bought about 850 units and MIT obtained 470 (Donham, 1972, 11). Enrollment in 1975 at Harvard was 15,000, up from 10,000 in 1960. MIT's was 8,000, up from 6,300 in 1960.

Since 1960, the enrollments of the two schools combined rose by over 6,500 students to over 23,000, with equally large increases in faculty and staff. Harvard and MIT students alone occupied about 3,000 of the city's non-university housing units (Barber, 1972, 89–90). Additionally, 8,300 Harvard and MIT personnel lived in town (McNally, 1970, 24).

The schools have also influenced the housing environment indirectly. In a sense they are "attractive nuisances" for the city. They attract numerous technological firms with affluent employees who can outbid local residents for scarce housing. Professionals, students, and others attracted by university life increase the housing competition in town.

HARVARD'S ROLE IN THE TRANSFORMATION:
THE "HARVARDIZATION" OF CAMBRIDGE

As the older, larger, and more centrally located to residential Cambridge, Harvard's role in the crisis in Cambridge (the "Harvardization" of Cambridge) is more easily recognized (Committee on Governance, 1970, 42). Telling alone is Harvard Planning Office Report's 1969 estimate that 6,850 Harvard personnel were living in Cambridge and occupying 3,500 city housing units—10 percent of the total supply. Of the 7,250 students living in Cambridge in 1970, over 3,000 attended Harvard and occupied 2,000 units of housing (Harvard University, 1972, 5, 6).[4] Harvard graduate students—particularly married ones—are a major competitive force in the city's housing situation: the University in 1972 supplied housing for only one-fifth of its married graduates. Fortunately, Harvard provides housing for almost all its undergrads, and was planning more campus housing facilities (Daly, 1972, 6, 7).

Harvard has also affected the city in a more visible way. Harvard had been buying housing and expanding in the residential sections of the city. Over the last decade, it bought 834 units, demolishing 202 (Donham, 1972, 11). While many of the units have remained in the housing market, their rents have risen. The effects of the acquisitions have been especially severe in the Riverside section into which Harvard had been moving for fifteen years.

The Riverside community has historically been a racially mixed, stable neighborhood, composed largely of families in low-rent, single-family homes (Donham, 1972). However, pressure from a large student influx, speculation, and rent increases at twice the city rate have brought a decline in its stability. Still, Riverside contains Greeks, Haitians. West Indians, French Canadians, Irish, Portuguese (largely Azorean), Puerto Ricans, and Blacks, "working-class and professional people, students, and natives, middle income and poor" (Harvard President and Fellows, 1949, 6). Riverside is also the home of a large and long-established Black community, which constitutes 20 percent of the area population. Such a mix of diverse people living together and cooperating is a source of community pride.

Riverside's problems come from Harvard's proximity and the resulting threat. Since 1965 both undergraduate Mather House and Peabody Terrace (499 mainly high-rise graduate apartments) have been built on university-owned land in Riverside. As *The Wilson Report* pointed out in late 1968, because the housing there is close and relatively inexpensive, "large numbers of students, many university-oriented persons and some faculty are now moving in" (*Wilson Report*, 1968, 44).

In the 1960s the number of unrelated households grew from 562 to 1,018 in Riverside as the number of families declined 32 percent (Shalom, 1969,

3). From 1960 to 1970 non-Harvard Riverside lost several hundred residents. The people of Riverside area have been angered at the University encroachment and contribution to their housing crisis. As *The Wilson Report* prophetically stated, "Riverside feels the University's presence keenly and is capable of articulating its concerns and methods for alleviating them" (*Wilson Report*, 1968, 44). The disruption of the 1970 commencement by Riverside residents concerned about Harvard's effect in the area bears this out! And in 1972 two city councilors represented the area; one was the vocal and increasingly well-known Black community leader, Saundra Graham, the other, conservative, white, Irish, Walter Sullivan, who became mayor, a largely ceremonial job, after serving as a council member for many years.

MIT AND THE TRANSFORMATION:
THE TECHNOLOGIZING OF THE CITY

The intellectual and industrial communities of Cambridge, long adjacent but seldom working together, provided a situation favorable to the establishment of research and development as an important aspect of the economy (Cambridge Historical Commission, 1965).

While Harvard contributes more to the simple supply and demand dynamics of a housing crisis in Cambridge, MIT's role in transforming the city is more structurally significant. Over 2,000 Institute affiliates occupy the same number of city dwelling units (Kaiser, 1969; CTOC, 1972, 3). As a major technological institution and a contributor to the scientific community, MIT and its personnel have created, cooperated with, and attracted many major technological firms to the city, including Polaroid, MITRE, General Electric, and Computer Corporation of America, and at least seventeen of the five hundred top defense contractors (Shalom, 1969, 5). A February 1966 MIT press release on its importance to Cambridge and the U.S. claimed that, "Between 200 and 300 new companies have started in this area in recent years, many of them 'spin offs'[5] from MIT research" (Shalom, 1969, 44). And many of the 574 firms on the "Golden Semi-Circle" of Route 128 were attracted there by MIT's presence nearby. MIT-related technological developments replaced industrial firms with research and development ventures, bringing more competitors for housing, and subtracting blue-collar jobs (Shalom, 1969). Since its opening in 1964 with four buildings, the joint MIT/Cabot, Cabot & Forbes development, Technology Square, brought over fifty R&D-related firms to Cambridge. MIT spin-off, Draper Labs, constructed a fifth building of 450,000 square feet in the Square. An unprecedented cooperative effort between a private university and a profit developer, the Technology Square development was the completion of the city's first urban renewal project in Cambridge.

Technology Square was built where the Lever Brothers' soap factory and five acres of housing used to stand. The housing destruction—including a spectacular D(emolition)-Day in November 1957—was part of the first urban renewal project in Cambridge. Actually five blocks of housing were demolished: the Rogers Block itself was a tenement (then meaning "apartment house") built in 1873 as low-cost worker housing for the period's industrial expansion (Shalom, 1969, 7). The 1950 census listed 189 dwelling units in the demolished area. A Cambridge historical commission director estimated 325 families might have lived there (*Cambridge Chronicle,* March 7, 1957). Destruction of the old, but low-cost, housing for Tech Square was described at the 1962 New England Regional Space Conference at MIT (to bring the Space Program to Cambridge and the MIT environs) by the Cambridge mayor as: "the blitzing out of slums" (Christopher, 1964, 51). The Citizen's Advisory Committee, headed by then MIT Chairman James Killian, chose this renewal site.

While urban renewal was a federal program, it was mainly because of MIT's presence and the powerful connections of Chairman Killian, President Dwight Eisenhower's science advisor, that the National Aeronautics and Space Administration chose Cambridge as site for a major research center in 1964. A thirteen-story building, which NASA only used for about two weeks, was the major fruit of a "Kendall Square" urban renewal project.[6] It displaced 94 industrial firms and 3,100 industrial jobs, while bringing 850 technical jobs (Rowland, 1973; Cambridge Tenants Organizing Committee, 1973). Then the Department of Transportation occupied the building, but paid no taxes, so the rest of the city subsidized its services.

The professional-oriented, high-rise, luxury housing planned for Kendall Square would be an especially visible and powerful part of the transformational trend.[7] Along with projects across the Charles River, Technology Square seems destined to become "the northern jewel in the crown circle of luxury redevelopment in Boston" (Metropolitan Area Planning Council, 1969). Such developments, by generating a "ripple effect" of redevelopment, raise land values in the surrounding areas, thus increasing property taxes and rents and encouraging speculation nearby (Cambridge Tenants Organizing Committee, 1971, 6).[8] Even when their construction does not involve destroying low-cost housing, the cumulative effects of development on the surrounding area contributes to "economic bulldozer," driving low-income people out of Cambridge.

Along with university expansion, the influx of R&D firms, and the high-rise trend, the presence of the universities has contributed significantly to changes in the composition of Cambridge and of the type of people seeking housing there. Students and other young people attracted to Cambridge by the university flavor increased tremendously as a factor both in the housing crisis and the transformation of the city. Over 3,000 Harvard and 1,750 MIT students live in town (Barber, 1972, 89, 90).

One-person households have grown 300 percent since 1950 and households of two or more unrelated people have skyrocketed 1100 percent. The only population group to grow at all from 1960 to 1970 was the eighteen- to thirty-four-year-old group, which increased by a quarter (Community Development Program, 1972a; C). In this context, the departure of families, who could not compete with the numbers and affluence of young professionals or students pooling rents, become understandable. *The Wilson Report* explained the situation succinctly:

> Persons connected with the university, or *seeking to live in its shadow*, have bid up the price of housing at an astronomical rate. Partly this is the result of the action of faculty members able and willing to pay higher prices than most other Cambridge residents for existing housing; partly it is the result of the influx of affluent business and professional persons who buy or rent that which even professors can no longer afford, and partly it is the consequence of students or others who . . . are prepared to join together in groups of three, four, or more to rent an apartment at prices far higher than one family can afford (Committee on the University and the City [*Wilson Report*, 1968, 33, 35, emphasis added]).

Moreover, "Landlords, once reluctant to rent to students, have in growing numbers been prepared to raise their rents in order to drive out family tenants so as to replace them with students." An ample supply of students willing to share apartments came from Harvard, MIT, Boston University, and other area schools to live in Cambridge (*Wilson Report,* 1968, 35).

The combined effect led to "Cambridge's becoming increasingly a city of transient renters and decreasingly a city of family home dwellers." From 1960 to 1970 renting rose by 9 percent, while owner-occupied households declined by 11 percent (Cambridge Community Development Program, 1972a, 24). The rate of increase in transients and renter turnover—results in increased wear on the housing stock and easier rent increases. They make it harder to keep a sense of community—and the decline in more stable family households. From all these forces, Cambridge has, in the words of the City Manager, "a markedly abnormal" market.[9]

> The "natural" forces of supply and demand—primarily for housing but also for commercial space—are such that it is only necessary for Harvard [and MIT] to do nothing for Cambridge to become a predominantly upper middle-class

community—that is to say, a community very much like Harvard itself (*Wilson Report*, 1968, 46) (quote marks added).

Left to the economic forces of Cambridge, only "market rate," largely luxury housing will be built, with serious implications for low-income people. From 1950 to 1970, when more than 200 low-income units were demolished, 1,900 luxury units were constructed (Pynoos, 1972, 419). The City Manager explained in 1969,

> More luxury housing will not relieve the pressure on the low-income housing market. The "filtering down theory" simply does not work here (Duehey, 1970a, 22).[10] In fact, the demand for housing in Cambridge has been so great that it has led to a filtering up of housing from less well-off working-class tenants to more well-to-do professionals and students (Pynoos, 1972, 419).

Such a remarkable seller's market could not exist without the tremendous demand the universities were instrumental in stimulating. In the City Manager's words, the answer was "more construction of subsidized low-income units" (Duehey, 1970a, 22).

More Problems than Answers?

Looking to the local government was not an answer in Cambridge. City government and agencies had hardly contributed to solving the problems. While scarcity of land,[11] resultant high unit costs, and community opposition were formidable factors, the fact that the Cambridge Housing Authority had built only 155 low-income units—all for the elderly—from 1954 to 1972 was an indication that the initiative and effort required was not available (Cambridge Community Development Program, 1972b, 18). The City Manager once described the Housing Authority as "the most lethargic agency in the city" (Cambridge Tenants Organizing Committee, 1972; Kaiser, 1969, 2).

The problem went further. Although the Housing Authority had received a government authorization for 1,500 public housing units of various types in 1966 from the Housing Assistance Administration of the then newly formed Department of Housing and Urban Development, by late 1969, largely because of lack of administrative commitment and development skills, only a small part had been utilized (Ad Hoc Task Force, 1969, 4).[12] The following September, the Ad Hoc Housing Development Task Force appointed by the City Manager in May 1969 wrote,

> The Cambridge housing problem is marked by the ironic situation that although additional low-income and elderly housing units are needed above and beyond the 1,500 authorized by the HAA, still the public agencies involved have not

begun to utilize the units currently authorized and may be in some jeopardy of having those units taken away by the federal government (Ad Hoc Task Force, 1969, 9).

Nor had the Cambridge Redevelopment Agency built any low-income housing, despite the Ad Hoc Task Force advising such action in its 1969 report (Ad Task Force, 1969, 52). The CRA continued to plan for upper-income housing. Even the City Council, other than setting up the Task Force under the City Manager in 1969 and pressuring Harvard somewhat, failed to take aggressive action to improve the housing situation.

While the city government had failed to act, policies, interests, actions and inactions of industry, banks, landlords, realtors, and developers, including MIT's partner, Cabot, Cabot & Forbes, had significant influences in the housing crisis and transformation of the city.[13] The universities were a major focus. "Harvard and MIT are the largest and most visible institutions in the city; not surprisingly, they have been singled out for special blame" (Harvard University, 1970, 35). As the Harvard *Wilson Report* admitted:[14]

> No institution of this size and with this purpose can be neutral about its environment. If it should act vigorously to secure land, erect buildings, and shape events, it will impose its preferences on others. . . . If it should be passive and let events take their course, it will implicitly choose a certain type of environment—one perhaps in which all Cambridge slowly becomes like Harvard and M.I.T. until we find that we are no longer an urban university but one which has allowed there to grow up around itself a kind of inner city suburb with a single life style, carried on by professors, students, psychiatrists, and the executives of electronic and consulting firms (*Wilson Report*, 1968, 7).

The report summed up the position both Harvard and MIT realized they were in. "By remaining inactive, the university is in effect contributing to the pressures on the housing market and hastening the transformation of the city" (*Wilson Report*, 1968, 3).

Whether by choice, or necessity, the universities had to act.

HOUSING DEVELOPMENTS

The contexts of the housing crisis and the transformation in Cambridge provide bases for understanding the history of how the universities became involved in community housing. A review begins in the mid-1960s with events symptomatic of the greater changes to come.

In 1964, Technology Square opened near MIT on the former site of a soap factory and blocks of in-expensive housing. In 1965, Harvard opened

Peabody Terrace, 499 units for faculty and married graduate students. On the former site of about 150 houses, the mixed low- and high-rise project is between the Charles riverfront and the rest of the politically sensitive Riverside neighborhood. Envisioning more campus housing soon, Harvard continued buying property in the area, where it would open an undergraduate residence, Mather House in 1970. By late 1965, the universities, too, were becoming more concerned with housing problems in the city—and the related community relation problems they created for themselves. At this point, the schools, along with some industry, began to support community-oriented housing efforts, most noticeably the creation of the Cambridge Corporation.

The turning point was 1966–1967. While housing problems had existed before, the worst effects would not be felt until the housing crisis hit Cambridge. In 1966, a credit crunch from the escalation of the Vietnam War virtually dried up money for financing new housing. Both new construction and vacancies almost disappeared.

Other aspects of the city transformation became prominent from 1966 to 1969: the displacement threat of the proposed Inner Belt highway, and the development of the Electronic Research Center for NASA as part of Kendall Square, across from Tech Square, created controversy—as well as community pressure on MIT. Housing and community pressures mounted in 1967–1968, while MIT was quietly working on housing schemes. In central Cambridge, Harvard, was not yet being confronted with its effect on the city, and remained traditionally aloof through the end of the 1960s.

In May 1968, Harvard took a step toward community housing. Sensitized by two traumatic events in April—the death of Rev. Martin Luther King Jr. and the Student Strike at Columbia University over expansion into Morningside Heights—then Harvard president Nathan Pusey commissioned the Committee on the University and the City to look at Harvard's role in Cambridge. Eight months later, a "Preliminary Report" would outline Harvard's role in the transformation and the housing crisis (Harvard University, 1970).

The climate for such a report and action on housing heated up as the housing crisis continued. Political organizing around the housing crisis began in summer 1968. In September, after a two-month survey of distressing elderly housing conditions and nine neighborhood caucuses, 900 Cambridge residents attended the first of three Cambridge Housing Conventions. Local leaders and area Congressman (and soon-to-be House majority leader) Thomas P. (Tip) O'Neill addressed "The Convention on the Crisis in Low-Cost Housing for the Elderly."

Convention members laid out numerous complaints about the housing situation and passed a hundred resolutions (Duehey, 1970a, 23). Ten of the resolutions and much of the debate dealt with the role of the universities in

the housing crisis. As a plan for future action, the Convention set up negotiating teams to meet with the universities and housing agencies to press for
solutions to the crisis.

COMMUNITY HOUSING INTRODUCED

On the day before the Convention the first university announcement on community housing occurred. MIT announced plans on September 13, 1968, to
build 150 units of low-income family housing on a site on Clarendon Avenue
in North Cambridge (*Cambridge Chronicle*, September 19, 1968). While the
project had long been planned for other reasons, the announcement was stra-
tegically timed to blunt Convention criticism of the Institute by clearly showing MIT's concern and actions. The announcement did not, however, discuss
the quite different relocation origins of how the project had come into being.

Interim Units: MIT, the Inner Belt, and Community Housing

Both the North Cambridge and the later-announced MIT projects need to be
viewed in the light of MIT's role in the Inner Belt controversy of the mid-
1960s. Planned since 1948 to parallel R&D-lined Route 128, the Inner Belt
(I-695) threatened to cut an eight-lane swath through low-income residential
sections of Cambridge and displace 1,235 families, more than 3,000 residents, and 2,116 jobs (Duehey, 1970f, 57–58). Citizens, City Council, and
Congressman O'Neill overwhelmingly opposed the road.[15]

Despite the potential destructiveness of the highway, MIT took no formal
position on the issue, its standard policy on public controversies. When an
alternate path was proposed to go through the western part of its campus,
however, the Institute in February 1966 publicly and intensively opposed
that routing, though still not the road itself. The MIT's attorney described
the route touching MIT as a blow to "a primary scientific arsenal of democracy" and "the Free World," and MIT's chairman Killian described it as a
"disruption [which] could affect the prosperity in the city, state and region."[16]
Though the route threatened Institute activities and expansion, the exaggerated and narrowly self-interested public stance raised criticisms of the image-
conscious Institute and changed many community residents' impressions of
MIT for the worse.

As an offshoot of the Inner Belt routing controversy, MIT was pressured
at the highest levels by the State in the summer of 1966 to provide relocation
housing for about four hundred of the 1,200 families facing displacement by
a routing that would not go through the Institute. To accomplish the housing

goal, the Institute Real Estate Office and Northgate Community Corporation, set up in 1965 to deal with MIT housing needs particularly to attract faculty and non-university personnel back to Cambridge, moved into action in late summer 1966. They began buying existing rental housing units, mainly occupied by students and for future building sites, generally near the highway route, for possible use by Belt displacees. By mid-1967, MIT had completed a relocation inventory of both existing units and new construction sites sufficient to house displacees by the Belt likely to require assistance.

By early 1968, however, while the likelihood of the Inner Belt was declining, the controversies surrounding the housing crisis and Convention were pushing MIT away from relocation housing for the Belt. Not only already sensitized by the Belt controversy and the realization that Cambridge overwhelmingly opposed the road to awareness of vulnerability to community protests, MIT, increasingly recognized the severity of the housing conditions that were producing the political pressures. During 1968, the Institute's housing plans and emphasis changed dramatically. By the day before the September Housing Convention, MIT would announce the first part of its housing program for Cambridge.

The Institute's commitment and plans for community housing were firm enough to announce that it would build new units in North Cambridge. This site, however, is three to four miles from the MIT campus, out of the way of the Belt and its environs. That move was timed to show MIT's concern and take the steam out of community criticism. This was before the April 1969, announcement of a complete "Housing Program in Cambridge" following long community negotiations and city pressures.[17]

After the Housing Convention

Following the Housing Convention in September 1968, negotiations with the universities and city agencies, along with a campaign for rent control in Cambridge, became parts of the major community movement for the fall. The Convention's university negotiating team met separately with MIT four times and Harvard three times to discuss the housing crisis, the universities' roles, and how they could help matters. They pressed for positive university commitments and action.

While MIT met willingly and cooperatively, Harvard had to be pushed by the City Council. Responding to community pressures, the Council called on the universities to explain their housing policies. In October, the Council also passed several resolutions toward getting the universities and sluggish city agencies to work on the housing situation and authorized a special investigating committee to study legislative methods to deal with vanishing low-cost housing. Also in October, a council committee presented a report endorsing rent control. A popular City Councillor recommended a "university zone" in the city to limit university expansion.

With negotiations ending, the year 1968 finished with another smaller and less successful, housing convention in December. This one reported on progress in the fall and planned to work on achieving a rent control ordinance.

The year 1969 began with Harvard issuing the *Preliminary Report of the Committee on the University and the City, The Wilson Report* (Committee on the University and the City, 1968). While commending the Harvard's community contributions, it criticized much of the University's effect on the city. It recommended more on-campus housing facilities for students and staff, and exploration by the university of ways to contribute directly to community housing units.

Specifically the Report suggested, "The proper role of the university in our opinion, is *both* to increase the supply of housing available for its own faculty and students and to serve as a catalytic agent which will facilitate efforts to increase the local housing supply generally . . . for persons of low and moderate incomes. . . ." (*Wilson Report*, 1968, p. 39, emphasis in original). The Report further recommended, "We would like to see the university, as part of this joint program [with the city], reconsider whether it might become the sponsor of one or more federally assisted housing programs" (*Wilson Report*, 1968, p. 40).

In late March 1969, however, the Report's author, James Q. Wilson, would publicly lament the apathy and silence with which the document was met at Harvard (*Cambridge Chronicle*, March 21, 1969). Local political organizing around rent control, as well as vocal attacks on Harvard, continued in early 1969 while MIT was working out details of its housing announcement for April. In March, the City Council began hearings on the weak housing efforts of the City Redevelopment Agencies. The Council was seeking more action and greater coordination in the housing area, as well as possible sites for publicly assisted developments. Later in March, responding to the overwhelming needs and growing community and Council pressures, the City Manager set up a Task Force on Housing. Composed of public and private agencies and the universities, the group was to coordinate efforts and develop short-range plans. In part, the Task Force had to deal with the embarrassing situation that Cambridge-in desperate need of more low-rent housing—had been unable to utilize 1,200 of a 1966 HUD allocation of 1,500 low-income units (Ad Hoc Task Force, 1969, 4). The Council pushed for a housing "expediter," and *The Cambridge Chronicle* called for a housing "czar" to bring action.

In late June, the City Manager made an extraordinary speech to a City Council hearing, presenting an interim task force report about housing (Duehey, 1970a, 18–25). His extensive presentation analyzed the housing problems in detail, outlining the weaknesses of past efforts and agencies. On a philosophical note, he claimed that "no market in a just society has ever been free to abuse the people it serves" (Duehey, 1970a, 19). He suggested that various groups could help get housing built. These included the universities, which should help in the housing situation "simply because they have resources to do it that no one else in the city has, and a clear responsibility to use them" (Duehey, 1970a, 21). He added that the Ad Hoc Task Force would issue a lengthy report in September 1969 on using the rest of the 1,500-unit HUD allocation and discussing how various agencies could increase the housing supply.

COMMUNITY HOUSING BECOMES A REALITY

In spring 1969, the pace of events at Harvard accelerated. In April, a Student Strike rocked the University. On April 9, by two hundred students led by the Students for a Democratic Society (SDS) occupied the University Hall administration building. Besides opposing the presence of the Reserved Officers Training Corps (ROTC) at Harvard, and university support of U.S. military activities, the group protested University expansion and its effects on the Cambridge and Boston communities. The next morning without consulting the faculty, University president Nathan Pusey called in the state police to clear the building, thus generating greater support and publicity for the strikers and their demands.

Though the occupation and the bust got most of the strike headlines, major issues involved housing and the community. Strikers demanded that Harvard roll hack rents in its Cambridge apartments to the 1968 level, that no University apartments be torn down to make way for the proposed John F. Kennedy Memorial Presidential Library, and that 182 houses in West Roxbury, near the Harvard Medical School, not be demolished (Harvard Strikers, 1969, 17–21). The demands by themselves "caused people to question attitudes and assumptions that had been taken for granted through the years; students, faculty, administration, and townspeople who had been indifferent to the problems of Cambridge began to re-evaluate the concept of a university and its relationship to its environmental context" (Duehey, 1970a, 56). Out of this controversy would come the community/university housing project in Mission Hill near the Medical School in Boston (see Part III here on Mission Park Housing in Boston).

Adding to these pressures on Harvard, MIT made a critically timed housing announcement the very day of the University Hall sit-in. Though the long-planned initial public statement was actually the evening before, some Harvard people found the timing "an unfriendly act." On April 9, at a major luncheon press conference, MIT Chairman James Killian and President Howard Johnson announced the Institute's "A Housing Program in Cambridge." For the next few days the newspapers simultaneously carried praises of MIT's housing plan and news of Harvard's strike. MIT announced a total target of 1,600 units of housing: 750 units at low income mainly for the elderly, and 850 units at market price. MIT would develop them on sites already under its control.

In mid-April, while the Harvard Strike continued, the Harvard Graduate School of Design (GSD) presented another demand. Ratified by a huge assembly at the University's Soldiers Field on April 14, the GSD proposal called on Harvard to build 3,000 units of housing in Cambridge, at least half of which would be for low-income families and the elderly of the city (Duehey, 1970c, 93ff). One month later students and faculty of the GSD proposed in great detail that Harvard build 500 units of housing, one quarter for low-income families, and one quarter for the elderly (Duehey, 1970c, 100+). A piece of ground near the Divinity School, which the University had been husbanding for faculty housing since 1955, the Sachs Estate was the proposed site for the 500 units. On June 2, at the instigation of the GSD assembly, the Cambridge City Council endorsed the Design School's proposal for the Sachs Estate.[18] Despite this political coup by the GSD, Harvard had no plans for community housing at Sachs.

Later in April, responding to the various housing pressures, Harvard hired a consultant to develop specific community housing proposals. Not to be outdone by MIT after the spring fiasco, in May 1969 the Harvard Corporation, trustees of the University, disclosed Harvard's preliminary plans for housing. It proposed eleven hundred low- and moderate-income units for both university and non-university personnel (displacees were given priority) for Boston near the Harvard affected hospital site. This enlarged upon four hundred units already planned for medical school-related personnel and included 30 percent low-income units.

A similar number of units, also for both University and Community personnel, were suggested for Cambridge. The numbers and plans remained unclear, though a community project at Mt. Auburn and Putnam Streets, as map 1.2 shows, at the edge of Riverside-Cambrideport, seemed certain.

In late June, University president Pusey told the City Council in an informal meeting that community housing would be built. However, he noted, the University's main emphasis would be on housing for faculty and graduate students.[19]

In summer 1969, the campaign for rent control in Cambridge intensified with meetings, protest and vigils at City Hall. In late June, the City Council

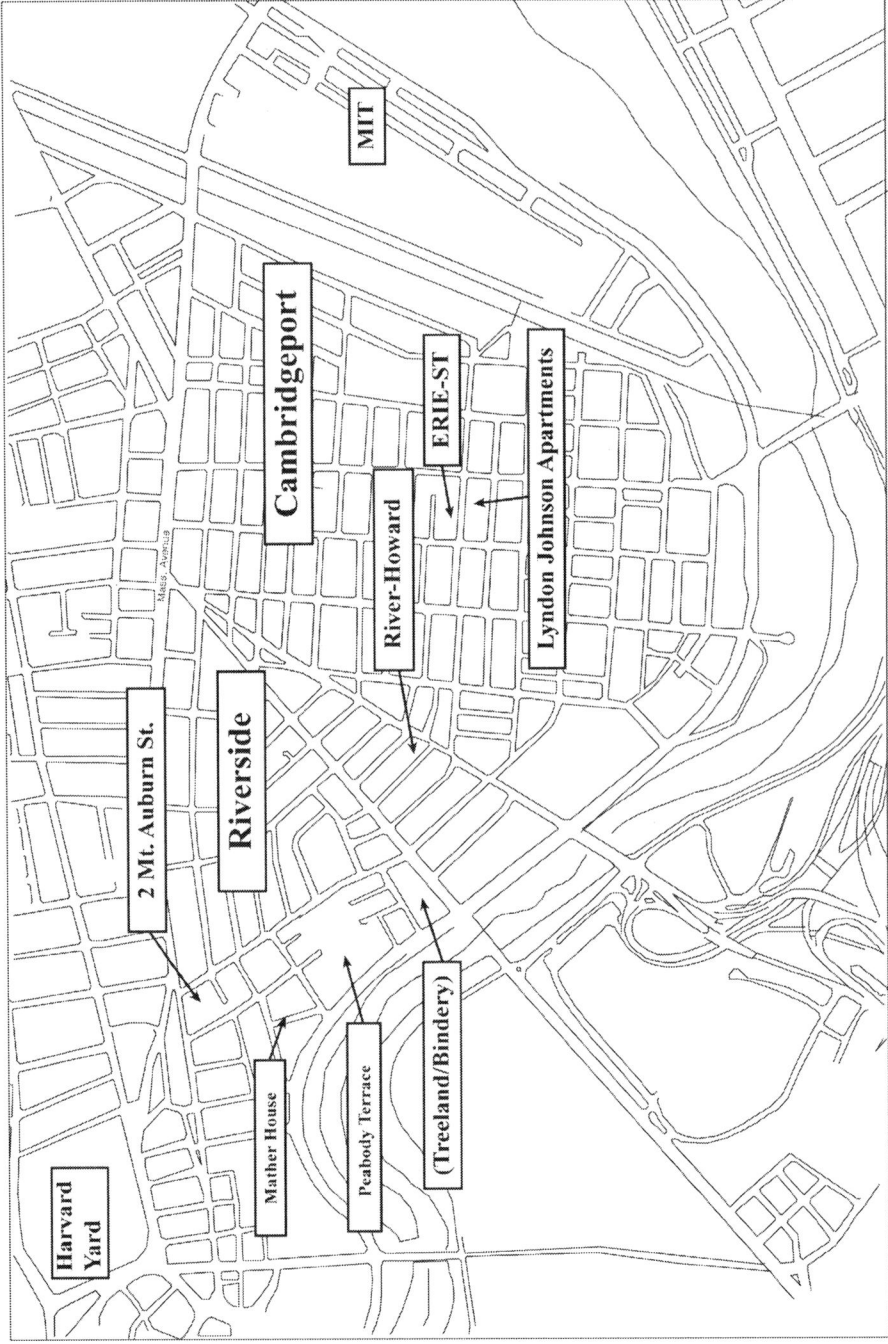

Map 1.2. Riverside-Cambridgeport
Credit: H. Kim

voted 5 to 4 against a Housing Convention-sponsored, community-drafted rent control ordinance. After further intense protests, the Council reaffirmed its decision at the end of July. Other community political groups, gathering signatures since spring, continued to press the rent control issue through a referendum petition for a November vote. Despite conflict among pro-rent control groups and some in anti-rent control groups (essentially landlord and property owner opposition), over 5,000 signatures were collected, where only 3,300 were needed. In a surprise ploy, the city solicitor ruled, not, as requested, on wording, but instead that the referendum should not occur. The election board and City Council supported this, thereby preventing the question from reaching the voters in November. Subsequent court and militant community action failed to change the situation. And tenant organizing soon replaced rent control as the new community organizational pursuit. A final Housing Convention on the issues occurred in November 1969.

In late September, Harvard finally made an official announcement on community housing in Cambridge. The September 25, 1969, *Harvard Crimson* revealed plans for 389 units for low and moderate income residents affiliated with Harvard and another 600 to 700 units for University and non-University residents. As a phase I, the University would develop the 389 low and moderate-income housing units on two sites which Harvard controlled. Coming out of a "crash program" since April, Harvard would help develop, along with the Cambridge Corporation and the Riverside Neighborhood Association, 64 elderly units (later increased to 94) on a university parking lot at Mt. Auburn and Putnam Streets. In West Cambridge, near Blair Pond, Harvard proposed 325 low- and moderate-income family and elderly units to be developed privately. Harvard's role in these would only be to sell or rent the land; others would have to develop and manage the projects (Galeota, 1969).

In late fall 1969, preliminaries were quietly worked on for the 2 Mt. Auburn and West Cambridge projects. In December 1969, there were protests about housing near Harvard Medical School in Boston. Little else was visibly happening on community housing in Cambridge.

The events in 1970 began with the late opening of Mather House, a Harvard undergraduate residential facility in Riverside. Built where homes used to stand at the edge of Riverside near Peabody Terrace, it provided partial relief for off-campus housing pressures. In late February, activity began again on community-related university housing at Sachs Estate. Harvard asked the City Council for a zoning change from single- to multi-family units to allow 300 faculty houses to be built. The Council passed the request onto the City Planning Board, which held turbulent hearings in March. Various groups opposed the plan, some wanting more, less expensive units, others wanting fewer, less densely placed ones to save green space. A few days after the hearings a group from the Cambridge Housing Convention demonstrated at Harvard to demand that the university build 3,200 low- and moderate-income units throughout Cambridge. This included making 40 percent of the West Cambridge development low-income. Harvard declined to commit itself. In any case, in late April the Planning Board gave a 3 to 2 OK to the rezoning petition, though it recommended changes in Harvard's plans to improve the project's impact. The City Council, however, did not act on the Board's recommendations, so Harvard lacked a zoning change for Blair Pond.

National events of that spring changed the context of housing politics. In late April the National Student Strike, in protest of the Nixon administration's invasion of Cambodia and the killings of students at Kent and Jackson State universities, broke out across the country. Harvard, which had its own version just a year earlier, was struck again. Neither community issues nor housing were featured in the national strike.

In May 1970, housing emphasis at Harvard shifted from the Sachs Estate to the Riverside Community to the southeast of Harvard. At that time, the Riverside Planning Team, an offshoot of the summer 1968 Cambridge Economic Opportunity Committee neighborhood caucuses, petitioned the Harvard Board of Overseers for help. The group wanted the last open location on the Charles riverfront to be devoted to community housing. They were seeking the 2.25-acre "Treeland/Bindery" site, next to Peabody Terrace in Riverside, for a 100-unit, low-income development. Harvard did not respond to the request.

Though the national Student Strike had dissipated, on June 10 a group of 300 people, including community members and some students, marched into Harvard Yard. They held an overnight "tent-in" there because of the unanswered demand that Harvard build community housing at the Treeland/ Bindery site. Again they were ignored. It was not until their leader, Saundra Graham, later a Cambridge City Councillor, and thirty others interrupted the Harvard Commencement ceremonies the next day that the University officials took heed. Nationally, their act drew unfavorable publicity. Graham made her point well when, to shouts of "go home," she reminded people that she and her group were home. In order to get her off the stage, she was permitted to address the audience and two Harvard Corporation members agreed to meet with the group immediately after the ceremony. Though they refused to give up the Treeland site as "too valuable for low-income housing," the Harvard officials did promise to buy a site for housing in Riverside by September 1970.[20]

Little occurred on community housing in Cambridge during the summer of 1970, though rent control became a reality. On August 30, the Massachusetts General Court passed enabling legislation for cities to implement the laws locally. In mid-September, the Cambridge City Council passed a form of rent control, which was under attack ever since from tenant groups as weak and landlord oriented, though landlords were not happy either. University housing, including some of MIT's Northgate Community Corporation units, was exempted from rent controls.

Also by September, Harvard had obtained a 1.6-acre alternate housing site to Treeland in Riverside. Located at River and Howard streets, it cost $540,000. About the same time, moreover, the University was asked by the Federal Model Cities program to acquire a piece of property just south of Somerville. Harvard obliged by obtaining a site on Inman Square where the Cambridge Corporation would develop elderly and family units.

In October 1970, Harvard also experienced difficulties with the city of Boston about the protested plans for an "Affiliated Hospitals Complex" (AFC) near Harvard Medical School. The Urban Renewal Committee of the City of Boston, which Harvard did not consult until then, called hearings on Harvard expansion efforts near the hospitals. Leading up to the hearings, in August City Councillors demanded that Harvard answer thirty questions about its role in the area, and clarify its plans or be denied zoning changes. Though Harvard, which was essentially land banking for itself and others, was slow to respond, this began moving Harvard to a more responsible position in the medical school area.

By late 1970, all the announced University/Community housing projects in Cambridge had been started and working out their details was proceeding. Though not as strong as Community groups wanted, rent control was in effect in Cambridge, and tenant organizing there kept housing in the news. In February 1971, Harvard asked for preliminary designs for 278 units of faculty and graduate student housing at Treeland, and in September promised the Riverside Community that nothing would be considered on the Treeland site for two to three years.

During summer 1971, office holders changed in various parts of Cambridge. Both Harvard and MIT had new presidents. The new Harvard administration brought a more responsive and politically sophisticated president in Derek Bok, former Harvard Law School dean and a labor mediations specialist. As one of his early acts, Bok created an Office of Government and Community Affairs, whose vice president, from the University of Chicago, another school with serious community problems, would deal with community affairs. Also in July, Jerome Wiesner replaced Howard Johnson as MIT president; Johnson became Chairman, replacing James Killian who became Chairman Emeritus.

In September, a liberal Cambridge Council was elected, including Saundra Graham, leader of the Riverside Community. An attempt to get a more responsive city manager failed, leaving the Council less able to act on the housing front. But with the Community-oriented Council in office, Harvard's chances for a zoning change to multi-family, faculty housing for Sachs Estate diminished. In fall 1971, however, the Harvard-assisted, 94 elderly-unit project at 2 Mt. Auburn Street became the first community housing project in Cambridge to be completed. In 1972, Harvard and MIT each abandoned one project, Blair Pond and Portland Street, respectively, because of Community opposition. For economic reasons, the original plans for River-Howard and 1000 Massachusetts Avenue were abandoned in 1973. The former was also a victim of the January 1973 Nixon administration housing freeze. In October 1973, MIT opened its first community housing project, the Lyndon B. Johnson Apartments on Hamilton Street. All the other ongoing Cambridge projects were completed by 1974, except River-Howard II, were done in summer 1981. The Mission Park project in Boston was finished in 1978.[21]

ON THE WAY TO COMMUNITY/ UNIVERSITY HOUSING DEVELOPMENTS

Community/University housing appeared in Cambridge prior to more formal developments. For several years, both Harvard and MIT had offered mixed community/university city apartments. Both were also sponsors of the Cambridge Corporation, which helped develop community housing.

University-Owned City Apartments: Northgate Community Corporation

Both Harvard and MIT own apartment buildings in Cambridge occupied by university and community members. This "organic" type of community/university housing occurs in non-university apartments, too. Through its housing office and a private firm, Harvard runs a rental operation for its city units. A major landlord in Cambridge, the University owns about 450 apartment units in Cambridge. They were obtained mainly in the 1960s for investment, faculty housing, and future expansion. Rented on a first-come basis, the Harvard apartments were about two-thirds community occupied.[22]

MIT had run a joint community/university apartment operation through the specially created Northgate Community Corporation. Begun in 1965, at the same time as the Institute Real Estate office started, Northgate was originally conceived to attract faculty back to Cambridge as part of a plan for a more residential campus community. In fact, MIT graduate and undergraduate students became most of the tenants. Yet, community members occupy about one-third of MIT's units, including about thirty-five units under a leased

Cambridge Corporation Developed Housing

a. Walden Square (240 units)
b. Harwell Homes (56 units)

Harvard-assisted Community Housing

A. Putnam Square Apartments (94 units)
B. Inman Square (116 units)
C. River-Howard (32 units)
D. [Blair Pond (248 units)]
E. [Sachs Estate (204 units)]
F. [Treeland-Bindery (278 units)]
G. Mission Park [Convent Site, Boston] (775 units)

MIT-RELATED COMMUNITY HOUSING

1. MILLERS RIVER [Gore St.] (304 units)
2. DANIEL BURNS APTS. [Clarendon Ave.] (199 units)
3. LYNDON J. JOHNSON [Hamilton St.] (181 units)
4. ERIE STREET (16 units)
5. 1000 MASS AVE. (250 units)
6. [PORTLAND STREET (800 units)]
7. [NORTHGATE COMMUNITY CORP. (470 units)]

Map labels

1. MILLERS RIVER [Gore St.] (304 units)
6. [PORTLAND ST.] (800 units)]
B. Inman Square (116 units)
b. Harwell Homes (56 units)
E. [Sachs Estate (204 units)]
A. Putnam Square Apartments (94 units)
5. [1000 MASS AV (250 units)]
C. River-Howard (32 units)
4. Erie St. (16 units)
3. LYNDON JOHNSON [Hamilton St.] (181 units)
E. [Treeland-Bindery 278 units)]
G. [Mission Park (775 units)
[In Boston, near Harvard Medical School]
2. Daniel Burns [Clarendon AV] (199 units)
a. Walden Square (240 units)
D. [Blair Pond (248 units)]

Somerville, Mass.
CAMBRIDGE, MASS
Boston, Mass.
Arlington, Mass.
Watertown, Mass.
Fresh Pond

MIT
Harvard
Radcliffe

Key

■ - Finished project
□ - Project developing or proposed
▨ - Project abandoned or stagnant
- Approximate boundaries or route

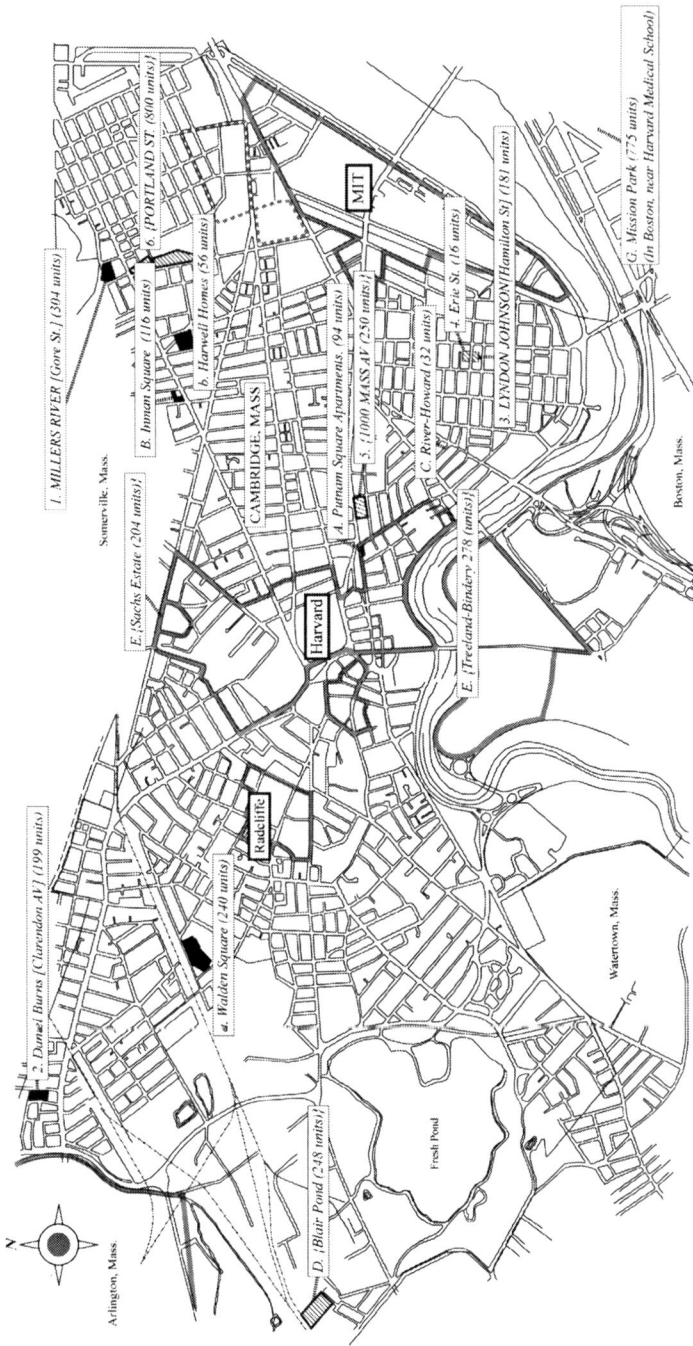

Map 1.3. Cambridge and Community/University Housing
Credit: H. Kim

public housing program. Besides providing housing, Northgate was planned to help Cambridge by building new units and paying taxes on the new construction developed at below market costs from favorable lending rates for an MIT-backed, nonprofit venture.

Harvard apartments have been a source of contention. Many are located in politically and racially sensitive Riverside, the site of previous University expansion. Harvard has torn down 200 units and let units slated for future demolition deteriorate as parts of its expansion program (Donham, 1972, 11). These activities incurred community antagonism for the University and charges of "slumlordism" during the 1969 Strike. Harvard began circumscribing its area of geographical influence and planned to sell some apartments. Relations among Community and University tenants have generally been "cordial." In fact, both groups of tenants have sometimes collaborated to fight increases in rents (Harvard University, 1972, 3). Some Harvard rents have been higher than the market, in part became the university overpaid for buildings.

MIT's landlord role has been less controversial, though not without problems. MIT keeps its properties in good shape and has made repairs for free. It subsidized controversial leased public housing units and avoided evictions and greater problems. But the location of some units in Cambridgeport—also a politically sensitive and racially area—contributed to tension. Neighborhood antagonism has directed toward MIT for moving students into previously community-occupied units and for a "MIT-style" of renovations that sometimes does not fit with traditional neighborhoods.

While Northgate has generally been successful at providing housing, it has run into financial problems. Over protest, it was granted an exemption from Cambridge rent control, which led to further protests, withholding of rents, and evictions. The exemption did not solve MIT's problems, however. With maintenance costs rising and a 30 percent tax bill (Northgate was set up to pay taxes and it did!), rents rose to a point where they could not compete with either urban or Cambridge rent-controlled units. Facing vacancy losses, rents had to follow the market, but did not produce adequate revenue to cover costs.

Though MIT bought several recently constructed buildings of ten to fourteen units and rehabilitated older ones, Northgate did not build the planned new housing. Hopes for favorable lending rates from MIT backing never emerged while construction costs rose 1 percent a month. So no new units were added to market supply.

While Harvard profits on its rentals, Northgate lost money, and MIT began selling its units. Though it still owned or leased about three hundred units, a substantial number were already sold to neighborhood residents and landlords.[23] Despite its problems, Northgate serves as a model for mid-income community/university housing. With the proper university or government subsidy—about $500,000 per year—and tenant participation in management, a Northgate-like program provided economically and socially-mixed housing.

THE CAMBRIDGE CORPORATION

For several years, both universities were also involved in the Cambridge Corporation representing a mid-point between isolation and involvement in community housing. Harvard, MIT, and Cambridge businesses created the Corporation in the mid-sixties to deal with problems, particularly in housing, in which the two schools later became directly involved.

The idea for such an organization was originally suggested in 1960 by then head of the Harvard-MIT Joint Center for Urban Studies, Martin Meyerson, later University of Pennsylvania president. Movement had begun in 1965, but accelerated when the Cambridge mayor wrote the presidents of both schools "living in Cambridge" that they were contributing nothing to the community but pressures on the city's housing problems (Duehey, 1970c, 8). The Cambridge Corporation began in 1966, mainly through the efforts of MIT Chairman, James Killian. The two schools largely funded it, though at lower levels than anticipated. Originally the Cambridge Corporation was supposed to get a lump sum of $100,000 to $250,000 from each University and the rest from business. In total, the Corporation got $300,000 from each school over six years through 1972, but little from industry. In 1974, it got another $15,000 from the schools for a total of $630,000. Both university presidents were on the Board. Its director, Oliver Brooks, and a small staff were quite involved in on housing issues.

Though the Cambridge Corporation was originally envisioned only as a "catalyst" for the solution of community problems, it by necessity took a more active stance. Faced with the question of "whether the community can find means for adjusting to change on its own terms, rather than purely on the terms that may be dictated by the economics of the marketplace or by the unrestrained collision of competing pressures" (Duehey, 1970c, 8), it had to go beyond the stage of being a source of seed money and "urg[ing] other people to make the effort" (Duehey, 1970c, 10). Conceived to get things started, provide insight, direction and coordination, it became more broadly involved as an instrument of physical, and socioeconomic development. It became heavily involved in housing problems and education and in launching the Model Cities program (McNally, 1970, 57).

Besides university-related work, the Corporation sponsored on its own two fairly successful developments in Cambridge, Walden Square and the Harwell Homes. Walden Square, as Picture 1.1 shows, includes 240 one- to five-bedroom apartments on a 7.5 acre site in West Cambridge. It is a federal Section 236 interest subsidy project, with about sixty low-income units at rent supplement levels.

The Harwell Homes project, shown in picture 1.2, is a Section 236 cooperative development for fifty-six homes, some subsidized further. Though Walden Square ran into some trouble, both Harwell Homes and it were helpful in providing badly needed family housing. Besides these new construction projects, the Corporation was involved in two rehabilitation/remodeling efforts, CAST I and II.

Despite vigorous attempts "to establish its credentials as an independent organization, the Cambridge Corporation's heavy dependence on the two universities for financial support has gave it the reputation as an agent of Harvard and MIT."[24] For instance, while commending the Corporation for "working with community groups, providing them with technical help in drawing up

Picture 1.1. Walden Square Apartments
Credit: Cambridge Corporation

Picture 1.2.   Harwell Homes
Credit: Cambridge Corporation

development plans," the community identified it as a "publicity agent for the institutions and big companies and also providing an intelligence network for them" (Ridgeway, 1968, 187). Its board, moreover, includes only university and business members, with no community group representation.

Although MIT's Chairman Killian was the driving force behind the Cambridge Corporation's start, he had to persuade Harvard to come along. Harvard has been much more closely associated with and dependent on the Corporation. For instance, when community pressures first built heavily on Harvard in September 1968, University president Pusey wrote to the Cambridge Housing Convention's University Subcommittee that he "had hoped the Cambridge Corporation, in which we are represented, was satisfactorily serving [to help alleviate local housing problems] with CEOC" (Kaiser, 1969; D-8) The Corporation's head found the suggestion distressing. The Corporation had, in fact, done the major development work on the two successful Harvard-related community housing projects at Putnam Square and Inman Square Apartments.[25] On the other hand, the Corporation also avoided involvement and thus the problems of the two more risky projects, Blair Pond and River-Howard I, which subsequently failed.

While associated with the Corporation, MIT's relations have been distinctly different. MIT indirectly contributed, more quickly than Harvard, to all the Cambridge Corporation's housing efforts. But the Institute had also been distinctly independent in its own housing efforts. MIT felt that the Corporation, with a limited staff and modest resources, was too small and undercapitalized to contribute significantly to a major housing effort such as MIT envisioned.[26] The Cambridge Corporation was very helpful to MIT in its North Cambridge project at Clarendon Avenue through community work and ideas. The Corporation might have been of further aid, but MIT chose to direct its own efforts. Relying on the Corporation, when the universities were being directly pressured to act, would have been "buck passing" by MIT, still the Corporation felt slighted by MIT's proceeding on its own. MIT got almost all of the public credit for its projects.

Not so much a failing of the Cambridge Corporation but an escalation of pressures on the universities for direct participation brought Harvard and MIT into the housing business. The Corporation—which had no part in creating a crisis the universities contributed to—could not solve the housing problems alone.

At the end of 1974, the Cambridge Corporation ceased its activities as an operational entity and the Harvard's Community Affairs Office took over it continuing functions. To a great extent, the Corporation's demise came from running up against inherent limitations. With the completion of university financial support and the national housing freeze in effect, it had developed as much low and moderate income housing as it could. The long-term responsibility for housing efforts, as table 1.1 shows, would fall to other hands.

Institutionally tied, yet a private entity, the Corporation's possibilities as a community conduit for funds—especially for community development revenue sharing—were limited. At times it was competitive with the universities over community relations, for instance, with MIT over housing development. It was almost confrontational with Harvard over development in Harvard Square and over the Kennedy Presidential Library, originally proposed for Cambridge, but ultimately built in Boston. And the Corporation's founder and strongest supporter, former MIT president, James Killian, was long gone. A relatively short-term director could only do so much, though Oliver Brooks accomplished quite a bit. As table 1.1, University-Related Community Housing Projects demonstrates, the housing problems in the Corporation's purview were not yet solved, however.

Table 1.1. University-Related Community Housing Projects

University Involvement	Project Name	Sponsors/ Participants	Number/Types of Units	Subsidies	Status	Comments
Indirect MIT/ Harvard Involvement	Walden Square	Cambridge Corporation Interfaith Housing Corp. DCA Development Corp.	240 apartments and townhouses (120 elderly, 120 family)	Section 236, 140 rent supplement/ public housing leases	Completed November 1972	Roots in 1967; part of an urban renewal project; neighborhood problems
	Harwell Homes	Cambridge Corporation Wellington-Harrington	56 co-op townhouses (40 family, 16 elderly)	Section 236 coops; Rent Supplements' Public housing leases	Completed April 1972	From Neighborhood Improvement program
Direct MIT Involvement	Daniel F. Burns (Clarendon Avenue)	MIT/Cambridge Corp./Local Community	199 elderly apts.	Mass Housing Finance Agency (M HFA), turnkey public housing	Opened November 1973	Announced September 1968 as 150 family units
	Millers River (Gore Street)	MIT/East Cambridge Planning Team/ Cambridge Council on Aging	304 elderly apts.	MHFA, turnkey public housing	Opened February 1974	Announced April 1969 as 200 elderly apts.

(continued)

Table 1.1. *(Continued)*

University Involvement	Project Name	Sponsors/ Participants	Number/Types of Units	Subsidies	Status	Comments
	Lyndon B. Johnson (Hamilton Street)	MIT/ Cambridgeport Planning Team	181 elderly apts.	MHFA, turnkey public housing	Opened October 1973	Announced April 1969 as 200 family and elderly
	Erie Street	MIT/ Cambridgeport Planning Team	16 family townhouses	MHFA, turnkey public housing	Deferred 1973 Abandoned	Planned to be adjacent to LBJ site, cost problems
	Portland Street	MIT/Private developer, local community	800 apts. (family and elderly), 600 market rate	200 subsidized	Abandoned 1972	Too costly, neighborhood opposition
	1000 Mass. Avenue	MIT/Private developer	250 market apts.	None	Deferred 1973	Has zoning change, seeks private developer
	Northgate Community Corporation	MIT (Institute and Community Apartments)	At one time, 470 community apartments now about 300+	Nonprofit, MIT backing	Being divested	Original plans for new units, too
Indirect Harvard Involvement	Putnam Square Apartments (2 Mt. Auburn Street)	Cambridge Corp., Harvard Univ. / Riverside Neighborhood Assoc. / Council on Aging	94 elderly apts. (efficiencies and one bedroom)	MHFA, Sec. 10c leases, Brooke Amendment, tax shelter	Completed September 1971	Announced as 64 units by Harvard Corporation in Sept. 1969

Project	Developer	Units	Financing	Status	Notes
Inman Square	Cambridge Corp. / Harvard University	116 units, 97 elderly, 19 family townhouses	MHFA, Sec. 236, 40% rent support, tax shelter	Completed November 1974	Begun September 1970, Harvard bought land, $253,000
River-Howard II (River-Howard Homes)	Riverside–Cambridgeport Community Corporation (RCC)/Harvard University	32 family (originally 36); 26 3- and 4-bedrooms	Section 8 leases, 221d4 MHFA	Proposed fall 1974; construction started 1976 for completion, spring 1977. Occupancy August 1981.	Follow up to River-Howard I
Direct Harvard Involvement					
Blair Pond	Harvard University/ Starret Corp	216 family apartments Starret Corp.	Sec. 236, rent supplements	Abandoned 1973	Announced September 1969 as 325 units, then 248
River-Howard I	Riverside Community Corporaton	102 family units	Sec. 236, rent supplements (10%)	Abandoned 1973	From June 1970 protest; Harvard bought land for $540,000
Mission Park (Boston)	Roxbury Tenants of Harvard, Harvard University, et al. (Mission Park Associates)	775 units (275 at market)	MHFA; 500 subsidized units under Sec. 236, 200 rent supplement	Start construction October 1975, completion, spring 1978	Plans begun 1969 after protests. University had plans for 400 institutional units
Harvard Housing					
Sachs Estate	Harvard University	204 University units, 144 apts., 60 townhouses	None	Abandoned	Needs zoning, 160 units, idea in 1955, revived 1970
Treeland-Bindery	Harvard University	278 units for faculty and married grad students	None	Abandoned	RCC sought Treeland Site in 1970

NOTES

1. Though the validity of the CEOC survey has been challenged (Slade, 1974), its story is essentially accurate. MIT officer Antony Herrey wrote, "Regardless of justifiable criticisms of the survey technique employed, there seems to be substantial human hardship behind the statistics." Besides confirmation in the 1969 Cambridge Community Development Program survey, "The general validity of these figures was confirmed by statistics that we were collecting at the Institute Real Estate Office" (Herrey, 1969, 30).

2. As with statistics on "voluntary" relocation before urban renewal dislocation (Rand, 1964, 7), it is hard to determine how many people high housing costs forced from Cambridge. A 1969 city survey found one-in-three residents expected to have to leave the city soon, four-fifths of them involuntarily (Pynoos and Mollenkopf, 1972, 401). A city-wide Sample Household Survey does not include expectations about leaving, but does show that 75 percent of Cambridge residents would choose to stay in the city over moving to any area suburb (Department of Planning and Development, 1973, 6, 17ff).

3. The analysis of Harvard and MIT's effects on changes in the Cambridge does not ignore the beneficial contributions the schools make to the city. Assistance to city and community includes in-lieu-of-tax payments by both schools since 1928 and the housing projects mentioned here. For more detailed information on the university-related community projects, see Harvard University, *Report to the Cambridge Community*, October 1972.

4. Harvard and MIT are not the only schools contributing to housing pressures in Cambridge. About 150,000 students attended college in Greater Boston (Levi, 1964). Boston University (about 800), Brandeis, Northeastern, and Tufts students also live there (Slade, 1974). Taking the total number of college students (graduates and undergraduates) from the 1970 census estimate of 19,000 and subtracting university-housed residents of Harvard/Radcliffe, MIT, and Lesley College (about 11,750) left an estimate of about 7,250 students living in town. Caroll, May, and Noe (1972) and Organization for Social and Technological Innovation (1970) cite 6,100 students from 5 of 65 local colleges, not including Tufts, Brandeis, Lesley, and the University of Massachusetts-Boston living in Cambridge units in 1970. The Cambridge Community Development Program (1972b, 37) found 6,600 full-time-student households in Cambridge in 1972. A likely estimate is probably about 7,500 to 8,000 students living in Cambridge in 1975. The 1972 Cambridge Community Development Program report suggested area universities build 1,700 units for students—perhaps combined with families—to reduce by 5 percent the pressures from student demand (CCDP, 1972b, 37).

5. The development of "spin-off" firms created by people and inventions developed out of the research work at universities, like Digital Equipment Corporation, was an indirect process until about 1972. In that year, MIT helped found the MIT Development Foundation to set up and profit from firms that turned the technology, developed at MIT into marketable products (*Business Week*, July 22, 1972). From 1957 to 1968, the number of high-technology, R&D-related firms increased by at

least eighty (Cambridge Community Development Program, 1972f) while 118 manufacturing firms left Cambridge (Barber, 1972, 3).

6. In July 1973, community pressures temporarily pushed the Kendall Square planning toward creating more blue-collar jobs. By cashing in on the good will of residents involved in the MIT Housing Program and some dislike of the style of radical opponents (Duehey, 1970a, 56–7), MIT prevailed. During the controversy, MIT said it might not certify certain Section 112 credits obtained by educational institutions for expenditures near urban renewal areas, if its Kendall Square plans were not approved ($6 million have been certified, $10.9 million were still uncertified). Concern then turned to the 24-acre Simplex Site MIT bought in 1969, probably for Institute housing or commercial development. To MIT's chagrin, the Cambridge City Council voted $10,000 to a community group for planning for the site.

7. A precursor to this trend occurred after World War II. Technology- and university-related professionals, who could not quite afford the huge homes of wealthy West Cambridge, dramatically affected the housing situation. What has been called "private urban renewal" (Duehey, 1970a, 16) involved remodeling, rehabilitating, and repairing whole blocks in less-expensive neighborhoods. In the process, old-time residents "who could not afford to refuse" (Duehey, 1970a, 16), sold their homes for much more than the previous value, raising property values and rents.

8. The ripple effect of development influenced other areas in Boston like the North Side of Beacon Hill through the creation of Government Center, and the South End through the building of the Prudential Center.

9. So devastating were the effects of these developmental forces on Cambridge that in the late 1960s many people believed in a "Master Plan" theory of development and transformation of Cambridge. "According to this theory the federal government has a Master Plan to transform Cambridge from a working-class city into the main national center for research and development of military and political technique" (Cambridge Tenants Organizing Committee, 1971, 3). Though unrealistically conspiratorial in terms of how and why changes are occurring (Cambridge Department of Planning and Development, 1973, 6, 17), the theory provides "insight into what is actually happening in the city" (Cambridge Tenants Organizing Committee, 1971, 8). *Suggested Goals for a Cambridge City Plan* (Cambridge Planning Board, 1965), moreover, which calls for decreased population, increased university and R&D sectors, and enlarged area to be occupied by such industry and schools (Shalom, 1969, 35, Harvard Strikers, 1969, 15). It claimed that "there is no inevitable 'market trend' to what the *Wilson Report* calls 'Harvardization'" (Harvard University, 1970, 42), but "that it must be deliberately encouraged." In support of this assertion, it mentions an unnamed Cambridge Redevelopment Authority study (which *Cambridge: Transformation of a Working Class City* claimed had a central role in "planning the entire process of Harvardization," producing "a class substitution process" in Cambridge (Harvard Strikers, 1969, 15, 1) on NASA plants elsewhere (in Cleveland, Pasadena, and San Francisco). It found the plants "have little effect on the surrounding town and industry," and brought no new industry, housing or services.

10. The "filtering theory" holds that building more market rate units will indirectly aid the poor: "through the efficient working of the 'filtering' process, newly

built houses will release older ones, which can then filter down to levels the poor can afford." Instead of raising incomes so low-income people can purchase adequate housing (or building more low-income units), the filtering process assumes prices of older housing will fall within the reach of the poor. The Committee for Economic Development (CED) adds, "Such an approach leaves the way open, obviously, to very low standards of housing for the poor, which even then may take a large share of their income" (1973, 20). A CED member added, "It has been repeatedly demonstrated that the 'filtering' theory simply does not work adequately" and urged a major program of housing allowances (CED, 1973, 57). See note 8 on filtering.

In the Cambridge situation, most tenants for new, higher-cost housing are moving from elsewhere and thus are not vacating present units that might serve in-Cambridge needs. Any housing vacated by people moving within Cambridge to higher cost housing, moreover, is usually quickly occupied by young professionals, and unrelated groups. who can afford high rents. This housing is typically at middle-income rents, which does not help low-income needs. In a tight market like Cambridge, both housing allowances and new subsidized construction are needed to aid low-income people.

11. Cambridge was the seventh most densely populated city in the United States, second in Massachusetts. Only two of its six and one half square miles are for residential use (Duehey, 1970a, 4). See data charts in Sobel (1975) for background.

12. In 1970, McNally and Mantel wrote: "The present Cambridge Housing Authority staff is only sufficient to do bookkeeping connected with rental and maintenance" (1970, 25). The CHA has a history of management and maintenance problems.

13. For a detailed discussion of the interrelations of various power and financial institutions on the housing situation in Cambridge, see Pynoos and Mollenkopt (1972) and Barber (1972).

14. Harvard President Pusey commissioned *The Wilson Report* in May 1968 to explore Harvard's relation to Cambridge and suggest ways to improve it. The 94-page report concentrates on the University's effect on the housing situation and recommends positive action in that area (Harvard University, 1970, 39–40). The report and committee take their name from the chairman and author, Harvard government professor, James Q. Wilson, a well-known, conservative author on city problems. See Wilson interviews 1973. Draft appeared late 1968; Final early 1969.

15. From 1961 to 1965, Massachusetts communities had a veto over highways planned to go through them. Diluted in 1963, it was removed in 1965 (Duehey, 1970f, 36).

16. From statements by MIT Attorney Edward Hanify and Chairman James R. Killian, February 20–22, 1966. The Hanify statement is now considered infamous even by Institute personnel: "Throughout Europe, the outlines of the great roads of ancient Rome are still visible, sad remnants of a civilization that has vanished, overrun by the tough invaders of its time. Will a traveler, centuries hence, trace the vestiges of the inner belt and sadly note that it was built at the cost of demolishing scientific facilities that might have effectively countered the blow that 'buried' us, to use Khrushchev's warning phrase?" The Killian statement (1966) also overstated the detrimental effects on MIT. That statement did, however, introduce the idea of Institute participation in relocation and community housing. "We stand ready to join

in sponsoring nonprofit, low-cost housing and in sharing in its financing if necessary. In addition, we stand ready to mobilize our own technical and professional resources to assist in finding solutions that will minimize problem created for displaced families and finding them in time, whatever the route may be chose" (Hanron, 1966).

17. In fact, three of the housing sites in East Cambridge and Cambridgeport fell in or near the proposed Inner Belt route. Commenting at the announcement in April 1969 on the connection to the Belt, MIT Chairman Killian said: "We are aware that the proposed Inner Belt Highway might touch several of our proposed projects. But we have been waiting twenty years on the Inner Belt and decided that it was not in the interest of the community to wait any longer" (*Boston Globe*, April 10, 1969). In giving intergovernmental acceptance of the MIT proposal in summer 1971, the Department of Transportation indicated that the Inner Belt was dead, though some Cantabrigians to this day fear resurrection.

18. Harvard's problems at Sachs Estate (also called Shady Hill or the Norton's Woods) were reflected in the fact that the only resolution defeated at the September 1968 Housing Convention was one in favor of the University's using the Estate for student housing to release other units for community use. That resolution was followed by a proposal that Harvard turn over the Estate for "use for low-cost public housing for elderly and families." Though Harvard faced opposition to its plans for use of Sachs Estate for from 60 to 300 houses as an attempted compromise, a group in Somerville opposed any housing on the wooded site. (Cambridge poet, e. e. cummings, who used to wander there, describe the Sachs Estate site, then called Norton's Wood, as a "mythical domain of semiwilderness separating cerebral Cambridge and orchidaceous Somerville" in his 1953 Harvard *i:six nonlectures,* p. 32.)

19. The approach of easing the housing crisis by building university housing has not worked well in Cambridge, where the number of university-related people is substantial. Donham reported in 1972, "Some pressure on local housing was removed by Harvard housing graduate students, but it is doubtful that the housing thus relieved reverted to community use." A study by the Department of Planning and Development in the City of Cambridge on secondary occupancy results from the occupancy of 94 new apartments at Putnam Avenue and Mt. Auburn St. revealed that students filled half of the vacated units "even though a careful selection process ensured that most of the tenants came from the Riverside area. Thus the construction of new subsidized units seems to increase the supply of private units available to University personnel" (Donham, 1972, 11).

20. This alleged quote has become infamous in Cambridge. According to the *Harvard Crimson*, George Bennet, University Treasurer and Corporation member actually said that Treeland was "too valuable to support practical low-income housing" (September 21, 1970). Ironically, the high cost of $540,000 Harvard paid for an alternate site at River and Howard Streets was an important factor in the demise of the first proposal for that site (see note 5, chapter 3).

21. A number of reports on housing became important during the 1971–74 controversy. In March 1971, a Harvard-issued report listed 4 projects and 520 community units it planned to help develop (Harvard University, 1971). In 1971–74, the Cambridge Community Development Program issued four reports on "Housing Needs

in Cambridge" (1971–73) about demand and markets in the city. These included a March 1972 report that recommended that "University housing might even attempt to combine student and family quarters in a single development" (Cambridge Community Development Program, 1972b, 37). In May 1972, the Committee of Concerned Alumni formed at a reunion meeting after the 1970 Student Strike, and subsequently supporting winning candidates for the Harvard Board of Overseers, issued a detailed critique of Harvard and a mixed housing proposal on "Harvard and Housing in Cambridge" (Donham, 1972). In October, the Harvard Office of Government and Community Affairs issued its own "Report to the Cambridge Community" (Harvard University, October 1972), concentrating on housing issues and their effects on Cambridge. And in June 1974, Harvard issued a preliminary Master Plan for review by interested people and community groups (Harvard Planning Office, 1974).

22. Harvard also owned the almost 200 rental units near the Medical School in Boston that became the focus of the Roxbury Tenants of Harvard/Affiliated Hospitals Complex controversy in 1969. Once guilty of neighborhood deterioration, the University, in response to community pressures, became a model landlord, even subsidizing rents for a period of time. (See Part II here, "Mission Park Housing in Boston.")

23. Finding responsible landlords is difficult because private owners typically invest in housing for profit rather than to serve a community need. This was especially so when many Boston area landlords were earlier converting apartments into condominiums, which pay better and involve less landlord-tenant conflicts. But most condo units are too expensive for low-income people. A vice-president said of Northgate's demise, "perhaps we're shirking an obligation."

24. Despite its close ties to the two universities, the Cambridge Corporation was different from "development" corporations like the Morningside Heights Corporation at Columbia University, University of Chicago's South West Hyde Park Neighborhood Redevelopment Corporation, or University of Pennsylvania West Philadelphia Corporation, whose main tasks have involved institutional expansion and related profit-making developments.

25. In the *Report to the Cambridge Community* in October 1972, Harvard wrote: "The University views the Cambridge Corporation—an independent organization operating with community participation and jointly funded by Harvard and MIT at a total cost of $600,000—as the vital element in Cambridge housing. In response to community wishes and in keeping with its own analysis, Harvard intends to relate to the Cambridge Corporation in a way that will minimize the University's own operational role in this field" (Harvard University, 1972, 9) (underlined in original).

26. Antony Herrey wrote, "There is no way that the Cambridge Corporation could have acquired the land, obtained the financial commitments, etc., for MIT's 1,600-unit proposal. No one—including the Cambridge Corporation itself—had ever envisioned it would undertake projects of this magnitude" (February 11, 1975).

Chapter Two

The MIT Projects

"A Housing Program in Cambridge"

In April 1969, with great fanfare, MIT announced "A Housing Program in Cambridge." The proposal provided for 1,600 units of community housing on five sites controlled by MIT. Developed by the Institute Real Estate Office after months of preparation, the proposal included 750 units for low-income elderly and families and 850 at market rates. The 1,600 units constituted a proposed increase of 5 percent in the city's housing stock. Included in this announcement were plans to lease fifty units of MIT-controlled, Northgate Community Corporation housing to the Cambridge Housing Authority for low-income tenants. The Institute also indicated it would build, or convert, space on campus for an additional 800 students. Anticipating little future Institute growth, MIT proposed the new university housing and increased on-campus facilities to lessen the housing crisis in Cambridge (*Boston Herald Traveler*, April 10, 1969).

The 1,600 community housing units in MIT proposals were divided into several projects. MIT proposed about 200 low-cost elderly and family units for each of three sites in North, Central, and East Cambridge. Also in eastern Cambridge on Portland Street, the Institute proposed an 800-unit mixed development of 200 subsidized and 600 market rate housing units. It proposed another 250 market rate units for a business area on Massachusetts Avenue, not far from the MIT campus. MIT owned or leased the land for the units and would be the developer in each case.

The main MIT projects were originally referred to by their street names: Clarendon Avenue in North Cambridge, Gore Street in East Cambridge, and Hamilton Street in Cambridgeport. They were subsequently renamed: Daniel F. Burns Apartments (Clarendon Avenue), Miller's River (Gore Streets), and Lyndon B. Johnson (Hamilton Street) Apartments. Because the Portland Street (800 mixed apartments) and Massachusetts Avenue (250 market-rate

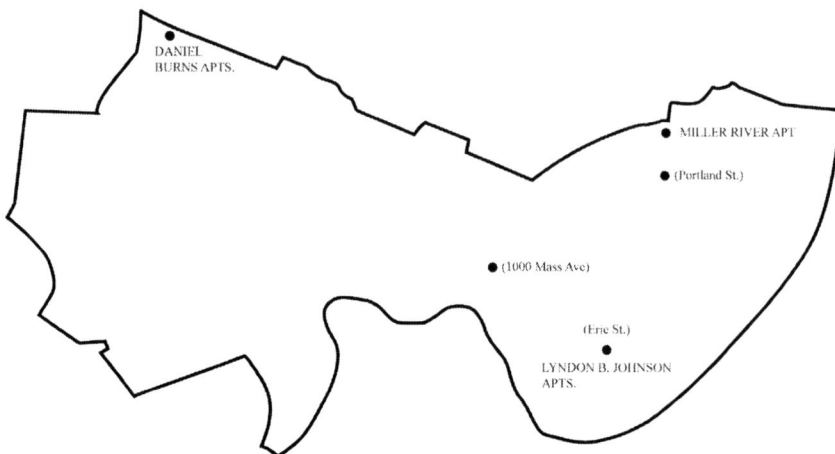

Map 2.1.   MIT-Related Projects
Credit: R. Sobel and H. Kim

units) were not built, this chapters focuses on the three main completed MIT projects.

In making its proposals, MIT indicated that the community would have to work with the Institute in determining the actual number of units to be built, the mix of elderly and family units at each site, and the physical character of the developments. Months of discussion with many members of the community, financing sources, and government officials changed the original proposal considerably. The formal submissions to the Housing Authority in January 1971 for 700 units in three developments was close to the 750 subsidized elderly and family units originally proposed but far less than the April 1969 announcement of a 1,600-unit development (MIT, 1971).

RESULTS OF THE HOUSING PROGRAM

What has been built, and how it was accomplished, are well worth observing. There are 684 elderly public housing units, built under the Federal Turnkey I Program, on three sites in different parts of Cambridge.[1] In North Cambridge on the Clarendon Avenue site, there are now 199 units of high-rise elderly housing in Daniel F. Burns Apartments. In East Cambridge on Gore Street sits the largest development, 304 elderly units in a nineteen-story building of Millers River Apartments, with a multipurpose center adjacent to the site. On Hamilton Street in Cambridgeport sit 181 elderly units in a six-story building, with a twelve-story tower, in the Lyndon B. Johnson Apartments. If plans for sixteen townhouses for families on the adjacent Erie Street had been realized, the 200-unit target at Erie and Hamilton Streets would have been reached.

Though heights, sizes, and building massings are quite different, the system of precast concrete is the same throughout. The light color, architectural style, details, and specifications on all three sites are identical. Each project has a medical clinic, activity rooms, including a large multipurpose space, and a lounge with TV. There are gardens and parking, and public transportation is nearby. The units are one-bedroom and efficiencies, designed so that both types have distinguishable bedroom and living room areas, adequate closets, kitchens, and balconies. Each has safety features for the elderly like emergency cords and grab bars in the bath. Though there are complaints about the small size (about 435 square feet for efficiencies due to federal maximum standards), most early residents were happy. Some of the elderly residents, used to three-story houses, were also disconcerted by the idea of living so high above the ground. The north and east Cambridge buildings seem huge in the scale of the surrounding neighborhoods.

THE ECONOMICS OF HOUSING

Under Turnkey I, MIT developed the three projects in accordance with requirements of the Cambridge Housing Authority and the federal Department of Housing and Urban Development (HUD). The Institute acquired the sites, did preliminary planning, obtained construction financing, worked with the community and hired the consultants and contractors who built the project. When each building was conveyed to the Housing Authority upon completion (Turnkey), it paid MIT the agreed price, designed to return MIT's direct costs. This ended MIT's role, except for a year's performance responsibility. The CHA selected tenants and managed the projects.

Rents were the same as other public housing projects. Tenants, who must have income below statutory maximums, paid 25 percent of their earnings for rent. The proceeds of long-term bonds, whose debt service was paid by the federal government, covered capital costs, and the rents cover maintenance expenses. Unit costs ran about $25,000, $3,000 more than the next bid, but the additional funds went into improved quality, not profit. Especially in family public housing, rents did not cover all maintenance costs, which had then to be subsidized, to prevent deterioration. Elderly housing is something of a profit center, on the other hand.

The total project cost was $17.7 million. Construction financing was obtained through a loan from the Massachusetts Housing Finance Agency at a below-market 5.05 percent. For obtaining sites, options, and preliminary architectural work, MIT had to advance at its own risk about $1.3 million. Direct costs of $17,092,000 were repaid at conveyance, but extensive staff, overhead, and miscellaneous cost—running over half a million dollars—had to be absorbed by the Institute. MIT went into the project with a "no profit/no loss" attitude. Property tax revenues to the City of Cambridge from the three sites were expected to total $250,000 more than the $65,000 for housing from previous uses. The increase in property tax revenue for this public housing was somewhat ironic since some urban renewal luxury developments return less revenue after tax abatements or because a site has lain empty for several years (Rowland, 1973, 10).

THE PROCESS AND COMMUNITY PARTICIPATION

Though specifics and problems for each site differ, the history of the development process for each of the elderly housing sites was very similar (Herrey, 1969; MIT, 1971; Mathiasen, 1971; Kaiser, 1969). MIT completed arrangements to acquire the sites and conducted detailed feasibility studies before involving the community or making its plans public. After announcing the proposal, Institute people spoke to many neighborhood, community, and civic groups about plans. They held open houses, gathered support for the zoning changes, which the City Council enacted almost unanimously, and took elderly citizens on information-gathering bus tours. They worked out design details, and adopted ideas from the community groups wherever possible.

This process accomplished much before the decision to build community housing was finally made and the housing program was made public. The Institute Real Estate Office began assembling sites by early 1967, before their specific future uses for a likely highway were precisely defined, and in secret to avoid escalating prices if MIT's role became known. MIT established its internal development approach, and targeted which community groups to contact. The Turnkey program, plus Massachusetts' Housing Finance Construction financing, was selected in late 1968 as a result of an intensive search by the Institute Real Estate Office for the most favorable financing of its proposal.[2]

MIT very consciously structured the development of the project and community participation. The director of the Institute Real Estate Office, Antony Herrey, created a "Development Team" approach to the planning process, with a clear "chain of command" (Kamilewicz, 1971, 6). Using this unique and effective, though rather overly MIT-controlled and preplanned method, a central staff with expertise in all areas of development—architecture, real estate, construction—work with consultants, support staff, and community in a systematically planned manner. Each central staff member, besides having responsibility for his technical area, was assigned Project Manager to know the people of his area and steward one of the housing projects to completion. All subsequent steps, from meeting community people, "educating the community," and working in planning sessions, to getting enough, absolutely necessary, community support for zoning changes were part of the system. A paper by an MIT project manager, "Relevant Housing through the Use of Information Systems" explained the details of the system (Kamilewicz, 1971). A noteworthy aspect of this system is that it allows for a two-way flow of education: "education [of MIT] by the Community groups," as well as "education of the Community groups" by MIT (Kamilewicz, 1971, 12, 14).

North Cambridge: A Start

Work with the residents near the site of the North Cambridge project for Clarendon Avenue began soon after they proposed the project in September 1968, eight months before the full housing program was announced. A Cambridge Corporation staff member, working with MIT, interviewed about fifty families to get their opinions about their area and its housing needs. In essence, he was doing community organizing for MIT, because a community group had to exist, or be created, for the MIT development process to work.[3] Such a group also had to be favorable, or at least neutral, to working with MIT on housing. While discussions with the North Cambridge residents continued, the September 1968 Housing Convention was also negotiating with MIT and Harvard on community housing needs of the city.

THE COMPLETE HOUSING PROGRAM IN CAMBRIDGE

Once MIT made the announcement of the complete Housing Program in Cambridge during April 1969, the Institute Real Estate Office and MIT Community Relations staffs began talking more widely. They told people in the affected communities and city agencies details of the program, and consulted them on their ideas. In East Cambridge especially, and also in Cambridgeport, the south central section of the city, U.S. Office of Economic Opportunity (OEO) planning teams already existed. Planning and participation focused on the groups and their executive committees. Near the site for the Portland Street project, which was eventually abandoned, Model Cities and local neighbors were involved in the planning. The North Cambridge process continued. Citywide groups, such as the Cambridge Committee of Elders, who would express major interest in the internal design, Model Cities, and the Cambridge Housing Convention, were contacted. Civic groups like the Cambridge Advisory Committee and the Cambridge Chamber of Commerce were also informed. MIT was in continual contact with federal, state and local government agencies, especially HUD, the Massachusetts Housing Finance Agency, and the Cambridge Housing Authority.

Achieving the community participation for the MIT projects was a delicate process. It involved not only overcoming initial suspicion about MIT's motives but it also required showing an appreciation for various community characteristics and desires. In East Cambridge, the Institute had to appreciate that the neighborhood was a very community-conscious, multi-ethnic area and home of a popular city councillor. Significant Italian and elderly groups live in the area, and both were socially and politically important in Cambridge. Both North Cambridge and Cambridgeport presented especially delicate problems for valid community involvement.

In North Cambridge, the Institute encountered suspicion because this was a "non-MIT" area. Another potential problem occurring was that one side of the Clarendon Avenue housing site consisted of white, middle-class families, while the other side was black families. The two communities had been separated since the nineteenth century by an old shoe factory on the site MIT acquired. Meetings and discussions were conducted with each group separately before they were joined at an open house in October. The potential divisive situation around class and race was somewhat addressed because the head of the Committee of Elders was both a senior citizen and a member of the Black community. The accomplishments should be viewed in the context of MIT and the Cambridge Corporation's organizing the community participation "from the ground up." Despite progress on many fronts, the North Cambridge communities could not be swayed from their opposition to low-income families in their area. So none of the family housing proposed there was built as part of Daniel F. Burns Apartments on Clarendon Avenue (30 Churchill Street) shown in picture 2.1. On the other hand, the community did agree to almost fifty more dwelling units than had been originally proposed there.

In Cambridgeport, though the existence of the OEO planning team helped, there was tension between long-established residents and recently arrived younger renters. As opposed to North Cambridge, where suspicion was aroused in a non-MIT area, Cambridgeport was close to the Institute and familiar with both unpopular Institute activities and the influx of MIT and Harvard students into the area. As picture 2.2 shows, this is where Lyndon B. Johnson Apartments were built at Erie and Hamilton Streets.

Picture 2.1. Daniel F. Burns Apartments
Credit: Cambridge Corporation

Picture 2.2. Lyndon B. Johnson Apartments
Credit: Cambridge Corporation

Mix of Housing

After initial information and discussion meetings followed the April 1969 announcement, regular discussions and neighborhood meetings continued in each area through December to work out plans and details for the respective sites. At the planning meetings, neighbors of each site discussed their preferences for elderly versus family units and what social and commercial facilities they wanted. They also expressed their feelings on size and heights of the buildings, shapes of rooms, amenities, materials, parking, and other details.

Support for the Projects

Following initial contact and planning, MIT organized an open house at each of the three housing sites. These colorful events were successfully held in large tents on three Saturdays in October 1969. Hundreds of residents had the chance to talk to MIT and city officials, view the building and site models, and ask questions. They also could sign petitions to change the zoning on each of the sites to permit the proposed housing. The zoning changes were from industrial or low density residential to high density residential, allowing more units per acre and reducing total cost per unit. Additional community meetings were held soon after this to officially endorse the MIT zoning petitions.

In a political city like Cambridge, zoning changes do not come easily, as Harvard well knows about its Sachs Estate Project, and zoning exceptions must have the strong community support which MIT carefully generated. MIT's efforts were so successful that the petitions were endorsed by each community organization involved, hundreds of residents, and the Cambridge Housing Convention's housing subcommittee. From November 1969 to January 1970, while the zoning changes were being heard and approved, the Institute sponsored bus tours for elderly community members to study the physical features of other housing developments in the Boston area. In December 1969, the City Council unanimously granted the changes.

THE PLANS FOR THE HOUSING PROGRAM

Though MIT's original projections included mixes of elderly and family housing, the final proposal would become entirely elderly units. North Cambridge residents expressed strong opposition to any low-income family development in their area, and only agreed to 199 elderly units in Daniel F. Burns Apartments on Clarendon Avenue. In East Cambridge, where a large elderly population resided, residents requested more than the 200 elderly units allotted and received 304 for the Millers River development for Gore Street (15 Lambert St.), shown in picture 2.3.[4] They also recommended that MIT buy an adjacent garage for common and commercial space, which the Institute staff believed was highly desirable.

In Cambridgeport, the community wanted a mix of elderly and family units, though heavily weighted toward the elderly. The plan for 181 elderly and sixteen family units reflected this in the Lyndon B. Johnson Apartments on Hamilton Street. The desires of the people near the Portland Street site were clearly for a low-density, low-rise development, which could not be made part of an economically feasible program and led to the eventual abandoning of the project. The site owners wanted a more economical and profitable high-rise development, which neighbors knew would change the character of the area. Opposition to low-rent family housing for the proposed sixteen unit development on Erie Street was less evident here, but the combination of economics and preferences made unfeasible family housing there and the 800-unit Portland Street project of badly needed, predominantly family units.

Interior Design of the Units

Community participation was less intense as the program moved to the internal design stage. In March 1970, the MIT Real Estate Office chose Benjamin Thompson of Cambridge as architect, after extensive interviewing of over fifty Greater Boston firms. MIT selected Thompson for his design ability and sensitivity to the environment. No community members were involved

Picture 2.3. Millers River Apartments
Credit: Cambridge Corporation

in this important decision. Thompson provided quality work, though some non-design problems arose.

The housing subcommittee of the Committee of Elders was particularly helpful in working out interior design features and amenities in a series of seven meetings with MIT from May 1 to July 1. Survey questionnaires by the Cambridgeport and East Cambridge planning teams also gathered design data. These meetings and surveys culminated in a detailed report on recommendations for housing features. Zoning restrictions, HUD requirements and the high preponderance of single elderly residents resulted in about 80 percent of the units being efficiencies. People wanted more one-bedroom units, which HUD rules prohibited single elderly from occupying and could not be changed. An idea proposed by an elderly resident to provide efficiencies with a sleeping "alcove"

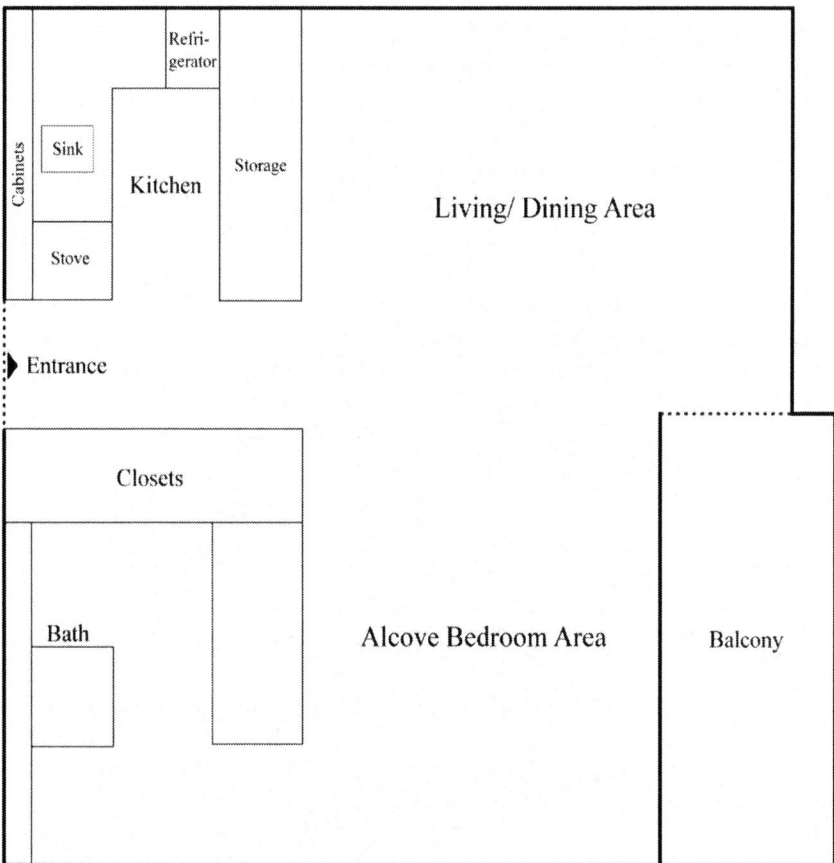

Picture 2.4. Schematic of Efficiency with Alcove Bedroom
Credit: R. Sobel and H. Kim

in place of a bedroom became a good compromise, as picture 2.4 demonstrates. Other design features suggested or required were emergency call buttons, closed circuit TV security, support bars for the bathtubs, balconies (a neighborhood desire), and communal space on the first floor. Ten percent of the units were reserved for those with disabilities.

THE BID

The Cambridge Housing Authority formally requested proposals for a "Turn-key" development in November 1970. Various developers, including MIT, made submissions in January 1971. While completing their submission, "A Housing Program in Cambridge: A Proposal for Turnkey Construction," the Institute conducted a survey in December 1969 and January 1970 to determine interest and demand for the housing. Though somewhat late to do a survey, the 500 questionnaires in Italian, Portuguese, Greek, Polish, and English served several purposes. It communicated the arrival of the project and encouraged sign-ups. It also rebutted skeptical cries of "too many projects" from opponents of low-income housing through a strong, positive response.

In April 1971, the Housing Authority recommended the approval of MIT's proposal for 684 units and in May HUD approved it. Despite the unit costs well above other bidders, the Institute had community support, sites in hand, hard-to-come-by zoning changes, and considerable stature in Cambridge and Washington, DC.[5] MIT's proposal also stressed opportunities for employment and training of low-income and minority residents as a selling point. The Cambridge Housing Authority might have preferred another bidder, but no one else controlled land or had the necessary zoning. Other developers suggested Kendall Square as an available site. The decision in favor of MIT caused some consternation among other bidders because of the higher costs and the feelings that politics affected the decision. MIT's additional costs, however, went into improved quality for the occupants, rather than increased profits by a private investor.

In June 1971, the Cambridge Housing Authority and MIT signed an agreement for the 684 units of Turnkey housing for the elderly on the three sites. About a month later, in the course of clearing the project with government agencies, MIT learned that plans for the Inner Belt, in whose route two of the MIT housing sites lay, had been dropped by the Massachusetts Department of Transportation. An official groundbreaking for the Housing Program in Cambridge, attended by hundreds of people, occurred on October 21, 1971.

Building Housing

During construction, community participation declined, while project teams continued their work and supervision. In January and February 1973, three open houses for a model efficiency apartment were held at the Gore Street site in East Cambridge. In spite of a blizzard, with bus transportation provided, several hundred city residents visited and commented on a pleasant model unit incorporating the alcove bedroom. Most people at the open houses seemed pleased. Another open house took place on August 9, 1973, at the formal dedication of the Hamilton Street site and over 2,500 people attended. A final open house after the completion in North Cambridge did not occur.

Occupancy began in October 1973 at the 181 unit Lyndon B. Johnson Apartments on Hamilton Street and in November at 199 unit Daniel F. Burns Apartments on Clarendon Avenue, after a slight delay for a ceiling leakage, problems that MIT addressed as part of their one-year performance responsibility. The largest project, Millers River (of 304 units) Apartments on Gore Street, was occupied in February 1974. MIT was to complete a multi-use center adjacent to the site by early 1976. But the center and the proposed 16 units of family housing for Erie Street were not built.

The housing units were placed under the management of the Cambridge Housing Authority. At one time, there was a proposal that a community management company work with the residents on participatory management. Though an MIT project manager praised the idea of "people beginning to control their destinies," MIT dropped the idea of community management because the Cambridge Housing Authority would likely not approve it. CHA would benefit, financially and otherwise, from running new and efficient projects like the MIT ones. And the decision to let the CHA manage the project turned out to be a point of contention, since the Authority had a history of problems in management and maintenance of other projects.[6]

PERSPECTIVE ON PARTICIPATION AND PARTNERSHIP

In the development process for community housing in Cambridge, the role of the community was inferior to that of MIT. The Institute made and controlled most of the basic decisions; the community fit into the MIT-defined parameters. MIT identified all possible groups to participate. MIT organized the entire process and said where and how the community would participate. MIT created the "development team approach." Through the Cambridge Corporation, MIT even employed community organizers to form a group for the MIT-defined process where no appropriate group existed in North Cambridge. Community organizing, however, is traditionally a method for powerless community groups to get something from an institution like a powerful university, and not to "manage" communities.

MIT proposed the target number of units and bought the sites for the projects before beginning to involve the community. Community discussion began in North Cambridge before the September 1969 MIT announcement, but this was after site acquisition and planning had begun. MIT involved the community, in segmented ways, in what was basically an MIT process; the community decided only the number and type of units, and what the design criteria would be. MIT allowed for community participation, but did not let the community set the scope, style, and mode. The community could not initiate new projects, though it could veto proposals, or deny support for zoning change. The community did not have a role in the crucial initial decisions and assumptions of the project. Even well into the process and after a period of working together, the community's role remained circumscribed: the community had no part in choosing the architect. These facts supported on an initial suspicion that "MIT came to tell them what MIT planned" (Shalom, 1969, 31).

Community Participation Not Totally Indispensable

The community's role, albeit an important one to MIT, was neither a totally involved one nor even indispensable. In the "development team approach" described in "Relevant Housing through Information Systems," community participation was to be included only at a point and style when MIT defined it as "necessary to go to the various groups in the community for inputs" (Kamilewicz, 1971, 9). Even after two years of work with the community, the MIT proposal to the Housing Authority (MIT, 1971) indicated that MIT did not see community participation as a *sine qua non*, but rather something of an appendage in creating community housing; while "sure" that community participation was of incalculable benefit, "it is possible that our development program could have been prepared far earlier in the absence of such efforts" in community relations. MIT did not say "we could not have built Community housing without community participation."

While MIT gave reasons for limiting community participation, they failed to deal with the inviolability of community involvement in community projects. For instance, while secrecy kept costs down when the university bought land for community housing, highway relocations, or university expansion, it also kept the community in the dark about the purposes of the acquisitions. This virtually eliminated the possibility of the community's initially affecting or protesting the purposes. Also, while housing was needed and demanded by Cambridge—and might have been built somewhat faster without community involvement—without community participation it might not have fit community needs in design or mix, or it might have been seen as legitimate. The community might even have opposed and delayed such housing as paternalistic. In terms of the "Ladder of Community Participation" (Arnstein, 1969), MIT allowed for community participation somewhere between "placation" (5) and "partnership" (6) (when "citizen control" is best [8]).

Human Concerns

There is no doubt, however, that MIT showed interest and concern for community members and their housing problems, and that the Institute helped solve the problems. MIT staff members were concerned about and developed rapport with the people they worked with, and the staff members devoted hundreds of hours to the project. The great affection and friendship that community members expressed for the MIT staff provided testimony to this.

But is concern enough when dealing with such a complex social process? Were there areas in which the community could not benefit because of the nature and style of MIT-defined participation? While the community was treated well and was provided with housing, did it get as much new confidence, technical skills, cohesion and power for future growth as it could have if it had participated thoroughly in all the development aspects? In terms of community development, could the participants in the MIT process repeat the development process without MIT's help? Did the community gain power for fulfilling its other needs?

The Limits of the MIT Process

Could MIT appreciate that it could not legitimately define all the limits and style of community participation? Did it treat the community as an equal partner to the technological Institute? Did MIT realize that it might exclude essential community perspectives, desires, and interests by defining the goals and process without a complete community role? In an aptly named thesis, "A Housing Program in Cambridge: A Management Problem," Karen Mathiasen questioned "whether or not community participation could, or should be a learning experience for MIT" (Mathiasen, 1971, 15). Because of important structural differences between a university and a community, "it is not clear to what extent MIT is organized to learn about [community desires and life style] or to what extent the Community is able to communicate them" (Mathiasen, 1971, 87).

How was this gap to be overcome? MIT's style toward the community was essentially a technical, professional, pre-planned "MIT-like" approach, though refined by concerned individuals. Was this enough to overcome, or to be sure MIT fully understood differences in lifestyle, class, culture, needs, and interests? Or was it essentially just enough to serve MIT's interests?

MIT relied heavily on professionals and favored fostering community participations just for housing development, as opposed to creating or strengthening autonomous community organizations, which might work on interests that did not include MIT's. While MIT was involved in community organization, the structuring of community participation generally precluded possible conflict with MIT. While this type of "organizing" might have saved MIT potential disagreements, it also means that people organized essentially to "participate" are less likely to be able to take future independent action on reforms or restructuring, like improving the city's housing function, which might help them and MIT.

While acknowledging that the positions here are stated "fairly—and eloquently" and "that all . . . comments are valid," Antony Herrey "cannot agree" with them (personal communication, February 11, 1975). While he feels the "position might have been more acceptable" if MIT had not risked its own resources ($1 million to $2 million), he feels "MIT should not be criticized for defending its own interests," which in this case were "construed as getting the housing built. . . . After all, MIT is not a public agency," he added and claimed "that no housing would have resulted if MIT had worked with the community before obtaining sites." From his perspective, in the 1968–1971 period "getting the housing produced was even more important than process." The point, however, is that MIT's interests—defined very much in MIT-credibility-supporting results—conflict with the community developmental process of genuine and total community involvement: authentic process and effective results.[7]

"A HOUSING PROGRAM IN CAMBRIDGE" IN OVERVIEW

As a first effort in building Community/University housing on a large scale, MIT's Housing Program in Cambridge was beneficial. But answering the questions and criticisms it generated, particularly about the limits of its approach, are crucial to creating co-equal participation in joint community/university partnership.[8] MIT built 684 elderly public housing units under Turnkey I on three sites in Cambridge. These include the 181 Lyndon B. Johnson units at Hamilton Street in Cambridgeport, 199 Daniel F. Burns units at Clarendon Avenue in North Cambridge, and 304 Millers River units at Gore Street in East Cambridge. While only 684 units of the announced 1,600 were realized, and the proposed low-income family units were eliminated, MIT's community housing efforts made a significant contribution to and created a model for university assistance in improving the housing problems in Cambridge.[9]

NOTES

1. The HUD Turnkey Program created in 1966 was intended to cut the inefficiencies and delays of direct government building by employing a private developer. The developer builds the project following government guidelines and "turns the key" and

project over to the local housing authority. MIT's requested a Turnkey I allocation of 700 units but they received 684 because HUD would not accept the high cost of the proposed sixteen townhouses. (Another local developer got a Turnkey allocation of twenty units on Clifton Street.) Deferred in 1973, it became doubtful that the sixteen townhouse units for families planned for Erie Street would be built.

2. The decision to employ the Turnkey I Program emerged from a thorough search by MIT of all possible options and approaches, many meetings with HUD, and consultations with numerous community people. In November 1968, moreover, the head of the Cambridge Corporation, Oliver Brooks, specifically recommended the advantages of the program in a letter to the presidents of both MIT and Harvard. The North Cambridge project, announced in September 1968, was originally proposed as a Section 221d3 subsidy project, but was ultimately included under Turnkey when the public housing approach was chosen.

3. This is at least the second time establishment groups used of a community organizer in Cambridge. In November 1963, after the recent defeat of urban renewal plans in East Cambridge, the Cambridge Redevelopment Authority hired Morris Kritzman to act as liaison and to organize in the community. His conditions for working, however, included, unlike the MIT approach in 1968, the option of organizing against urban renewal if the citizens opposed it. His efforts helped to create a successful urban renewal process (Duehey, 1970b, 37). See note 8 below on community organizing.

4. In March 1969, East Cambridge voters passed a referendum 423–3 asking the Wellington-Harrington Urban Renewal Citizens Committee, Model Cities, and the Housing Authority "to construct a great many units of low-income housing for the elderly." This vote addressed a four-acre urban renewal site where 54 houses were scheduled, but it indicated sentiment about the need for elderly housing in East Cambridge (Duehey, 1970b, 62). Two hundred elderly units were suggested at the time, but only 56 units of family housing, Harwell Homes, were ultimately built on two acres at the site. The Wellington-Harrington story includes the community defeat of urban renewal in 1962, followed by a successful community-directed neighborhood improvement after 1967 (see Duehey, 1970b).

5. MIT's unit costs were unclear. The 684 units at $17.1 million cost $25,000 per unit. Yet Mathiasen (1971, 55–56) claims the unit costs were $27,700, about $5,000 above other bids. This suggests the total project costs would have been almost $19 million.

6. The generally discredited CHA was in some danger of being taken over by the Commonwealth. An example of the problems created when an old agency runs an innovative project was the lack of a CHA preoccupancy program for a smooth transition for the elderly into the MIT projects. The CHA, moreover, was no more able to deal with housing problems after MIT (and Harvard) helped it. In fact, the universities assistance took much pressure off the CHA and the City to improve their own capacities to solve problems.

7. As the Mission Park project shows about community involvement there from the start and fulfilling the need for both elderly and family units, process and results can occur together. Just concentrating on the physical results alone loses the importance of the human development of a community and its members. See Curvin, 1975.

8. Another important point about the MIT-created structure of community participation is elucidated in Fish (1973) about The Woodlawn Organization (TWO) and the University of Chicago. Willard Congrieve of the University of Chicago wrote about a joint education project: Where a strong community organization "does not exist, we doubt the wisdom and integrity of the professionals alone will do the job. . . . Where a community organization does not exist, one of the first things . . . a university interested in local reform should try to do is help create such an organization, with the full knowledge that it will eventually create conflict with the very institution which helped it come into existence" (Fish, 1973, 198). See also note 3 above on organizing.

9. In June 2000, MIT reported on continuing community housing efforts. "Affordable Community Housing, MIT's commitment to enhancing the affordability of housing follows from a history of contributions made over the past three decades. In the 1970s, MIT constructed 700 turnkey units of housing for the elderly in three neighborhoods in Cambridge. During the 1980s and 1990s, as part of the University Park development, MIT made a commitment to build 400 units of housing, including 150 units of affordable housing. The total number of units has climbed to 650—over 50 percent more units than originally proposed. The affordable units are distributed among the buildings along Brookline Street" (MIT, 2000), web.mit.edu/president/ communications/Building.pdf.

Chapter Three

Harvard-Related Community Housing Projects in Cambridge

In September 1969, Harvard proposed four major university-assisted community housing projects for Cambridge. First, it planned to build 94 elderly units at 2 Mt. Auburn Street in the Putnam Square Apartments. Second, it proposed 116 mixed family and elderly units at Inman Square. Third, it planned 36 mainly family units at River and Howard Streets in Riverside. Fourth, it developed proposals for up to 325 family and elderly units for the Blair Pond area in West Cambridge.

Two of the four planned projects were ultimately built there: the 94 elderly units at Putnam Square Apartments at 2 Mt. Auburn Street and the 116 mixed family and elderly units at Inman Square at Cambridge and Prospect Streets. After the 1973 U.S. housing freeze killed its first conception, the Riverside development later made progress. Blair Pond housing was stopped on environmental grounds, though local opposition to low-income family housing was also a major factor in its demise. Two other preliminary proposals for the Sachs Estate and Treeland-Bindery sites were abandoned earlier in the planning process.

PUTNAM SQUARE APARTMENTS
AT 2 MT. AUBURN STREET

The first completed community housing project in Cambridge was the Harvard-assisted Putnam Square Apartments for the elderly at 2 Mt. Auburn Street. The 94 units at public housing rents of one-quarter of monthly income are in a twelve-story tower on the north edge of Riverside. The Harvard Corporation requested a proposal for the project soon after the Harvard Strike in 1969. By the end of that summer, the Corporation approved the project, and

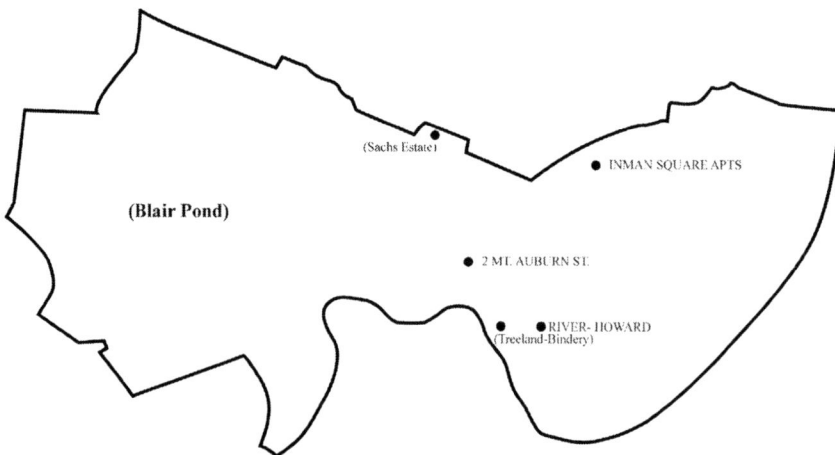

Map 3.1.　Harvard-Related Projects
Credit: R. Sobel and H. Kim

leased the land for fifty years at $500 per year. Developed by the Cambridge Corporation, construction began in November 1970. The project, shown in picture 3.1, was completed a year later in November 1971.

Community Role

The Cambridge Corporation carried through the major responsibilities for 2 Mt Auburn, including working with the community groups. The housing subcommittee of the Riverside Neighborhood Association (different from the Riverside Community Corporation) and the Council on Aging worked with the Cambridge Corporation on development and design. Obtaining public housing rent-levels through federal leases, the Riverside Neighborhood Association and the Cambridge Corporation conducted tenant selections, with first priority to the elderly of Riverside. A private management firm, Saunders Associates ran the project.

Physical Features

The 94-unit building, now called Putnam Square Apartments, is a pleasant, gray, corrugated-concrete structure. Twelve stories tall, it blends fairly well with its rather high surroundings. Though some find it unattractive, it has a nice scale and is comfortable inside. A game room and lounge adjoin the lobby, and a laundry room is located on the top floor. There is also a com-

Picture 3.1. Putnam Square Apartments
Credit: Cambridge Corporation

munity room/terrace at the top, with a good view of Cambridge and Boston. The 84 one-bedroom and ten efficiency apartments are slightly awkward in design; kitchen cabinets are high and electrical outlets are low. As in the MIT housing, there are safety features like emergency call buttons. Most residents seem to enjoy the facilities and what goes on inside. A social worker helps them with their needs.

Financing

The financing of the project through a $2,130,000 mortgage loan came from the Massachusetts Housing Finance Agency (MHFA) by sale of tax-exempt State Bonds. The MHFA loan was at 5.915 percent, 1.25 percent below the market, and would be repaid over forty years until 2009 from rents and government subsidies for costs, that the rents do not cover.[1] Though a 90 percent mortgage, it would cover all the construction costs ($1,830,000) because the gift of land covered 10 percent of the equity. Harvard contributed the land for about 10 percent of its market value, cutting project costs by over 10 percent. The three-tenths of an acre site, bought by the university several years before, was made available at $500 per year for fifty years through 2019, $25,000 in all, on a $250,000 property. In making the land available, Harvard and the Cambridge Corporation incurred $25,000 in expenses for removing houses and preparing the site. These costs were regained through selling tax shelters.

Basic to the project was the federal rent subsidy. The program used was Section 10(c) leasing in the 1937 Public Housing Act. These forty-year leases permitted tenants to pay public housing rent levels, 25 percent of their available income. Some tenants of 2 Mt. Auburn earn so little that the "Baby Brooke"[2] subsidy had to make up the difference between what Section 10(c) pays and 25 percent of income. The average rent was about $50, which called for an annual federal subsidy of $129,500. Sensible and effective, these subsidies were difficult to obtain; now they are no longer available. The head of the co-developer Cambridge Corporation estimated it took twenty trips to Washington and New York to get the leasing subsidy approved.

Federal income tax shelters covered part of the equity and other costs. This was the most innovative, technical, and somewhat controversial aspect of the subsidy. The general partner in the development was a profit-making subsidiary of the nonprofit Cambridge Corporation. It syndicated tax shelters through a brokerage firm under the tax law of 1969. Wealthy individuals became limited, non-controlling partners to defer income taxes by "buying" depreciation from the project. In this way the Cambridge Corporation raised about 14 percent of the project cost, just under $200,000 net. This money covered overhead amenities and staff expenses on this and future projects.

Finally, a substantial savings was also obtained through tax abatement. The City receives only 10 percent of total annual shelter rents averaging about $35 per unit or about $3,300 in yearly taxes, on a $2 million project, and a $257,000 lot.[3]

INMAN SQUARE

The other Harvard-related community housing project completed in Cambridge is Inman Square, located at the northwest corner of the Cambridge Model Cities area, at Prospect and Cambridge Streets. It consists of 116 units of low- and moderate-income housing units for families and the elderly finished in early 1974. This twelve-story tower, here in picture 3.2, includes nineteen townhouses in one-, two-, and one four-bedroom units, topped by eight floors for 97 units of elderly housing.[4]

The Housing Committee of the Cambridge Model Cities Program conceived the project about 1970. The group was concerned both with the need for housing and with the possibility of a fast-food outlet being built on the Cambridge and Prospect Street site. Model Cities approached Harvard in mid-1970 to buy and carry the land and help with the development. Harvard obliged and obtained the 35,500 sq. ft. corner site for $259,000 in September 1970. Working through the Cambridge Corporation, Harvard also provided funds for relocation of existing commercial residents, demolition of vacant buildings, design and technical assistance. The Corporation did most of the work, by creating the development plans and funding. The Corporation worked with the Model Cities program, neighbors, and Better Cities, Inc., a group of nine banks. The Model Cities board approved the project in December 1970 and the Cambridge Planning Board agreed in April 1971. From 1970 through midsummer 1972 the Corporation staff met extensively with Model Cities and concerned neighbors. In December 1972 ground was broken.

A problem with rent levels and communications surfaced in early 1973. The head of Model Cities accused the Cambridge Corporation of a "glaring lack of communication" concerning the project. "Although Model Cities is not opposed to the construction of housing," the rental scale "is too high." He indicated that the agency had expressed its agreement about rent levels in the past but had received no response from the Corporation. He also complained that the building "had too many costly extras like parquet floors and central air conditioning when low rents were the key concerns" (*Council Communicator*, January 1973). The Cambridge Corporation responded that all these aspects of the development had been brought up at a June 1972 meeting without complaint.

Picture 3.2.   Inman Square Apartments
Credit: Cambridge Corporation

Besides poor communications, the core problem apparently was the difficulty in getting rent subsidies, though some features of the building may have added costs. One week after the financing had been settled in December 1972, President Richard Nixon imposed a housing moratorium, which cut rent supplements from 25 to 10 percent. This meant only twelve low-income units could be included in the 116-unit project. In January and February 1973, the cost controversy surfaced. But by March, subsidies rose up to 25 percent again and by fall to 40 percent.

The Inman Square project was completed in November 1974. The twelve-story building has a pleasant brown facing, and landscaping has increased its overall attractiveness. Unfortunately, the project is out of style and scale with the rest of the low-rise neighborhood and lacks open space for children. It is too tall for the area, an impression accentuated by the large land coverage on a small site, close to its neighbors. The Model Cities Housing Committee was worried about height, but neighbors approved it at a community meeting because it allowed more housing. The only building of similar size and scale in East Cambridge is the MIT Gore Street project, a mile away but clearly visible. Controversy erupted in the neighborhood over high-rise commercial development at Inman Square, which would transform the physical and economic character of that area. The Inman Square housing appeared to be part of that physical trend. In any case, the project provided a large number of low-income units, including several badly needed ones for families.

Satisfaction with the project was high, but there were problems, for instance, with leakage. The family and elderly sections act virtually as two separate buildings. While there is no open space for children, the common space on top of the elderly units was generally unused except for occasional evening meetings by the families, with special arrangement since most occupants prefer to congregate on the ground floor. Although there was user participation in the design, the elderly apartments lack adequate closet space and kitchen cabinets are too high. While the management was in good hands, one of the elderly units became the office.

Financing

The basic financing program for Inman Square created a moderate income development. The $3,350,000 project was financed through a $3 million mortgage loan from the MHFA at 5.77 percent (1.25 percent below the market). It came into the moderate rent range through Section 236 of the 1968 Housing Act, which subsidizes the interest to a net of 1 percent. But by itself, Section 236 could create low-income housing. As the Model Cities board complained, the standard rents for this project were too high for low-income renters from $130 for an efficiency to $241 for a four- bedroom unit. Under Section 236, a family must pay at least 25 percent of their monthly income for rents. To afford the above rents, families would have to earn $6,250 for an efficiency and $11,500 for a four-bedroom to pay only 25 percent of income for rent. But about one-third of all Cambridge families had incomes less than

$6,000 (Housing Needs in Cambridge, 1972, 1). Most elderly in Cambridge earned less than $3,000 per year. Lowering rents further required greater rent supplements. After considerable effort, Harvard and the Cambridge Corporation obtained a guarantee that 47 units (about 40 percent) would be at 25 percent of the income of the eligible tenants. This covered all the family units and some for elderly. These 40 percent subsidies were achieved by combining rent supplement and the MHFA leasing program.

Harvard was reimbursed for the $259,000 land costs. But it did forgo a 4 to 5 percent return on the money for three years, about $30,000. The co-developers and general partners, the Cambridge Corporation and Better Cities, Inc., also sold tax shelter for about $350,000 to cover part of the equity, overhead, and amenities.

RIVERSIDE: RIVER-HOWARD HOMES

Coming out of the disruption of the 1970 Harvard commencement was a pledge by the University to the Riverside community that the University would provide land and assistance for building low- and moderate-income housing (Harvard press release, June 10, 1970). The process ran into numerous frustrating problems, but ultimately made progress (*Harvard Gazette*, June 10, 1970).

At the commencement, the community demanded about 187 units of housing on the university-owned Treeland/Bindery site on the bank of the Charles River next to Peabody Terrace, a complex for married graduate students. Responding that the 2.25-acre Treeland site on the riverfront was "too valuable for low-income housing," the University rejected the demand, but promised to obtain another site[5] (*Cambridge Chronicle*, June 18, 1970). By September 1970, Harvard had bought the 1.6-acre River-Howard site for $540,000.

The meeting planned for Harvard's announcement of the purchase of the River-Howard site was highlighted by a walkout of the Riverside Planning Team. The community left when they were not guaranteed control in choosing the developer and tenants. For several months the group worked rather unsuccessfully with a Harvard-suggested developer. In March 1971, the Riverside Planning Team took a major step by creating the Riverside Community Corporation (RCC). In September 1971, the University promised it would not plan development for the Treeland Site for at least two years. A month later Harvard suggested the City of Cambridge allocate to the Planning Team $20,000, part of a $200,000 community development fund Harvard had earlier given to the city. At the same time, Harvard agreed to sell the River-Howard site to RCC for $270,000, half of its cost.

Working with their own developers and advisors, Greater Boston Community Development, Inc., and with Harvard, RCC developed a proposal for 102 units of Section 236 housing, with a goal of 40 percent eligible for rent supplements. After a year and a half of planning, major community involvement, and $16,000 in preliminary expenses, the Treeland proposal was abandoned. The excessively high cost of the small site and difficulty getting enough rent supplements to make the project work were difficult enough problems. Then the U.S. housing subsidy freeze in January 1973, along with escalating construction and operating costs, finally killed the Treeland proposal in April.

The River-Howard Homes II

The plans for River-Howard Homes were originally for a development of 36 (later 32) units for families rather than the elderly. Originally conceived as a Turnkey III project, the River-Howard Apartments could reach public housing rent levels through Section 8 leases. Mainly meant for 12 three- and 4 four-bedroom units, the $1+ million project was for five rows of two- and three-story townhouses, 31 of which were will have direct access to the ground, and include community and possibly commercial space. The Riverside-Cambridgeport Community Corporation (RCCC) was the main community agent.

A Cambridge resident and Harvard alumnus, Brett Donham, of Donham & Sweeney Architects was selected as architect in December 1974, and application for a mortgage made to the Massachusetts Housing Finance Agency in May 1975. Donham was experienced in working with community groups, and used a process of extensive user participation in design. In a series of six to eight meetings, he and an RCCC committee developed specifications on density, height, open space, unit types, and interior layout. RCCC and Harvard, which had to write down land costs totally to make the project work, were co-developers. Planned to begin in spring 1976 for summer 1980 completion, construction on the homes shown in picture 3.3, began in spring 1980 and was completed in summer 1981 at a cost $2 million. Harvard president Derek Bok attended the dedication ceremony (Donham, 2013).

In August 1981, 32 townhouse units opened in four three-story buildings. This includes 7 one-bedroom units, 9 two-bedroom, 12 three-bedrooms, and 4 four bedrooms (Donham, 2013) for a total of 77 bedrooms. In 2002, modernization of the units was scheduled, but the $3.5 million project did not begin until 2006 and was finished in November 2007 (*CHA Bulletin*, Winter 2007). Currently it comprises 7 one-bedroom, 10 two, 11 three, and 4 four, for 76 bedrooms (CHA website, 2013).

Picture 3.3.   River-Howard Homes
Credit: Brett Donham, Architect

Though creating a smaller number of 32 units, rather than the 36 originally planned, this project directly serves the biggest need in Cambridge—for family housing at low cost. In retrospect, a fully low-income project at the level of MIT's subsidized housing units, but for 36 families, would have provided more family housing. Since a Section 236 development required rent supplement to reach low incomes, the entire 36 low income units became impossible when only 11 low-income units could be assured. Section 8 now provides the subsidies for the 32 unit family housing project.

Treeland-Bindery

Between the initial and final plans, there developed another proposal for Treeland-Bindery. In April 1973, after the 102-unit project died, a technical advisor to RCC suggested the possibility of a joint community/university development for both the Treeland and River-Howard sites. Harvard responded with an interesting proposal, but it had strings the community could not accept. Harvard proposed a package "combined development" of 300 units, 200 at Treeland and 100 at River-Howard. One hundred and fifty units at Treeland would be for faculty and married graduate students, while fifty units there and all at River-Howard would be for the community.

Harvard suggested that the Cambridge Corporation become the developer, with MHFA, federal and private funding. But this package involved a deal in which Riverside would help Harvard get a zoning change for the Sachs Estate. There the University wanted to build 204 faculty and married graduate units, sixty townhouses and 144 apartment units in an eighteen-story tower. But RCC rejected the deal and the combination project idea was dropped. While community housing was not to be built at Treeland, the community carefully watched the University's plans, especially for high-rise conceptions, which could cut Riverside off from the Charles River.[6]

Blair Pond

Another development planned for community housing in Cambridge was a Harvard-related project at Blair Pond that failed for problems in the development process. Announced with 2 Mt. Auburn Street in September 1969, the original plan was for 325 low and moderate family and elderly units to be developed privately. In 1970, Harvard bought a seven-acre site for $600,000 at Blair Pond in West Cambridge on which it planned to build 248 units of low- and moderate- income housing under Section 236.

After local opposition surfaced, the project was scaled down to 216 and then 200 units. The project died in 1972, because the site was so far from central Cambridge; it was a poor place for low-income housing under any circumstances. In addition, local groups vigorously opposed low-income family housing. The issue that surfaced, however, was the environmental impact of filling in part of Blair Pond. Despite Harvard's efforts in scaling down the proposal to lessen its environmental and social impact, it never developed.

HARVARD'S CONTRIBUTIONS
TO HOUSING IN CAMBRIDGE

In short, Harvard contributed to 210 units in three of four proposed university-aided community housing projects for Cambridge. The University assisted in the building of the 94 elderly units in Putnam Square Apartments, and 116 mixed family and elderly units in Inman Square Apartments. It helped develop the plans for 36 family units, of which ultimately 32 were built, at River and Howard Streets in Riverside. Its proposals for up to 325 family and elderly units at Blair Pond went unrealized. While not as major in scope as the MIT Housing Program, Harvard did help the community improve the housing situation in Cambridge.

NOTES

1. Forty years from 1969 means the subsidies would end in 2009. At that point, the Putnam Square project faced loss of subsidies and reversion to market rate housing. A March 22, 2013, Harvard news release about a property transfer to Homeowners Rehab, Inc. noted, "Harvard has required HRI to preserve the 94-unit building as affordable housing for senior citizens for a minimum of 30 years, and ensured that residents' eligibility and their rent calculation will not change" (*Harvard Gazette*, 2013).

2. The Brooke Amendment of the Housing and Urban Development Act of 1969, named for then-Massachusetts Republican senator Edward Brooke, provides that rents of a public housing tenant may not exceed 25 percent of family income. "Baby Brooke" subsidies provided the difference.

3. In a September 21, 2001, letter to Cambridge City Manager, Robert Healy, about "Other Contributions to Community Housing," a Harvard planning officer wrote that Putnam Square Apartments "is a 94-unit building for elderly and disabled persons. It was built between 1970 and 1972 on Harvard-owned land, has a fifty-year ground lease, is HUD subsidized and administered by the Cambridge Housing Authority. The designated managing agent was Harvard Planning and Real Estate Office (HPRE), and in 2000, Harvard initiated a $3 million renovation" (Harvard University, 2000–2001 Town-Gown Report).

4. In 2011, Homeowners Rehab, Inc. purchased Inman Square Apartments to preserve the apartments as affordable housing under Chapter 40T (an Act to Preserve Publicly Assisted Affordable Housing). See Herzog and Brauner, 2013.

5. This quote was "too valuable to support practical low-income housing," according to the *Harvard Crimson*, September 21, 1970. The Treeland Site, owned by Harvard for years, was undoubtedly obtained for less than the $540,000 paid for River-Howard. But Treeland's value also lies in its prime riverfront location and contiguity to Peabody Terrace (see note 20, chapter 1).

6. In November 1973, the Riverside-Cambridgeport Community Corporation (RCCC), of which the Riverside Community Corporation (RCC) was one of 22 members, announced plans to renovate thirty family units under Turnkey III. In this program, families rent with the option to buy, with no down payment. Rents do not exceed 25 percent of income and families do their own maintenance, for which they receive credit.

Chapter Four

Looking Back on Cambridge and Community Housing

The MIT and Harvard community housing efforts with neighbors in Cambridge are in many ways distinctive and impressive. By 1975, 875 units of elderly housing and nineteen units of family housing were been built in five university-sponsored developments there. Including Cambridge Corporation projects, the figures reach 1,190 elderly and 179 family units. Another 32 family units joined them at River-Howard Homes. While recognizing the great value and lessons of the contributions, these efforts fail to live up to the universities' public statements both in terms of the number of units proposed and the contributions to diversity in Cambridge.

EVALUATING THE MIT PROJECTS

The MIT "Housing Program in Cambridge" largely completed the Institute's proposed low-income elderly housing component. Through an effective, though MIT-controlled, four-year process, the Institute built 684 of 750 planned units of pleasant, and badly needed, low-income elderly housing. MIT involved hundreds of community residents in various stages of development. Also important, Institute people learned from community members, who in turn learned about housing development and MIT. However, the planned 850 market units, largely focused in the 800 unit Portland Street proposal, among the 1,600 units originally announced, were not built, nor the 16 planned for Erie Street. In fact, no MIT family housing was produced.

MIT's role essentially ended in turning over its three elderly projects and their management to the lackluster Cambridge Housing Authority. At the time, there was only a small possibility that 16 units of family housing at Erie Street, or 250 units at market rates on Massachusetts Avenue, which already has a zoning change, would be built, and neither was ever developed. The 800-unit Portland Street market-rate development was also dropped. A promise that fifty MIT-owned apartments would be available under the leased housing program only led to acceptance of about 35. MIT offered more than fifty, but many did not fit the leasing cost guidelines While MIT has certainly produced positive results, it still fell far short of its much publicized goal of 1,600 units, though closer to its original low-income goal of 750.[1] The Institute then began addressing its on-campus housing needs.

HARVARD-RELATED CONTRIBUTIONS

Harvard contributed to 210 units of community housing on three sites at Putnam and Inman Squares. And it assisted in the proposal of the Riverside neighborhood for a 36-unit development, of which 32 were built, at River and Howard Streets. Harvard participated in community housing only in response to community pressures and requests. Community groups came directly to Harvard for assistance, and the University's involvement in the projects was indirect and limited. These are important distinctions from MIT. Responding to the community, Harvard has essentially provided land, and some financial and technical help. Cambridge Corporation and community groups did the development work.[2]

The indirect Harvard role was generally beneficial. Where Harvard was directly involved—Blair Pond and River-Howard I—and paid too much for land, the projects were unsuccessful. While the university participation has been minor in successful projects, community involvement has generally been strong, particularly at Inman Square and in Riverside.[3] Harvard, however, has failed to define clearly what beyond start-up aid its role would be so community groups could use the University most effectively as a resource. The University has also fallen short of the suggested May 1969 Boston goal of about 1,100 units, or even the 389 units announced in September of that year. A March 1971 university brochure described four projects for 520 units (Harvard University, 1971).

DIVERSITY: A STANDARD

The diverse natures of the City of Cambridge and its population have been characteristics of Cambridge to which many people, including university spokesmen, have paid homage over the years. Both universities have come out publicly for the importance of maintaining the diversity of Cambridge.

Several months before announcing its housing program for Cambridge, for example, MIT Corporation Chairman Killian praised the diversity of the city:

> Our conviction [is] that Cambridge should maintain a balanced distribution of population. We need to maintain conditions whereby different ethnic, racial, income and age groups can find humane living conditions in Cambridge and at prices they can afford to pay. . . . Cambridge is a Community of exceeding richness in the diversity of its population, and our city gains great strength from this kind of well-balanced diversity. . . . Maintaining those distinctive qualities [is] uniquely essential to a great educational institution (Killian, 1960, 1).

Just after the April 1969 Housing Program announcement, Chairman Killian reaffirmed, "Cambridge is and should be a mixed Community—including University people and other residents—rich, poor, middle class and various ethnic groups" (*Boston Herald Traveler*, April 11, 1969).

Harvard, too, saw the importance of differences. *The Wilson Report* held that "diversity and even conflict are relevant to the intellectual life Harvard wishes to sustain. . . . A diversified city has, to us, considerable appeal." (*Wilson Report*, 1968, 43).

The Report also maintained that

> Narrow self-interest requires, we believe, Harvard . . . to ally itself with those who wish to preserve, for as long as possible, a measure of diversity and heterogeneity. But enlightened self-interest should lead us to cherish, not simply tolerate, that diversity as useful to the educational purposes of the University (Wilson Report, 1968, 46).

The success of the housing projects by the universities can be measured then, at least in part, by the extent to which they help the diversity of Cambridge continue to flourish. A city gains its vitality much from its families and children. Integral to maintaining this nature is keeping working families in the city. It is here that the universities' contributions fail to pursue aggressively the goal of maintaining diversity. Both schools praised the importance of diversity in Cambridge, yet each failed to support the flourishing of that quality by significantly increasing the family housing stock, while continuing to attract affluent singles and the housing pressures they bring.

Diversity involves more than providing reasonably priced housing, though that is a major part. Jobs for working people must exist in town, or nearby. Schools and other facilities must attract and hold people. Fortunately for the elderly, jobs and schools are less of the question, and the elderly units built will allow many of them to spend the rest of their lives in their home city. Of course, too, the universities are not solely responsible for contributing to diversity. This is an area where government and industry should make the major contributions.

The point is that universities especially should follow practices that contribute to the goals they espouse. A university's responsibility for providing housing might roughly be gauged from the number of families and elderly its pressures on the housing stock displaced by the demand for housing of students, faculty and other personnel, plus some percentage of the professionals from university-attracted, or spin-off, companies. "Housing Need in Cambridge," also points out that a university could contribute numbers of units to remove demand pressures which force rents up (Housing Needs in Cambridge, 1972, 37).

The 8,000 families leaving Cambridge from 1960 to 1970 and 4,500 families needing lower-rent housing became overwhelming concerns. The realities were that nothing will solve the low-income housing problems in Cambridge, or contribute to keeping families a part of Cambridge life, except aggressively building or subsidizing more low- and moderate-income family housing.

"Homes for People" added, "merely building additional housing units does not itself solve the problem. Simple net additions to the inventory do not necessarily meet the requirements of those families who suffer the greatest pressure or have the least range of choice. What is needed is housing that is specifically fitted to the needs and the aspirations of those families" (Ad Hoc Task Force, 1969, 2).

While this is fundamentally a government concern, the universities have recognized the problem and stated they would responsibly contribute to really solving it. Yet, even including their contributions to the 160 Cambridge Corporation family units, neither school significantly assisted in solving the family housing problem. Perhaps if MIT had worked from the very start with community groups interested in family housing, as Harvard had to in Riverside, and chosen sites in Cambridgeport where family units were wanted, the results could have been different.

This does not suggest that MIT itself should have imposed family housing on unwilling areas. But it might have been more persuasive and persistent in stressing the major need for such units. It could have sought to work with groups favorable to family units, in trying to overcome the biases against family housing. If the image-conscious Institute had been willing to weather some of the almost inevitable controversy and bad publicity involved in actively supporting family units, results might also have been different.

FAMILY HOUSING

While there are numerous factors involved in diversity and many reasons why family housing is difficult to build, the fact remains that a city is diminished in diversity without families. While the elderly units are truly important, the universities have not supported their rhetoric of the importance of maintaining diversity in Cambridge—the "Universe-City"—whose destiny they integrally affect. And, unfortunately, with the changes in the times, pressures, and actors, the universities appear finished with their community housing efforts.[4]

Though at one point a major part of all MIT's planned units—200 of the low-income units—were for families, the Institute built no low-income family housing. The 16 units at Erie Street became doubtful, then were dropped. Harvard helped complete 19 subsidized family apartments at Inman Square. As the River-Howard project reemerged, 32 more (of 36 planned) units were developed in a part of the city where they are badly needed. Yet these 51 units total still only provided a small contribution to a huge need for family housing.

The opposition of various groups to MIT and Harvard's proposals for family units, of course, complicated attempts at solving the family housing problem. Harvard's Blair Pond project had to be abandoned because of this community opposition in their neighborhood. MIT ran into stiff opposition to family units in a number of places and would not proceed in face of it. The realities are that many people oppose the building of low-income family units, sometimes for valid, but often for biased reasons around race and class, and that sophisticated political capital needs to be invested to counter it successfully.

With its ability to devise a complex system its original goal of 200 low-income family units, and its fine performance on building elderly housing, MIT's failure to produce any family housing is disappointing. Harvard was somewhat more successful when working with community groups that wanted family units. Ironically, MIT's failure came to a large extent from its desire to be responsive to all types of community feelings.[5] The Institute was certainly responsive to those communities in support of low-income elderly housing. Otherwise, it could have never gotten the zoning changes needed for the 684 units. But it was unwilling to press forward in the face of some neighborhood opposition especially in North and East Cambridge to family units to assist the more complex need for family housing in the community.

Nonetheless, both MIT and Harvard contributed to innovative Community/University housing projects and provided models for others. These contributions on a variety of sites in Cambridge provide instructive comparisons to another large development near Harvard Medical School in the Mission Hill neighborhood of the Roxbury Tenants of Harvard beyond the Charles River in Boston.

NOTES

1. Head of the Institute Real Estate Office, Antony Herrey (1969, 32) stated under "Paramount Objectives of Proposal," Number 1: "A massive increase in the Cambridge Housing stock was essential for a turnaround in the housing situation.

Minor efforts of a few hundred units would not do it. Hence our proposal was to set a target of 1,600 units, representing a five percent increase in the housing supply." In the Turnkey proposal to the CHA, MIT states "The 1,600 units have been increased to 1,800, of which at least 900 are to be subsidized" (MIT, 1971, 1). The number of elderly units built by MIT has substantially increased that housing stock.

2. In retrospect, the Cambridge Corporation, MIT, and Harvard found that contributions to solving the housing problems in Cambridge removed pressures on them and brought positive publicity. But the developments have not prevented further criticism or lack of appreciation of the university efforts, nor have they made government more responsible, responsive, or capable.

3. Community participation at Inman and Riverside through Model Cities and RCCC, respectively, has been strong and legitimate. Essentially, this is because the community initiated the contact with Harvard and thus could define how community members would be involved. The community, moreover, has been involved in all phases of development. At Putnam Square Apartments, Harvard and the Cambridge Corporation involved some community members, yet left out the Riverside Planning Team. Awkwardness in the design of the interior rooms there indicates a failing in user participation. Unfortunately, the completion of Inman Square reveals similar problems. Learning from Putnam Square's problems, like kitchen cabinets that were built too high, would have prevented their recurrence at Inman Square. A feedback mechanism for improving user participation, and perhaps a checklist of commonly occurring problems to insure good results, could prevent these mistakes elsewhere.

4. Harvard and MIT may build market rate or faculty/married graduate student housing in the future, but it is doubtful that these will help the low-income family needs because there is little "filtering-down" effect in Cambridge (see note 10, chapter 1). MIT planned 250 market rate units at 1000 Massachusetts Avenue and an undetermined number on the former Simplex Wire and Tool Co. site, purchased in 1970 and under discussion with the future of Kendall Square. Harvard planned faculty/graduate housing on Sachs Estate and Treeland. Fortunately, some lower cost family units were otherwise built in Cambridge during the period. The two schools also indirectly contributed to about 175 family units at Harwell Homes and Walden Square apartments through the Cambridge Corporation (besides 19 family units at Inman Square and 32 at River-Howard). The Cambridge Corporation, along with Northgate Community Corporation and the Community Housing programs, however, went out of business in the 1970s. Both MIT and Harvard planned more on-campus units, which might somewhat reduce off-campus demand; if enrollments did not rise too greatly. But this would do nothing to increase the supply of low-cost family housing.

5. Some call Cambridge the "St. Petersburg of the North"—for "overbuilding elderly housing, not its revolutionary traditions!" In fact, besides the additional need for more elderly housing, there is a greater necessity for family housing. The Massachusetts Department of Community Affairs Survey (*Cambridge Chronicle*, April 18, 1974), indicated there were still a need for 3,500 elderly housing units, and a greater need for 5,000 family housing units.

Part II

MISSION PARK
HOUSING IN BOSTON

Chapter Five

Mission Park

A Development of the Roxbury Tenants and Harvard

In Mission Hill, a working-class neighborhood of the West Roxbury section of Boston, just south of Harvard Medical School, a 775-unit project arose out of joint efforts after strong community opposition developed to Harvard's role in the creation of an Affiliated Hospitals Center (AHC). After much groundwork, the Roxbury Tenants of Harvard Association and the University[1] constructed a major community/university housing development as well as community and hospital facilities.[2]

The story of the Roxbury Tenants of Harvard (RTH) and Harvard Medical School is an intriguing study of conflict evolving into cooperation. The project and its development involved major issues and facets of community/university housing and politics. It is an example of how a community—with student, technical, press, and city assistance—brought a university to successful cooperation in development. In particular, it shows how independent access to excellent technical assistance can be a boon to a community group.

The example also demonstrates the extent of cooperative development possible between community and university. It shows the degree of influence a strong community can have on helping or hindering institutional plans. And it highlights the numerous, often avoidable, problems university expansion involves. While Harvard has contributed financial support and technical help to the Mission Hill community housing development, the community has maintained major control in choosing the developer and having the right to approve all housing plans. This is a dramatic shift from earlier instances where the Mission Hill community was excluded from planning for this area.

The development of Community/University housing in Mission Hill has been a lengthy process, with many ups and downs, arguments and agreements. But it shows what can be done. And not only is Mission Park an innovative housing development, it addresses major community and university needs.

BACKGROUND TO THE RTH CONTROVERSY[3]

The controversy and planning for the Roxbury Tenants area began in the early 1960s when Harvard started land acquisition and institutional planning in the Mission Hill area.[4] In 1961, for $1.5 million, Harvard bought the former site of the Convent of the Good Shepherd, south of Harvard Medical School and the RTH neighborhood. The huge ten-acre "Convent Site" was turned into a parking lot. A year later, Harvard and three local research and teaching hospitals, which were affiliated with the Harvard Medical School (the Peter Bent Brigham, Robert B. Brigham, and Boston Hospitals for Women), met to discuss developing a new research-oriented joint facility, the Affiliated Hospitals Center (AHC). They decided to develop a complex south of the Medical School. Harvard was to acquire the land, which it would lease to the Affiliated Hospitals Center (AHC) (Winkeller, 1971, 91).

Plans for the center began to take form for hospital facilities, housing for institutionally related personnel, parking, and a power plant. In 1963, without a master plan or provisions for relocating displaced tenants, Harvard began obtaining residential property in the RTH neighborhood (Sharratt, 1970, 12).

Harvard acquired the housing *sub rosa* by using a number of real estate agents. By 1964–65, the University owned 67 structures in the area, acquired 35 in 1966, and added 20 more by May of 1969. The prices paid were very high: between $12,000 and $60,000 for the wooden houses. One brick building cost $100,000. All told, it cost Harvard $3 million for 182 structures (Harvard Strikers, 1969, 4).

The RTH area remained a healthy residential area throughout the early 1960s. As Harvard real estate managers rented increasingly to transients, however, by mid-decade the neighborhood became less stable and unsatisfactory for permanent residential tenants. The sidewalks were cluttered, and maintenance of university-owned buildings declined (Office of Community Affairs, 1971).

In April 1965, an Affiliated Hospitals Complex master plan report proposed city use of eminent domain to obtain dwellings and provided them to the hospital center. It would have destroyed the entire neighborhood. In June, the Boston Redevelopment Authority issued a Greater Neighborhood Redevelopment Plan (GNRP), compatible with the AHC plans, which encompassed Mission Hill and the RTH area. The GNRP was a preliminary step to getting federal urban renewal approval and monies—including Section 112 credits. The resident fought vigorously: the RTH area was subsequently excluded from the urban renewal boundaries.

In 1967, the Affiliated Hospitals Center was incorporated. In April 1968, a new Boston urban renewal plan for the Mission Hill area was issued. While responding to protest by leaving out the new RTH neighborhood, it gave so little attention to the expansion plans of the local medical institutions that even they did not support it. Though removed from the urban renewal threat, the RTH area was also excluded from federal and state planning and funding areas. That left the area open to speculation and further institutional land acquisition. Obtaining mortgage financing soon became difficult. By winter 1968, Harvard had acquired most of the neighborhood. In fact, only two houses were not institutionally owned (Winkeller, 1971, 92).

The Initial Shock

Toward the end of the 1960s, residents were becoming increasingly disturbed that a university with Harvard's reputation was letting their neighborhood decline. But their first major shock came in January 1969 when Harvard sent letters to 182 tenants in Roxbury informing most of their evictions in two years, while warning the rest of likely displacement within five years. Rents were being raised, too. An AHC statement in February promised 400 new apartments nearby to be available prior to the start of Center construction. The goal was 20 percent low-income units, and priority would go to displaced (and employees). No details or promises were provided, however.

In early March, plans for the AHC and support facilities were officially announced at a gala dinner. A 910-bed unit, the largest private hospital in the U.S., would bring three Harvard-related hospitals together in an essentially teaching and research-oriented center. Along with the $50 million AHC, there would be an ambulatory care center, nursing school, and doctors offices to be served by a power plant and the 400 apartments. Construction was to begin in mid-1971, with a late 1974 opening.

THE HARVARD STRIKE

The first shock to Harvard about its actions near the Medical School came in the Student Strike of April 1969. One of the demands of the 250 students occupying University Hall on the Cambridge campus was "that houses in Roxbury not be torn down to make room for the Affiliated Hospitals Center" (Harvard Strikers, 1969, 19). The University's reaction was to deny the problem. "How can one respond to allegations that have no basis in fact. . . . There are no . . . houses being torn down to make way for the Harvard Medical School expansion" (Harvard Strikers, 1969, 19). The students quickly refuted this, to the embarrassment of Harvard. And later in April a research team of striking students issued a detailed report on the situation called "The Affiliated Hospital

Complex: A Critique of Harvard Expansion" (Harvard Strikers, 1969). It enumerated the problems that Harvard had caused in the area. The report showed clearly that details on the proposed relocation housing had not been worked out and that, because of a housing authority backlog, the 20 percent low-income units might be impossible to obtain. It also explained that the teaching and research-oriented AHC would probably not serve the health need of the Roxbury community.

Soon after the Strikers occupied University Hall, the Roxbury Tenants of Harvard was formed. It began with the aid of students who had come to the area to inform the residents about Harvard's plans. With the assistance of students in getting organized, an advocate planner, and a handful of sympathetic medical school faculty, RTH began to complain vociferously and asked for redress of its problems with housing and the AHC plans.[5]

After the Strike

The residents of the area became angry about other concerns besides maintenance problems. Their declining faith in Harvard was shattered when they discovered that the University owned two other sites nearby, big enough for the new hospital center. Both the Convent Site and the Quarry Site, just across Huntington Avenue, could have been the location for the Affiliated Hospitals Complex. But Harvard considered them too inconvenient (Sharratt, 1970, 12).

The protests during the Strike quickly produced result from the RTH area. On April 15, 1969, the Dean of the Medical School, Robert Ebert, announced that Harvard was prepared to build low-cost housing for relocation for families to be dislocated by the Affiliated Hospitals Center. But this housing, actually the same 400 units planned previously for the Convent Site, would be available to students and employees at the Medical School, as well as to area residents (*Harvard Gazette*, April 17, 1969)

A few days later, the Medical School formed the "Fein" committee to work on questions of relocation, housing repairs, new construction, and health care. But no community members were named to the group, a problem Harvard would have to confront later in the summer. Student strike-related demonstrations continued in April. On May 6, 1969, the Harvard Corporation announced that there would be no residential demolition or displacement in position until relocation housing was available nearby at comparable prices. To facilitate this, the Corporation announced that it would build 1,100 units of housing in Boston, 700 more than the 400 units previously planned for hospital-related personnel. Planned for the Convent and Quarry sites, 30 percent would be at public housing levels. The University hoped to have community participation in the process (*Harvard Crimson*, May 7, 1969).

Progress toward Agreement

Further changes came in early August 1969 at a meeting of community members, the Affiliated Hospitals Center president, F. Stanton Deland Jr., who was also president of the Harvard Board of Overseers, and other Harvard officials. Announced then was a smaller, 870-bed AHC. It would not be in the original area, but on the site of the Peter Bent Brigham Hospital north of the east section of the RTH area. The hospital complex itself would require destroying no housing, though fifty units would probably still be razed for an ambulatory care center. Community members protested that even fifty houses would not have to be destroyed for an AHC built on the Convent Site to the south. But they were told that this would be too geographically inconvenient and costly.

The Harvard committee chairman did promise repairs, at no cost and no rent increase, for community houses and a fulfillment of University commitments to the area. He asked for community input in the planning for the 1,100 previously promised units of housing, though he acknowledged little historical basis for trust. By the end of the meeting, some community members were open to joining the committee (Harvard University, 1970, 126–29).

Another optimistic note came in August of that year. A meeting between Harvard officials and Department of Housing and Urban Development secretary George Romney brought a commitment of 400 units of Section 236 housing funds for the RTH area from the Secretary's discretionary fund. At this time also, the Community made specific its housing demands on Harvard (Winkeller, 1971, 94). RTH wanted joint University and Community approval of a developer, a cooperative management agreement, and Community role in tenant selection and management policy. In mid-November, a Harvard dean wrote RTH that January 1973 (not April 1971 as originally indicated) would be the earliest that part of the RTH neighborhood would be required to move by Harvard (Sharratt, 1970, 68). In any case, two years notice would be given on the plans.

Maintenance Still an Issue

Harvard worked through the early fall on the application to HUD for Section 236 funds. RTH then rejected the proposal the University made, however, after a series of community meetings in November. The rents were too high for the potentially displaced, and there were not enough apartments projected for large families. This created a disappointing, but not unforeseen, delay. The group and Harvard had recently signed an agreement stating that RTH had to approve all plans; and RTH had both the right and opportunity to insist that proposed plans fully fit the community needs (Tenant's View, November 6, 1969).

Even while the problems of building new housing were being worked on, the maintenance of existing units remained an issue. In mid-December 1969, one hundred students, faculty, and community members demonstrated at the Medical School against Harvard's maintenance policy. They complained that university-owned buildings were still being allowed to deteriorate and that rents were being raised for filling vacant apartments. They demanded immediate repairs and control of rents (*Harvard Crimson*, December 18, 1969).

In early January 1970, residents took the Dean of the Medical School on a tour of the area to see maintenance problems for himself. A further protest by medical students about maintenance occurred a week later in the Dean's office. Students pressed the Dean for action on the community's demands. The students, faculty, and employees were also challenging the validity of the AHC complex and whether a specialized research facility would serve the health needs of the people of Boston. On January 21, the director of real estate at Harvard sent a letter to RTH president, Robert Parks, explaining Harvard's delayed acquisition plans. He explained how Harvard would deal with relocation, and affirmed that it would do the area maintenance including for housing (Sharratt, 1970, 68–72).

THE ROXBURY TENANTS OF HARVARD PROPOSAL

On March 20, 1970, the Roxbury Tenants of Harvard with their architect, John Sharratt, issued a major proposal for the area: *The Relationship of Harvard University Medical School and Affiliated Institutions to the Neighboring Residential Community: Its Problems and a Solution* (Sharratt, 1970, 12). Describing a "trial attempt on our part to deal with the members of Harvard as reasonable people," the eighty-six-page document proposed in detail a redevelopment of the RTH area, including upkeep and rehabilitation of existing units and construction of new housing.

The five-phase RTH plan called for total neighborhood redevelopment. In housing, it called for adequate maintenance of existing community units and for the building of 1,300 new units. This would include 400 units (200 family, low- rise and 200 high-rise) on the Convent Site and 400 for families on the Quarry Site across Huntington Avenue. New shopping facilities and new schools, as well as a cultural center, were parts of the plan. Also proposed were health facilities for the community, along with appropriate and necessary growth of area hospitals. The plan included support facilities for parking and a power plant. Thus the imaginative plan took care of both Community and University needs.

Repairs of Existing Units

Harvard announced in late March 1970 that it had completed repairs in the first of three RTH areas. At a cost of $25,000, it repaired the units in the first area, and provided land plans for rehabilitation work in areas two and three. Moreover, rents would not increase because of the work. Families in the first area, who would not have to move until at least 1973, would be encouraged to relocate into the third area, which was not in danger of being demolished. Rents for people moving there would remain the same for six months (*Harvard Gazette*, March 27, 1970)

Progress continued. By May 1970, the University and RTH had an agreement on the importance and future of the Mission Hill area as a stable residential neighborhood. Harvard would maintain and repair existing housing until the removal of any particular house was justified, and the tenants relocated. The University also agreed to a relocation rent "bridge" for the 400 units to be built on the Convent site. Harvard would "bridge" the gap between a tenant's rent in the old housing and the new housing; the new rent would gradually increase over a period of five years during which time wage increases might decrease the burden of higher rent. Site rents, rejected by RTH in November 1969, were still too high. Harvard also planned to seek 20 to 40 percent rent supplements to ease the rent strain. Finally, RTH got the right to choose a developer, though the summer proved frustrating as the group was unable to find a developer who served the community's needs until 1972.

During summer 1970, a year after the Harvard Strikers first raised the Mission Hill housing issues, and just after the commencement disruption brought the Riverside concerns forcefully to Harvard, too, the Affiliated Hospitals Center was again considering building in the full RTH neighborhood (*Harvard Crimson*, October 1, 1970). At this point, however, the Urban Renewal Committee of the Boston City Council got involved in the controversy, at RTH's request. In August 1970, the Council asked Harvard for its plans, and for information on the impact of the AHC on the area and on tax revenues. In October, the Council held hearings. The mayor of Boston also issued a "Medical Institutions Policy Statement" on limiting institutional development in the Mission Hill area. The Boston Redevelopment Authority issued expansion guidelines. After the city's intervention, Harvard dealt systematically with community grievance.

By November 1970, in fact, the Dean of the Medical School, Robert Ebert, acknowledged the seriousness of the resident's plight in a speech to the school. Realizing it was possible to live in the shadow of a major medical school without getting any care from the institution, he suggested giving members of the community a share in the decision-making process, as it affected their destinies. Yet in June 1971, the architecture firm of I. M. Pei issued an "Interim Study" for the Mission Hill area, which, despite all the protest and discussion that had gone on before, was oriented to institutional and traffic needs and neglected the community (Harvard Planning Office, 1971; *Harvard Gazette*, October 8, 1970).

After a period of few notable events, AHC activity began again in early 1972. In February, Harvard, the three-area teaching hospitals, and the AHC Corporation signed a Memorandum of Understanding on basic concepts for the new Center (*Harvard Gazette*, February 4, 1972). Including housing, it covered hospital siting, ambulatory care and neighborhood services, parking, a power plant, and finances. The signers also agreed to try to provide for the housing needs both for persons displaced by hospital-related developments and hospital personnel. Stores, offices, restaurants, and other services were also to be built for area residents and employees. In March, the details of the plans for the RTH project became clear: about 800 units of mixed housing would be built, along with parking and commercial space (*Harvard Gazette*, March 3, 1972).

In August, a coalition of Mission Hill groups, the Circle Federation, issued a report on joint community/institutional cooperation in area planning (Sharratt, 1972). "Alternatives for a Community-Institutional Area Plan" critiqued past institutional plans, but also proposed in detail ways of solving both community and institutional needs. Stressing the need for area-wide planning and community/institutional cooperative efforts, it asserted, "vital elements must cooperate in order to survive." Though supported by the Boston Redevelopment Authority, an effort to set up a joint community/institutional planning organization (the Mission Hill Planning Commission) was not endorsed by the medical area institutions. Map 5.1 shows the relationships of Mission Hill and Harvard Medical School.

By 1973, however, the situation in Mission Hill had stabilized. Amidst setbacks, there was progress. RTH had developed a full plan for housing and redevelopment. The AHC was not under construction. And the future plans of the larger area were still under consideration. Two blocks had also been rehabilitated in Mission Hill.

In mid-1974, the unit totals rose from 800 to 864, but then dropped to 774 by the end of the year. The plans for the larger number of units, and one mid-rise building, were dropped for cost reasons. While much of the area has already been reshaped, lack of funds has also contributed to plans for demolition of about 100 units, whose sites would become part of the overall project area.

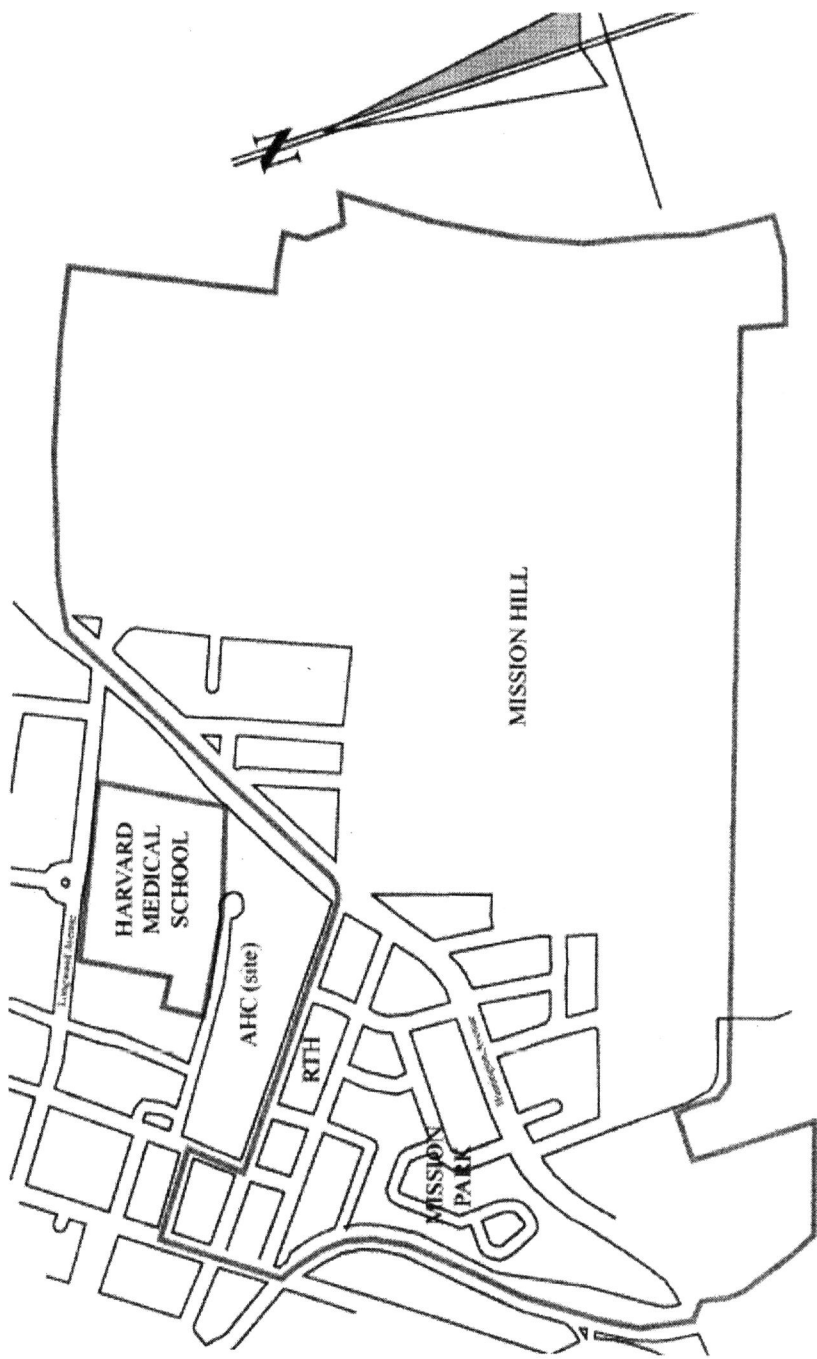

Map 5.1.   Mission Hill and Harvard Medical School
Credit: Walter H. Sobel FAIA and Han Gyeol Kim

THE PLANS FOR MISSION PARK[6]

Mission Park became a 775 unit of mixed housing[7] built on the Convent Site and part of the RTH neighborhood. The development also includes a mix of a high-rise tower, mid-rise and low-rise buildings, subsidized and market units, with supporting community facilities; 500 of the units were to be financed under Section 236 through the MHFA, with basic rents from $125 for one bedroom to $175 for four. In order to provide housing for families with low incomes, 200 (40 percent) of the Section 236 units were planned under the rent supplement program. Harvard also agreed to a "rent-bridging" agreement for relocated families who would be adversely affected by the higher rents, but were ineligible for rent supplement. This mixed occupancy development also included market rate units. While some were available to Harvard Medical students and institutional staff, priority went to RTH area families (*Harvard Gazette*, October 17, 1975).

The final project of a 27 floor tower, three mid-rises (from four to 13 stores) and 147 townhouse units included 391 one-bedroom, 228 two-bedroom, 128 three bedroom, and 28 four-bedroom units. Rents were 30 percent of units for low incomes (one quarter of tenants' incomes), 65 percent for moderate incomes (a quarter of tenant income), and 15 percent at market rates (from $425 for a one-bedroom to $625 for a four-bedroom townhouse) (Sharratt, 1977).

RTH, Harvard, and private developers were involved in developing the $48.222 million project, with construction costs of $36.032 million (Sharratt, 1977). The MHFA mortgage was about $40 million. Harvard, which is absorbing $620,000 in renovations and relocation costs, wrote down $3 million of land to $1 million. The project would generate $600,000 a year in taxes.

Harvard relocated about 100 families and rehabilitated the exterior of about 27 wood homes, among 75 dwelling units. The first 100 units at Mission Park, shown in picture 5.1, were ready about two years after construction began in 1975.

The housing project is in a high-rise tower, three steeped mid-rises, and townhouses, also included are a community center, a swimming pool, tennis and basketball courts, and medical office space for Brigham and Women's Hospital.[8] Groundbreaking for Mission Park was on October 17, 1975, and the project opened in January 1977 (Gonzales, 1976), and was completed by spring 1978 (Sharratt, 1977). John Sharratt Associates was the architect, and Cornu Corporation became the management agent at the end of 1978.

In 1999, RTH raised $70 million to buy Mission Park from Harvard and undertook $20 million in repairs. In 2000, RTH became the owner of Mission Park (www.missionpark.com/history.htm). Mission Park is now 90 percent affordable housing occupied by household with income below 60 percent of

Picture 5.1. Mission Park Apartments
Credit: John Sharratt Associates

the median income. It has also been involved in restoration housing in the Fenwood Road and Francis Street areas (Epsilon, 2009, appendix A).

Other parts of the $200 million developments for the medical area include a $50 million energy plant. It provides power for Mission Park and eleven area medical institutions, and paid $960,000 in lieu of taxes. There is also commercial space and underground parking for 1,300 to 2,000 cars. After the January 1975, merger of the three hospitals into the AHC, the 680-bed, $129 million Affiliated Hospitals Center was built on the Peter Bent Brigham parking lot just outside the RTH neighborhood's north border. The five-year process of AHC construction began with groundbreaking in December 1975 (oasis.lib.harvard.edu/oasis/deliver/~med00055). In 1980, AHC was renamed the Brigham and Women's Hospital.

A Dramatic Finale

The few weeks before the Mission Park groundbreaking in 1975 were almost as eventful as the weeks in April 1969. Following successful completion of widely attended hearings on forming a development corporation, an environmental impact statement and the energy plant in late summer 1975, all appeared set. RTH was even able to get higher Section 236 funding than normal. Unfortunately, $500 million of MHFA bonds were not selling in the spillover from New York's financial crisis, and funding for Mission Park and other projects was in doubt.

Sponsored by the RTH area State Representative, the legislature approved a bill to put Commonwealth backing on the issue. Then, ironically, it appeared that Mission Park, requiring $40 million of only about $65 million available for new projects, might not get funded (*Boston Globe*, October 12, 1975). Some MHFA officials felt the money should be spread out on more projects, and that, with Harvard backing, the project could get private money. While Harvard could not perform a financial miracle, the project was high priority for numerous Massachusetts and Harvard officials: On October 15, the MHFA board approved the $40 million mortgage. (Funding was assured, but if MHFA covered find alternative funds for Mission Park in ninety days, the $40 million could be used elsewhere.) On October 17, 1975, with the Mayor, Lieutenant Governor, Harvard President, and numerous neighbors looking on, ground was broken for the Mission Park project at 835 Huntington Avenue, it opened in 1977. In 2000, the Roxbury Tenants became owners of what today is a Section 8 development.

RTH IN RETROSPECT

The story of the Roxbury Tenants of Harvard provides an excellent example of a community group's successfully altering institutional planning and coming out with a major redevelopment plan. In a politically sophisticated and technically-detailed way, the Roxbury Tenants halted Harvard and Affiliated Hospitals Center encroachment. It thereby ended community exclusion from the planning process. By surmounting significant obstacles with their supporters and technical assistants, the Roxbury Tenants and Harvard have created and brought to the implementation a total community plan.[9]

The process created Mission Park as a mixed 775-unit community/ university housing development within the preservation of the Roxbury Tenants' neighborhood. It also provided for commercial, educational, and institutional developments in the area. The project produced redevelopment of the Roxbury Tenants of Harvard community, while accommodating medical area needs.[10]

NOTES

1. This chapter concentrates on the relations between Harvard Medical School and the Roxbury Tenants of Harvard community, two of many area groups and institutions. In the larger context, besides Harvard Medical School, the Affiliated Hospitals Center encompassed the Peter Bent Brigham, Robert B. Brigham, and Boston Hospital for Women. The Mission Hill Community group, the Circle Federation, had fifteen members. The Harvard Medical Area Planning Commission included fourteen institutional members. MASCO (Medical Area Service Corporation) runs food services, parking, shuttle-buses, and power services for eleven medical-related area institutions. City-backed attempts to develop an area-wide joint community/institutions planning organization had little success (see p. 119).

2. The central Harvard administration "outranks" the Medical School's and, after an initial period, the central administration handled details of the medical area project. The Office of Government and Community Affairs helped coordinate the project. The Medical School campus also includes the Harvard School of Public Health, School Dental Medicine, and the Countway Medical Library. Other medical area hospitals, including Mass Mental Health Center (MMHC), are also affiliated with Harvard but were not part of the Affiliated Hospitals Center, now Brigham and Women's Hospital.

3. This history derives from several sources cited here, and relies on Winkeller (1971, VI), with the author's permission.

4. About ten years earlier, there was a preview of this expansion controversy in the RTH area. At that time a group of neighbors mobilized, through political and legislative channels, to thwart an attempt by the Massachusetts Mental Health Center (MMHC) on Fenwood Road in Boston to acquire house and land for expansion through eminent domain (*Boston Globe*, 1963). In 2010, plans for the area for a Brigham and Women's clinical and research building included a 15 story high rise for at least 136 affordable apartments and condominiums (Rocheleau, 2010). Though the ultimate plan included 158 housing units (Taber, 2011), MMHC's redevelopment from its existing 113,769 sq. ft. building would be relocated to 76,540 sq. ft. in Brigham and Women's Hospital and a "Partial Hospital/Fenwood Inn" building (Development Plan, 2010) (see note 9).

5. Most area residents gradually came to support and join RTH. It is doubtful that a group without this broad base of support or the democratic orientation of RTH could have maintained its credibility with both the University and Community through five years of difficult negotiations. The Harvard students originally assisting RTH in community organization included Doug Levinson, Jeanne Neville, and Hayden Duggan, www.missionpark.com/history.htm.

6. Designated "Mission Park" in late 1974, begun in October 1975 and finished in spring 1978 (Sharratt, April 77), three of its buildings would be named for the community organizers, Doug Levinson (260 units in a high rise tower), Jeane Neville House (154 mid-rise units), and Hayden Duggan House (129 mid-rise units), who helped create RTH in 1969 and win the battles against Harvard. In addition, there were 85 units in mid-rise Flynn House and 147 two to three story townhouses (Sharratt, 1977) (see note 5).

7. Begun in 1968, the Massachusetts Housing Finance Administration (MHFA) was created by the State to build mixed-income (i.e., low, moderate, and middle) housing, like Mission Park. Projects begun earlier, like Putnam Square Apartments, River-Howard, and Inman Square, involved only low or low and moderate units. A social audit of mixed-income housing, "All in Together, An Evaluation of Mixed-Income Multi-Family Housing" (MHFA, 1974), found tenant satisfaction at all economic levels greater in mixed developments than in single level projects; design, sound construction, and proper management were crucial determinants of tenant satisfaction. Mission Park is an inner-city mixed-income development, not full Community/University housing. But as a mix of low, moderate, and market rent units, it was an important test of the MHFA program. It is now largely a Section 8 project [lihtc.findthedata.org/l/10316/Mission-Park].

8. Besides the 775 units of housing, there was an underground parking garage for 1,274 cars, 40,000 square feet of medical office space, and 6,000 square feet of neighborhood shops and recreational facilities, including a separate community building and play area, on the 13.5 acre site between Huntington Avenue and the Riverway next to Harvard Medical School in Boston. Thirty-nine of the housing units were handicap accessible (Sharratt, 1977). Total building space was 1,310,328 sq. ft., 639,462 sq. ft. residential, and 477,279 sq. ft. commercial. Construction cost was $27.48/sq. ft. and development costs $36.80/ sq. ft.

9. Reconsidering a 1969 critique of the Affiliated Hospitals Complex plan provides perspective on the progress accomplished during six and a half years of what at first seemed a hopeless situation. "[B]y failing to maintain the buildings in the Affiliated Hospitals area, and by favoring transient tenants, Harvard destroyed a once-strong community that now lacks the power to refuse to accept Harvard's expansion" (Harvard Strikers, 1969).

10. In 2010, plans for redevelopment of the former site of the Mass Mental Health Center included a clinical and research building for Brigham and Women's Hospital and a 15 story high rise of at least 136 (and up to 165) affordable housing and condominiums to be developed by the Roxbury Tenants of Harvard. At least 66 affordable apartments and 70 condominiums, half affordable were part of the plan (Rocheleau, 2010). Construction of the tower at the Riverway and Fenwood Road was to begin in 2013 for the tower then to include 158 units, the planned 66 affordable rental units and now 47 affordable condominium units and 45 market rate condos. It was planned to be completed by 2015 (Taber, 2011). Affordability would be available for households with incomes below 60 percent of the area's median income and widely marketed to neighborhood residents (Epsilon Associates, 2012) (see note 4).

Chapter Six

University Responsibility and Community Housing

What is a University's responsibility to the community in which it lives? While this is not a simple question, it is a particularly relevant one to the study of community housing. Did the universities espouse a responsibility in Cambridge and Boston that they met or not? Were the rhetoric of responsibility and talk of "diversity" mere discussions without results, or precursors to concrete action?

While University responsibility is a complex subject, the *Boston Herald Traveler* effectively summarized it in an editorial on MIT's 1969 housing announcement:

> A University's central function is academic, as MIT Chairman James R. Killian said this week. But when this function attains the scale and scope it does at institutions like MIT, there is bound to be an effect on the environment. The effect is usually a constructive one, but it can create or contribute to problems. And a University, it seems generally agreed today, has an obligation to help solve those problems (April 11, 1969).

The Report of a Presidential Committee at Stanford University summed up responsibility a year later: "The Committee believes that when the University (or any other institution) contributes to creating a severe social problem, it has a responsibility for contributing to a solution for that problem" (Shipler, 1968, 4).

How close did Harvard and MIT come to these simple standards in Cambridge?

THE UNIVERSITIES' VIEWS OF RESPONSIBILITY

Beginning in 1968, both MIT and Harvard started to speak the rhetoric of responsibility about community housing. MIT broached the subject at its

91

first negotiation with Housing Convention representatives in October 1968, a month after announcing plans to build housing in North Cambridge:

> We share your concern about the housing shortage and the escalations of rents, and we feel an obligation to help find remedies. Our sense of responsibilities is not limited to our internal needs; it extends to the city. We want to be a good institutional citizen (*Tech Talk,* 1968).

After the announcement of the full housing program in Cambridge, the head of the Institute Real Estate Office, Antony Herrey, justified MIT's actions by the intolerability of economic forces driving people out of Cambridge and the need for MIT to face its responsibility since: "Exaggerated and simplistic though they may be, accusations that our academic personnel were forcing out old Cambridge residents contained certain elements of truth" (Herrey, 1969, 29). In retrospect, Institute Chairman James Killian made an equally important point:

> It was . . . clear that the demand for housing on the part of the MIT Community itself had served to increase demand for housing in Cambridge and that we had a responsibility to help in dealing with the shortage (Killian, May 2, 1973).

MIT also felt another type of responsibility, one arising from its capability: "[If] MIT's willingness to exercise leadership, to provide the necessary resources, skills, and organizational capabilities, might . . . be the key to producing the needed housing. . . . Perhaps, notwithstanding the questions whether housing actually was our 'business,' [a leadership] obligation was ours. . ." (Herrey, 1969, 30).

Harvard also talked about its responsibility to the community in a cogent manner, though it initially failed to act on it. It was also mindful of the pragmatic considerations involved. In *The Wilson Report,* an official university document, though not reflecting University policy, the Committee on the University and City stated, "Harvard has a responsibility for helping improve [its] environment . . . in part because Harvard's presence is a significant determinant of the shape of that environment..." (*Wilson Report,* 1968, 11–12). "The university, because of its visibility, its symbolic importance, and the standards of conduct . . . has a special obligation to behave in exemplary ways" (36).

In the area of housing, the *Wilson Report* was quite specific, "We cannot assume that the local housing problems are someone else's affair if, by attracting more and more students, we have contributed to driving up rents and breaking up old neighborhoods" (*Wilson Report,* 1968, 12). It further stated, "we believe that Harvard, along with other local institutions, has a responsibility to join with public authorities to devise ways of increasing the housing supply or of subsidizing the cost of housing" (*Wilson Report,* 1968, 35).

The Need for Pressure

While MIT's Real Estate Office began charting the progress and causes of the housing crisis in 1966, and *The Wilson Report* identified in 1968 the problems of Harvard's role in Cambridge, neither school responded directly to housing needs nor their stated conceptions of responsibility though both began to contribute indirectly through the Cambridge Corporation. Facts, surveys, reports, the housing crisis, the Columbia Strike, and talk of responsibility set the stage. But it took direct pressure and demands from the community to get the universities directly involved in alleviating the problems they helped create. In 1967, MIT's Northgate Community Corporation planned to build additional community units, but did not produce them.

MIT INTO ACTION

MIT did not have to be physically confronted on the housing issue, but the Institute took a rather circuitous route to direct involvement. While MIT was conscious of housing problems early on, contributed to the Cambridge Corporation, and provided some community units and proposed further housing through Northgate Community Corp, even these limited Northgate plans were put aside for relocation work for the Inner Belt.

In any case, MIT was moved from its resolve to provide relocation housing for a highway by the intensity of protest against the Inner Belt, the increasing housing pressures of 1968, and the devastating evidence of the elderly housing survey. The September 1968 Cambridge Housing Convention and negotiations brought MIT to major action without need of a cataclysm. Had the community known of MIT's relocation-type housing role in assisting the hated Inner Belt, the Institute might have suffered more direct pressures at an earlier point. Had MIT not begun plans for a major relocation program, whether the housing crisis alone would have brought the Institute, typically more responsive than Harvard,[1] into building more than the few Northgate Community units planned, is difficult to say.

In retrospect, pragmatic self-interest had a central part in bringing MIT into a major housing contribution.

> This housing shortage and rent escalation hurts us too. [Because] not only teachers [and their recruitment] and students but also our many employees—were seriously affected by the housing shortage . . . the housing situation [in Cambridge] posed a genuine threat to the institution and the welfare of its members (Herrey, 1969, 28).

Moreover, Antony Herrey added,

> The disorders at Columbia that spring, involving University/Community rela-
> tions as they did, further fanned the flames of debate concerning the proper role
> of urban educational institutions. For us they confirmed the conviction that a
> University ignores the Community at its peril (Herrey, 1969, 29).

Made easier by its earlier relocation plans, great technical sophistication,
and a conducive philosophy, MIT made a major contribution in the Community housing area, essentially out of pragmatism.[2]

Harvard Action after Confrontation

In Harvard's cases in Boston and Cambridge, only the 1969 Strike and the
Commencement disruptions of 1970 brought results. In 1968, neither the
exhortations of *The Wilson Report*, City Council intervention, nor forceful
negotiations with the Housing Convention brought much change in the University's aloof attitude toward the housing problem or its role in Cambridge.

Harvard's more recalcitrant position is reflected in a general approach.
Achieving the University's primary objectives required "that the University
(or its principal officers) take seriously into account the concern within and
without the university for the consequences of the institution's behavior on
those who live near it or are affected by it" (*Wilson Report*, 1968, 10).

> [T]he citizens of our urban environment expect the University to act as a re-
> sponsible and enlightened landlord, employer, and neighbor. Little more than
> a legitimate concern for its own self-interest will lead the university to reflect
> seriously and act positively on the obligations of its urban citizenship (*Wilson
> Report*, 1968, 7).

The Report warned Harvard that, "The legitimate grievances of community
groups will increasingly be amplified and articulated by students and faculty,
partly because they share their problems and partly because the education the
university has helped provide leads them to conclude that these concerns are
morally right" (*Wilson Report*, 1968, 31, 7, 8). Moreover, the Report held,
"the students and faculty increasingly feel that having due regard for their
environment is one of the responsibilities of universities generally and of
Harvard in particular" (*Wilson Report*, 1968, 31).

Despite comments about responsibility and diversity, an understanding of
the pragmatic considerations[3] and warning in *The Wilson Report* and from
protesters that "Harvard will stop Harvard, if we have to tear it apart like
Columbia and San Francisco State" (Duehey, 1970a, 51), it was only crisis
at Harvard that brought a squaring of rhetoric and reality in the building of

community housing. It was dismaying that an educational institution that so clearly espouses responsibility to the community has to have its self-interest threatened and its image tarnished before it will act. Some argued that because of its character, a university will adhere to a higher standard. Others say that, despite its purposes, a university is like all other institutions and moves only when pushed or when its self-interest is threatened.

Again, both dismaying and encouraging is the realization that the crises Harvard experienced concretized its views on responsibility. *The Wilson Report* (1968) could be viewed as an attempt to convince a Harvard audience to do something, by approaching this in the way the audience could really understand—through self-interest, albeit enlightened. While *The Wilson Report* is directed to Harvard, one must search for a cogent statement of responsibility to the community.[4] Four years later another report "to the Cambridge Community" on the University's community efforts, particularly housing, stated clearly:

> The report recognizes that, although Harvard is neither a charity nor a social-action organization, it has a responsibility to the Community in which it is a substantial resident. This responsibility reaches beyond Harvard's primary function of research and teaching. It is based upon moral commitment, and enlightened self-interest and the knowledge that today urban institutions neither can nor should live in isolation from their surrounding Communities. Within the scope of its role and capacity, Harvard already has accepted much of its responsibility (Harvard University, 1972, 11).

How far the University came by the early 1970s, at least verbally, appeared more clearly in contrast to a statement by the president Nathan Pusey in 1967: "Our purpose is just to invest in places that are selfishly good for Harvard. We do not use our money for social purposes" (Magid, 1975, 41).

EDUCATIONAL VALUE IN COMMUNITY HOUSING INVOLVEMENT

Indirect Benefits to the University

A university's involvement in solving community housing problems can contribute to addressing its central role—education—in a number of ways. In a broad educational sense, for instance, because "diversity and even conflict are relevant to the intellectual life Harvard wishes to sustain," *The Wilson Report* advised contributing to housing development to support a "stimulating and heterogeneous environment" (*Wilson Report*, 1968, 43). For these reasons and to avoid housing-related disruptions, the Report supported development of student, faculty, and community housing on university lands: "We believe that it is in the educational interests of the university to seek out, actively, ways of increasing the supply of moderate-income housing in those areas of Cambridge and Boston on which the University impinges" (*Wilson Report*, 1968, 68).

True, the intellectual life of the university alone may prosper in a tight housing situation by the building of university apartments near campus for off-campus students who could not otherwise afford comfortable quarters with adequate study space, or for faculty who would not find suitable residences convenient to their regularly being on campus: Yet joint Community/ University housing development can create a learning experience about differences and similarities for university and community people who live together. The possibility of living/learning academic programs—courses offered at the housing, continuing education opportunities—occurring in such projects could also be great.

For the Academy

Developing community housing can also be tied directly to a University's main educational roles—teaching, scholarship, and service—occurring on campus and elsewhere to the benefit of both school and community.[5] Courses relevant to "Communities"—when the schools see themselves also as local institutions, make local concerns part of university lives. A "double play" of university and local community has been a long time in coming and a vital "symbiosis" is yet to be realized.

The development process in architecture, planning, and engineering, especially if the community participates, can be part of classes; social sciences and economics courses can also deal with relevant issues. MIT, for instance, had good success with civil engineering courses' working on ideas in pre-fabricated concrete for the MIT Housing Program. Because of its many facets, moreover, community housing may be the focus for interdisciplinary work, and the coordination of a number of subject areas around a central theme. In all these ways, courses become more relevant from combining real world problems and solutions to academic study and research. Besides learning the subjects and working out innovations, of course, students can also get experience performing surveys or providing technical assistance.

Research by professors and students on programs and processes to assist the projects can also be worthwhile. The building of community housing, and the related topics of Community/University relations can also be research and teaching subjects (see Mathiasen, 1971 and Slade, 1974). Such research on the development process, when presented to the community and not just in academic journals, and coordinated with the ongoing work, can provide great contributions. Research, however, is best done with the approval, respect for privacy, and sustaining of integrity of the community, otherwise people may become research "guinea pigs." Merely academic exercises, starting a project out of academic interest then dropping off when the tedious but necessary parts arrive, or because a preferred theoretical or policy approaches is not adopted, have to be avoided.

For the Administration

University officials working on community housing can learn and teach, too. For instance, from the start of its involvement in Community housing, MIT's staff found the sometimes frustrating negotiations with the Cambridge Housing Convention "mutually educational" (Herrey, 1969, 30). In retrospect, moreover, an Institute official saw community-housing planning as "a process of two-way education": "education of the Community groups" and "education by the Community group" (Kamilewicz, 1971, 21, 14). The Institute Real Estate office and Community Relations staff taught community members some of the possibilities, complexities, and tradeoffs of housing development, while learning much in return. The administrators learned about the problems community members face and came to respect the points of view of people in very different situations. They also learned about the realities of the problems their institutions were causing neighbors, and the anger and frustration such situations create. Besides receiving effective planning ideas and advice, the professionals acquired greater respect for community people, their problems and concerns.

A related educational aspect of community housing is that MIT felt its participation required the same level of standards as it had for education:

> MIT's role had to be consistent with its profound responsibilities as an educational institution. Every policy and every action . . . would have to meet the high standards that a center of learning like MIT must maintain. . . . In practical terms this meant that honesty and candor at all times in dealing with all parties, openness to new ideas, eagerness for innovation, intellectual discipline, thoroughness of workmanship and the highest standards in planning, design, management and the other fields involved (Herrey, 1969, 31).

To a great extent, MIT succeeded.

FOR THE ENTIRE EDUCATIONAL ENTERPRISE

Finally, a university's participation in community housing can in itself be educational. University members can learn from the process by participating or observing. When a school or community reports through the media about the college's involvement, or word travels widely, the details of university involvement can in themselves educate others. The lessons about what individual administrators, students, professors, and community members have done, and how the work contributes to education, both directly and through sustaining a stimulating campus and community environment, can inform others.

Retelling the stories of the successful and unsuccessful Community/ University housing efforts in Cambridge, Boston, and beyond can inform participants and other individuals of the value of fulfilling university responsibilities by providing community housing assistance. In short, a university's contributions to Community/University housing are intimately related to its educational goals and most fundamental concerns.

NOTES

1. There was enough difference in MIT's responsiveness for the Cambridge Housing Convention to distinguish between MIT's consultations and Harvard's "aloof" approach (Duehey, 1970c, 19). In June 1969, however, a participant in negotiations felt "the comparative results of the meetings with the two Universities showed MIT coming out far ahead in attitude but only slightly in specific policy commitments" (Kaiser, 1969, 21). As the author of *The Wilson Report*, James Q. Wilson, said in an interview, "MIT always won the battle of the press releases with Harvard," as it certainly did with its announcement of 1,600 units of low-income housing on the day of the Harvard bust. But he was skeptical about MIT's ever building the 1,600 units since the Institute was the "prime mover behind the Kendall Square land clearance project" and "wanted the inner belt" around its campus, which would have torn down hundreds of housing units (interview, February 26, 1973). MIT built 684 of 850 promised elderly units.

2. A different type of pragmatism, or practicality, brought MIT into community housing, too. The Massachusetts Institute of Technology is a "can do" school, both as a teaching/research academy and a corporation. Special talents allow special, or unusual, activities. MIT has the "necessary resources, skills, and organizational ability" (Herrey, 1969, 30), including the "special resources of talent" (Killian, May 2, 1973). The Institute went further, and sought "to find ways for an educational institution to take initiative in assisting the Community in meeting critical housing needs . . . without distorting its central academic function" (Killian, 1969).

3. "Preserving the Urban Fabric" (1966) sums up concisely how "City universities can no longer hide behind the walls that edge the campus. If the city beyond the walls is deteriorating, then the urban university will deteriorate too. They share a common fate." Moreover, "This new community concern is inspired not only by the nightmare of Morningside Heights [during the Columbia strike in 1968], but by the students themselves, who are moving out into the city to live, to study and to work. This fact alone links the university and the city together in a symbiotic search for survival" (Cummins, 1973, 51).

4. Harvard in particular, but similarly, MIT, has conceived of the "community" in too narrow, or too general, a sense by including all of Cambridge and the universities' contributions there. Harvard, and MIT to a lesser extent, have concentrated on the academic and technical world, on and off campus, using the nation or world as references. Both schools see their roles as creating leaders for world affairs and technological developments. The nation and world are places from which they draw, and to which they send their students. MIT especially does major research for industry and government, particularly the Defense Department. Killian once called MIT "crucial [to] the defense requirements of our country and the free world" (Killian, 1966). Figures like Henry Kissinger and Killian strive toward national and international, not local, stature.

As a "national institution [whose] talents and resources are dedicated to the national interests" (Killian, 1966, 11), MIT's main concerns are for "the 'symbiosis' of education and business, the 'triple play' of government, to education, to business" (Christopher, 1964, 51) on at least a regional level. By Community, MIT essentially means New England or the R&D industry, and feels a leadership responsibility as "a major resource" to the professional, scientific, and engineering community (Cabot, 1965, 9). As "Harvard and MIT define their constituencies in national and even worldwide terms, inevitably Cambridge affairs are considered relatively insignificant within that broad context" (McNally, 1970, 51). In 1966 for instance, MIT did not protest Inner Belt destruction of a large part of Cambridge housing; however, a threat to an edge of the nationally important Institute brought MIT into the fray. Never an ivory tower, MIT, became more open to outside service and local concerns than Harvard. The Universities' definitions of role and Community to which they are responsible, then, have retarded their responses to local problems. It has only been in large part because of local pressures that might affect their abilities to serve their other "Communities"—that the schools have seen themselves also as local institutions, where closer-to-home concerns must be part of their lives. A "double play" of University and local Community has been a long time in coming and a vital "symbiosis" is yet to be realized.

5. Some argue that universities should not be involved in the "housing business" at all. This argument might be valid if universities did not help create the problems they are called on to solve, and were not involved in non-educational ventures like Stanford Industrial Park, Technology Square, the Forrestal Center, the Cambridge Underpass, or pharmaceutical research and development. Moreover, most schools already are involved in the "housing business" through college housing, faculty mortgage programs, owning city apartments, investments in real estate, and, like Princeton and Stanford, having private profit making apartments on university lands. A 1972 EFL report, "Student Housing," adds a relevant point, too (Educational Facilities Laboratory, 1972; see Magid 1975a, 51). At the beginning of a section called "Preserving the Urban Fabric," it reports "Whatever means a college takes to realize its responsibility for housing students, it still faces a responsibility for preserving or improving the neighborhood around it." "In Pursuit of Shelter—the Housing Crisis at UMass" makes another important point: "Human services are a responsibility of an educational institution" (Magid, 1975a, 5).

Part III

COMMUNITY/UNIVERSITY HOUSING ELSEWHERE

Chapter Seven

Other Joint Developments

While Cambridge and Boston have the greatest concentrations of Community/University housing projects, other universities and communities have been involved in building, or planning, community housing. As table 7.1 at the end of the chapter summarizes, there is a wide variety of community housing elsewhere: some new construction, some rehabilitation; some planned, but not yet built; still others planned but abandoned. While most involve universities, communities and local governments, other institutions like hospitals and planning organizations have participated. Looking at other joint development projects provides beneficial insights.

MIDDLETOWN AND WESLEYAN UNIVERSITY

One of the most interesting community projects is in Middletown, Connecticut, where Wesleyan University and the Middletown Housing Authority built adjoining university and public housing projects midway between the campus and downtown. The sixty-unit, mixed high- and low-rise, family public housing was completed in fall 1972. The 341-unit, $3.9 million undergraduate Wesleyan housing was completed in fall 1973. The Wesleyan units were built under the HUD College-Housing program.

The original conception was to develop totally integrated graduate and public housing apartments. Because of projected shifts in graduate enrollment and the housing authority's immediate desire for relocation housing, Wesleyan changed to undergraduate housing and the Housing Authority went ahead independently. Despite these changes and the physical separation of the two projects, this is a joint institutional venture. Both projects share a redevelopment site. The University, in fact, retained an architect to develop an integrated site plan for the two projects. The University's participation in the redevelopment generated for the city almost $2 million of Section 112 housing credits.[1] An important distinction between the two projects is that, while the University involved students in the interior design of their future housing, the authority did not involve future residents. This difference contributed to the Wesleyan project's being more attractive and flexible. This lack of user participation in developing the public housing means that this development constituted more of City/University housing than a Community/University joint project.

Why did Wesleyan, which already makes in-lieu-of-tax payments, participate in such a project? Community pressures similar to those in Cambridge were absent in largely middle-class Middletown. The motivation basically came from within the University. Besides a desire to gain favor in the city and maintain stable neighborhoods, student housing was seen as a mechanism to integrate the low-income families into the fabric of the larger community and thereby avoid the traditional isolation of residents in public housing projects.

The project also tied in with a philosophy that few other institutions hold: "that it is not enough for the University to be a critic of society, however useful and constructive. The University also has an obligation to be a vital part of its Community." Though the hope that undergraduates would help public housing tenants may involve a rather idealist conception of community service, the project is a revealing model of University/Community cooperation. Interestingly, the Wesleyan architect felt it would be possible to create a totally integrated college/public housing project, where there is a sufficient conviction to overcome bureaucratic and political inertia.

What is especially encouraging about the Wesleyan case is that this joint Community/University project at Williams Street is not the University's first venture in Community housing. In 1966 the school capitalized the Hill Development Corporation and transferred 288 acres of Wesleyan-owned land to the Corporation for a 1,100-unit Planned-Unit Development south of the city. Mainly a middle- and upper-income development, the six-year project was planned to include 100 low-rent units. And in 1968, Wesleyan announced a $1 million revolving fund program of low-interest loans to help stimulate housing for low- and moderate-income families.

THE WOODLAWN ORGANIZATION AND
THE UNIVERSITY OF CHICAGO

After attempting to expand into and displace the nearby community through urban renewal, the University of Chicago was pressed to provide housing assistance to The Woodlawn Organization (TWO) of Saul Alinsky fame. TWO has built about 900 units of housing, some with University assistance. The University provided a $500,000 loan for architectural, legal, and other technical services in order to get full federal financing. It has also leased some of the land obtained under urban renewal, but would not need in the foreseeable future, to TWO for housing sites.

The first TWO development, Woodlawn Garden Apartments, was constructed on land the University had sought to obtain. Built under Section 221d3 low-interest loans, the mixed high- and low-rise project of 504 units (now Grove Parc Plaza Apartments) was completed in 1969 by TWO alone. The housing complex also includes a 54,000 square feet shopping plaza and supermarket. In succeeding with the $9.5 million project, TWO's executive director said, "We proved that a Community organization could build housing."

The second project, Jackson Park Terrace, was completed in the spring of 1974. It was built under Section 236, with university aid and on university urban renewal land. A residential project including day care and a commercial complex, it contains 312 units of housing and cost $8 million. Both projects were "economically integrated" through rent subsidies from the Illinois Housing Development Authority (Winkeller, 1971; Brown, 1970; *Chicago Tribune*, 1974; Fish, 1973; *Cleveland Press*, 1974; Student Community Housing Corp, 1971).[2]

SYRACUSE UNIVERSITY

A four building complex near downtown Syracuse, New York, is one of the earliest joint Community/University housing projects. Toomey-Abbott Towers, a 24 story elderly public housing project adjoins two Syracuse University dormitories, Brewster and Boland Halls, twelve and eight-story dorms, respectively, originally one each for men and women. About 400 elderly and 750 students share facilities for eating, shopping, and recreation in Brockway Hall, too. The complex also contains dining halls, health center, library, snack bar, and a 250-car underground garage. The development is a joint project of the University and the Syracuse Housing Authority.

Planned in 1961, the project grew out of a compromise in a land use controversy between the university and the city, and was completed in 1969. The complex also houses the All-University Gerontology Center, begun in 1972 to run academic and service programs for the elderly and to provide a focus for community/ university interaction. Particularly successful has been the "Tower Topics," continuing education program for elderly residents, which makes use of Syracuse facilities and personnel. Elderly residents have

University ID cards and can use other campus resources. The Ittleson Family Foundation conducted an evaluation of this intergenerational mixing (Klemesrud, 1970; *The Gerontologist*, 1971; *Apartment Construction News*, 1972; Hedden, 1974).

NEW YORK UNIVERSITY

Built in 1968, Silver Towers on 120 Bleecker Street is a three-towered, Mitchell-Lama project sponsored by New York University in Washington Square, Manhattan. Designed by I. M. Pei, the Towers (once called University Plaza) consists of two NYU faculty apartment buildings and 505 LaGuardia, a middle income cooperative originally used for relocation for the other two buildings. Though Mitchell-Lama is a New York State "moderate" income program, rents are only moderate for New York City. NYU also owns a mixed, luxury building in Washington Square, built in the late 1950s, called Washington Square Village.

DAVENPORT COMMONS AND
NORTHEASTERN UNIVERSITY

Northeastern University and the Lower Roxbury community in Boston developed Davenport Commons on a two and a half block site in Lower Roxbury adjacent to the Northeastern campus. Ultimately it became a 595 bed student housing complex and 75 home ownership units near Northeastern in Boston. Originally proposed in 1997 for 835 student beds and 50 community units, half home ownership and half rental, community pressure lead to an additional 10 community units at the site and 15 residences at another location in a deal agreed to in late 1998 for a $51 million project including commercial space (Bluestone, et al., 2003, 11–13, 21–22). The community was concerned about the process of decision making, the unit mix and type of housing, and the impact on the Lower Roxbury community. Both groups worked with Madison Park Community Development Corporation. The project fully completed and occupied by August 2001. The 75 condominiums and townhouses are at or below market rates. It is essentially two projects of dorms and family housing on one extended site. Northeastern and the Roxbury-Dorchester communities were also involved in developing what was called "The World-Class Housing Collaborative" (Bluestone, 2003, 22–24).

TALLADEGA COLLEGE

Talladega, a century-old, small Black college in Alabama, built low-cost housing on college lands in the early 1970s. The Talladega College Hills Apartments is a 40-unit, Section 236 project begun in September 1970. On a ten-acre site, the project mixes a few faculty units at market rates with lower-income family units, including 20 percent under a rent supplement. The housing was completed in June 1971 and cost $540,000.

PROJECTS PLANNED[3]

The Talladega and other cases show that it is not just big schools that can achieve Community/University housing. At least two other small colleges worked on the problems. In Fulton, Missouri, William Woods and Westminster Colleges cooperated with the city in a joint College/Community development in a deteriorated neighborhood between the two schools. Based on a Community "spine" design and including a College/Community center, the Fulton Plan Project (Urban Design Associates, 1972) was designed to include about 150 new units of housing, for a net gain of about 110. Scattered site and infill predominantly, the housing would be mixed graduate student, staff and market units, and all the non-student housing would be for families. How much would be low-income housing was unclear.

STANFORD AND COMMUNITY:
A PROJECT AFTER PROBLEMS

Stanford University in Palo Alto, California, and the Mid-Peninsula Urban Coalition worked on the "Frenchman's Terrace" community housing project for campus lands. While Stanford had already leased lands for middle- and upper-income housing, this was its first low- and moderate-income project. The Report of a Presidential Committee at Stanford summarized the University's responsibility in 1968. "The Committee believes that when the University . . . contributes to creating a severe social problem, it has a responsibility for contributing to a solution for that problem" (Shipler, 1968).

The 1969 *Moulton Report: Low Cost Housing Committee Report* set the stage for Stanford's participation. It recognized that the University helped produce the area's low-income housing shortage both by demand generated by its students, faculty, and staff, and "because of its land development program . . . significantly increased demand for local housing." University-related industrial development and population growth had helped create disproportionate middle- and upper-income housing demand; housing prices had risen beyond the means of families earning $15,000. The report estimated that 70 percent of the 4,000 low-income unit shortage was "directly attributable to University operations or the developments on Stanford lands." While the problem was aggravated by the restrictive zoning of adjacent communities which are beneficiaries of the University and its developments' policies, and share responsibility for acting on housing, the University had to face the fact that low- and moderate-income families, including University affiliates, were "being squeezed out of the area."

In May 1970, *The Wright Report: Final Report of the President's Ad Hoc Housing Advisory Committee* called on Stanford to act. Reflecting familiarity with Harvard's *Wilson Report on the University and the City*, the Cambridge housing situation, and the MIT and Harvard projects, the report written by Professor Gordon Wright recommended developing, at the earliest possible date, several hundred of Stanford's 8,168 acres of land for 600 to 2,000 units of low- and moderate-income housing. Besides housing, the report recommended physically integrating schools and Community facilities like recreation and day care into the projects, and involving the community in planning, design, and management (Caldwell, 1970). The report cited four reasons why Stanford should involve itself in Community housing. First, the University owned the largest piece of undeveloped land in "an area with little suitable land for lower-income housing." Second, "Stanford's leadership role in the area" and its moral force would be seriously impaired in failing to act and leading others to act. Third, the self-interest of the University was involved in solving the housing problem for university employees and affiliates. Finally, "The Committee believes when the University (or any other institution) contributes to creating a severe social problem, it has some responsibility for contributing to a solution to that problem."

The Stanford Trustees approved the 225-unit "Frenchman's Terrace" project in September 1971. Its course had been slowed by intense area discussion and debate about low-income housing-related issues and by the 1973 Nixon housing freeze. It was also delayed by disagreement with HUD over the inclusion of middle-income units in a Section 236 and rent-supplement project. The family development with 20 percent low-, 40 percent moderate-, and 40 percent middle-income (market) units was to be developed on twenty acres of Stanford lands by the Mid-Peninsula Urban Coalition. Half its occupants were to be Stanford employees, a quarter employees of firms on Stanford lands, and the rest from the wider community. Set for bids for the $5 million development in mid-1975, the project could have been finished in 1976.

In the meantime, the project failed when the federal government declared a moratorium on housing loans in 1973 and then withdrew funds two years later. Although a May 1974 Stanford trustee statement found it inappropriate to use the significant amounts of university lands for non-university-related housing, more joint housing remained possible. In 1979 the project was revived and a new plan was developed for 200 units combining townhouses and apartments for the twenty-acre site on Frenchman's Hill. The project was scaled down to 140 units ranging from 1,200 to 1,500 square feet (Wright, 1970; Moulton, 1969; Stanford University 1971; Student Housing, 1972, Joncas and Newman, 2006).

PRINCETON: COMMUNITY HOUSING AND LUXURY DEVELOPMENT

In a town experiencing university-generated housing problems similar to Stanford's, Princeton University announced in mid-1971 plans for 1,500 units of low- and moderate-income housing. In 1973, it proposed instead a 600-unit luxury development. The University, which owns about 3,000 acres, proposed to build some subsidized units near its research campus and in the town center.

Community Housing in 1971

Following a 1970 land use and housing study (Brown, 1970) noting five possible university sites for community housing and a consultant's report with housing recommendations (Landauer, 1970), the University learned that the area housing need was 4,500 low and moderate units (Landauer, 1970, 17). In May 1971, then University president Robert Goheen announced that Princeton "is now prepared to seek to bring about, on land which it owns, the construction of 1,500 units[4] of low and moderate housing, to be available to the general public" (Princeton University, 1975). Plans were announced for a 250 to 300-unit project on University lands of middle- and possibly lower-income apartments as part of an extension of a university-owned commercial development in Palmer Square in the Central Business District.[5] The rest of the 1,500 units would be built on university lands in four townships over five to seven years. The University also planned in 1971 to sell Palmer Square, as it was felt inappropriate for the school to control so large a part of the town's center.

Even before their community housing announcement, the University was indirectly contributing to the development of subsidized units through membership in a local housing coalition, Princeton Community Housing. By 1970,

PCH was working on 78 subsidized apartments above parking in the Central Business District near Palmer Square and about 240 units in outlying sections of town. The 78-unit project died in 1971 but 239 units of Section 236 housing, including 24 low-income units, "Princeton Community Village," opened in September 1975.

The Phase I Plan

By September 1971, a local developer presented "Phase I" proposal for 300 low and moderate units. Low-rise townhouses and garden apartments would have been built on thirty acres of University land near a graduate student Lawrence Apartments complex finished in 1966. The $5.4 million Section 236 project would have included 20 percent rent supplement, recreational facilities and parking. It was planned for 1973 especially for elderly and institutional employees who were experiencing increasing difficulty finding housing in the area. A 1971 consultant report (Citizens Housing and Planning Association of Metropolitan Boston, 1969, 5) suggested 150–170 units, with 60–65 subsidized. In March 1972, following an interim Central Business District report (Moulton, 1969) calling for 150 mixed income units, and 180 luxury ones nearby, the Princeton Planning Board raised the low-income housing limit from 200 to 550 to accommodate the University's Phase I project (*The Daily Princetonian*, January 14, 1972). By early 1972, the University announced plans for 276 units and the "necessity" of developing low and moderate housing at Palmer Square "to stem the exodus of low-income residents."

Plans Change

In July 1972, however, the projects were stopped when the University administration changed from Robert Goheen to William Bowen as president. As an offshoot of another University land use study it conceptualized a doubled student body, a law school and two other professional schools (Rein, 1973, 10), Princeton announced a delay for "some months" in the plans for community housing (*Princeton Packet,* 1972). Though the University had only promised to lease land and provide seed money, and the developer was willing to proceed, the delay was explained as a need to examine financing, management, and sponsorship. By January 1973, with the questions of July unresolved, the Nixon administration's national housing-freeze halted university plans for the community Phase I project.

In late 1973 the University no longer planned to sell Palmer Square and announced a proposal to add more stores and apartments just north of the Square. Coinciding with Town Central Business District planning, in early

1974 the University suggested building 80 to 100 apartments, including some with subsidies (*Princeton Packet*, 1974, 1). The Central Business District plans were formally adopted in July 1974, but poor economic conditions led the University to defer downtown housing development. The project was not dead, however, and the University reexamined it in the near future.

From Community Housing to Luxury, and Back?

In October 1973, the University announced plans for the Princeton Forrestal Center, a 1,607 acre planned multi-use development of an office- research center and residential village near Princeton's James Forrestal research campus (Princeton University, 1973). The Center was publicized as a development both to preserve and enhance the quality of the local environment and generate income for the University (Princeton University, 1974). It was a joint venture with private industry, perhaps the most lucrative since Technology Square in Cambridge to generate perhaps a million dollars a year (Rein, 1973, 13). Included in the plans were 600 acres of corporate office-research space and 500 acres of open space. The first plans called for the creation of a 190-acre Residential Village of 600 luxury townhouses, averaging $60,000, along with a 200-room hotel and small shopping center. Despite the area housing crisis and the 1971 promise to assist in its solution, the original plans did not include any subsidized units. [6]

After pressure from local officials, criticism by alumni and the Princeton Housing Group (1974), and coverage in the press, the University decided to include units "materially below market prices for the area." Now the 600 townhouses and apartments on 86 acres "will be designed to meet a spectrum of income needs. The University sought a housing developer willing to obtain subsidies for up to twenty percent of the units." Though the University did not promise any low-income units, university officials discussed with developers and evaluated subsidy programs, like Section 8 leases and state financing. Of the 600 units, about 200 were expected to be occupied by Forrestal Center employees. The Center was expected to generate 1,150 new households and the University expected a nearby moderate-income 3,000 unit Twin Rivers development would absorb much of the new demand (see Keller, 2003).

Delayed until late 1974 by sewerage restrictions, Princeton hoped to begin construction by fall 1976. In general, the Center's progress was slow. Housing plans included about 100 units a year until 1982. Princeton was also holding out the possibility of making more of its lands available for development, possibly fulfilling the 1971 pledge of 1,500 subsidized units. It was awaiting an improvement in the housing climate and the issuance of a Princeton Township Housing Master Plan for guidance.

Just south of the Forrestal Village site is an earlier commercial housing development on university lands. In 1962, the 120-unit Millstone Apartments were built privately under conventional financing (Landauer, 1970, 25). Princeton Theological Seminary owns the 200-unit Princeton-Windsor Apartments, ninety of which are open to the public (Landauer, 1970, 25).[7]

UNIVERSITY OF MASSACHUSETTS/BOSTON: PUBLIC UNIVERSITY INVOLVEMENT

The University of Massachusetts in Boston is the urban branch of the Commonwealth's system of higher education. For most of its first decade, UMass/ Boston was located in a number of buildings in downtown Boston. In January 1974 it moved to its new "Harbor Campus" on the Columbia Point Peninsula (Sobel, 1974). The community relations situation for the new campus was complex and tense. The super-block campus shared the peninsula with a 1,500-unit, predominantly Black and Puerto Rican, public housing project. The closest neighborhood, Dorchester, is a large, working-class community concerned about the ill effects on its housing situation of a growing university. Plans projected 12,500 students and 1,600 faculty.

Residents of the housing project feared that the University eyed their homes for students housing. A daily influx of commuters and a residential immigration of students and faculty boded havoc for the residents of Dorchester. Residents opposed a "Cambridgization" of their area, fearing real estate speculators would push rents up and community residents out. The community brought pressure on the university and city to prevent a detrimental impact on the area. Following this pressure and a Task Force report that clearly spelled out the magnitude of the impending influx, the university discouraged students from living in the local "impact area." In January 1974, the University and City of Boston announced plans for a major Community/ University development for the peninsula (Greenhouse, 1971).

The development proposed for Columbia Point would be a "New Town for the Peninsula." Plans included a revitalized commercial center, recreational facilities, a town center, and up to 1,000 new, upper- and 2,000 middle-income units as part of a 4,000-unit housing program. The economically and socially integrated in-town plan reversed the idea of dispersing low-income people to the suburbs while bringing upper-income people to the city. Plans for taking over and rehabilitating part of the public housing project created controversy, however. Though 1,000 public housing units would have been renovated, several hundred vacant units would be demolished. This move would reduce the available low-income supply and confirmed project residents' fears.

The proposal, especially notable because a public university and a city government were involved in major roles, faced a tough test in a delicate

Community/University situation.[8] Others looked suspiciously at support by community groups, which co-sponsored the proposal report. By 1975, the $150 million project was not funded. According to one city hall source, "It's a statement of desire, rather than a statement of reality" (University of Massachusetts, 1974).

In February 2005, UMass Boston and the Harbor Point Apartment Company signed an agreement to provide for university access to housing at Harbor Point and community access to UMass services. Harbor Point was a mixed income housing community of subsidized and market housing. The agreement permitted 10 UMass faculty and staff and 600 UMass students to live at Harbor Point. It was partly funded by HUD and the Commonwealth (Harbor Point Agreement, 2005).

In Worcester, Massachusetts, site of the University of Massachusetts Medical School, the Worcester Higher Education Consortium stimulated private developers to provide housing for students and the community. Downtown offices were being remodeled for about 75 apartments; with new construction a possibility. Home of eleven schools, before the full opening of the Medical School in 1975, Worcester faced a housing crunch.

Community/University housing might also be a possibility for Amherst, home of the 25,000 student main UMass campus, and Amherst College and Hampshire College. "Rural Amherst Has an Urban Problem" and "In Pursuit of Shelter—the Housing Crisis at UMass" explained the situation (Magid, 1975a, 1975b): vacancies at about one percent under a construction moratorium. A transformational trend of students displacing lower-income residents had begun and the possible lifting of dorm requirements for 11,000 students became a campus and town issue. University of Massachusetts president Robert Wood, former Housing and Urban Development secretary and architect of the Model Cities program, or campus leaders could have presented a UMass/Boston-like plan in Amherst. Community/University housing might have been a solution there and in Worcester when UMass Medical School opened. Wood offered a campus site in Boston near the new UMass Boston Harbor campus when a Cambridge location for the John F. Kennedy Presidential Library was rejected.

DREAMS DEFERRED

Columbia University

Growing out of community opposition to University encroachment as a demand during the 1968 Student Strike, Columbia University worked on a "Pharmacy Site" project for both rehabilitation of existing units and construction of 140 to 200 new apartments for community members and Columbia personnel. Sponsored under the New York Mitchell-Lama and Section 236 programs but seeking other subsidies, the high-rise construction was to include a Community service program and facilities, and commercial space. It was deferred after the 1973 Nixon housing freeze (Fried, 1969).

Columbia Teachers College[9]

In November 1968, Columbia Teachers College announced a $60 million campus expansion program to include 1,000 units of Community/University housing. Planned to complement new academic facilities, a library, an arcade and shops, the housing was to be in two forty-story towers, one for community members including subsidized, low-income units, graduate students and faculty, the other only for students. The announcement followed by six months the conflict over expansion by Columbia University (CTC is related but separately run) was met with community approval, and featured in front-page *New York Times* coverage (Shipler, 1968, 27). Community members were consulted on the housing plan, and the development was scheduled so the 200 families on the target block could stay in other apartments there until the new housing was ready. CTC owns about 400 city units, mainly community occupied.

Though an academic building has been finished and library construction is planned, the CTC project conceived in 1966 for a 1971 start was dropped because of the more restrictive economy for both universities and housing development.

University of Pennsylvania

The University of Pennsylvania and the local community in West Philadelphia negotiated the construction of 85 new, low-cost units as a follow-up on a February 1969 trustee commitment for a $10 million revolving housing fund. Originally planned as a Section 236 development, this route for the "Unit III" housing was killed by the 1973 housing freeze. The Community then approached Penn for university funding in 1974. The University refused but offered technical aid and services of their real estate consultant to see if a project could be developed.

UNFULFILLED PROMISES

Cornell University

Still other schools have talked about community housing projects. In Ithaca, New York, in 1969, Cornell University began discussions with TOMCO

Better Housing for about 100 detached houses for low-income families. The University would sell the land at a low price. Unfortunately, according to the University, TOMCO "had more good will than experience in building housing" and the project failed to materialize. Cornell, however, also contributed to a feasibility study for scattered housing and sold land for a project in cooperation with the city of Ithaca and the New York Urban Development Corporation (UDC).

Manhattanville College

In Purchase, New York, in early 1971, Manhattanville College planned to sponsor academic and staff housing. Trying to solve the problem of near-campus housing for faculty in an expensive suburban area, the College proposed, with New York Urban Development Corporation aid, about 200 low-rise, garden apartments for faculty, staff, and student housing. Up to 30 percent of the low- and moderate-cost units in the $3.4 million project would have been for local residents, possibly teachers at elementary and secondary schools. Despite strong on-campus interest, the plans had to be abandoned because of intense local opposition to subsidized housing and Urban Development Corporation involvement in wealthy Westchester County (Greenhouse, 1971; *The New York Times*, 1971, 47).

VARIATIONS ON THE THEME

University Circle Cleveland

Case Western Reserve University in Cleveland, Ohio, has been indirectly involved in developing community housing. The University Circle, Inc., a University co-sponsored organization, was involved in three housing projects in the nearby Hough neighborhood. Along with Citizens for Better Housing and the Hough Area Development Corporation, UCI completed Community Circle Estates in eastern Hough. The 160 units of middle-income housing under Section 236 were begun in 1971 and completed by 1974. The $3.25 million project includes 116 smaller units and 44 town-houses on two sites.

Two other projects were planned. Antioch Apartments would be 170 low-income units built under FHA Section 221d3, with 100 percent rent supplement. Community Circle II was planned for about 120 townhouses on urban renewal land. They would also be 221d3 with 100 percent rent supplement. University Circle, Inc. also worked on a New-Town-In-Town concept for Cleveland (Cleveland Press, 1974).

Presbyterian-University of Pennsylvania Hospital

An especially interesting community housing project that shows what other types of institutional sponsors[10] can do was co-sponsored by Presbyterian-University of Pennsylvania Medical Center, a university related, but separate institution, in west Philadelphia. Center Post Village, 84 garden apartments in eight buildings, was completed in February 1973 after five years of preliminaries. Built on land once slated for hospital expansion, the Section 236 project, with 20 percent rent supplement, is predominantly family housing. There are only eight single units. Previous residents of the site and people displaced by government action received priority. A few hospital employees also live there. The medical center provided seed money and created a sponsoring organization of hospitals and community. The Center saw the housing as part of its preventive health care program, since good housing reverses the cycle of poor housing's contributing to strain and poor health (Cummins, 1973).

Student Community Housing Corporation

In New Haven, Connecticut, the Student Community Housing Corporation, with no direct ties to Yale, rehabilitated old apartment buildings for community use. In 1970, Yale announced the Yale-New Haven Community Housing and Economic Development Corporation, with funding from a Yale donor. But it did not move in the community housing direction (Student Community Housing Corporation, 1971).

IDEAS WHOSE TIME MAY BE COMING

A promising new way to look at Community/University co-development appeared in a report by Educational Facilities Laboratories urging university leadership in the revival of the cities (Withers, 1970). "A College in the City" presented the idea of a new "community college" in Bedford-Stuyvesant in Brooklyn, whose programs and physical facilities would become integral parts of the community and contribute to the renewal of the city. Creating the College would help regenerate the city, rather than annihilating whole blocks as new college construction or expansion typically does. College facilities like libraries, classrooms, and cultural centers would fill in vacant spaces and upgrade existing buildings. This urban mix of joint uses—an exciting physical interpretation of the authentically urban educational concepts of a true community college—was envisioned for major regenerative effect on the part of Bedford-Stuyvesant.

Table 7.1. Community/University Housing Elsewhere

Project Name/Description	Sponsors/Participants	No. of Units	Subsidies	Cost $ Millions	Completion Date
Williams Street Apartments	Wesleyan University	341	College Housing	$3.9	Fall 1973
Travis Square Apartments	Middletown Housing Authority	60	Public Housing	$1.5	Fall 1972
Woodlawn Gardens	TWO	502	221d3, Rent Supplements	$9.5	Fall 1969
	TWO/University of Chicago	318	236, Rent Supplement, University of Chicago	$8.03	Spring 1974
Twomey-Abbott Towers	Syracuse Housing Authority	364	Public Housing	$6.65	January 1969
Brewster-Bolland Dorms	Syracuse HU/NYS Dorms.	400	NY State College Housing	$5	January 1969
Silver Towers(U Plaza)	New York University	180 x 2	Mitchell-Lama	$8	Late 1968
505 LaGuadia Plaza	New York University	180	Co-op		
Talledega College Hills	Talledega College	40	Section 236	$.54	June 1971
Fulton Plan	William Wood/Westminster	150		$2.5	
Frenchman's Terrace	Mid-Penn. Urban Coalition/ Stanford University	225	Section 236, Rent Supplement	$5	(due 1975–76 Dropped 1976)
Lawrence Golf Course	Princeton/Kendall Dev. Co.	275	Section 236	$5.4	(dropped 1973)
Palmer Square Extension	Princeton University	90	leases?	?	(proposed May 1971)
Forrestal Center	Princeton University/private devel.	600	120 subsidized	$36	(proposed October 1973)
Columbia Point New Town	Boston/University of Massachusetts-Boston/ Community	4,000	1,000 public housing	$150	(proposed January 1973)
Pharmacy Site (?)	Columbia University	140/200	Section 236, Mitchell/Lama	$5	(proposed 1968)
Unit III	Unit III Housing/ University of Pennsylvania	85	Section 236, Rent Supplement	$1	(proposed February 1969)
Tomco	Tomco Better Housing/Cornell Univ.	100	Section 236?	$1.5	(proposed 1969; abandoned)
Manhattanville College Apts.	UDC / Manhattan College	200	Section 236?	$3.4	(proposed 1971; abandoned)
Teachers College Project	Columbia Teachers College	1,000	500 Subsidized	$60	(proposed November 1969)
Community Circle Estates	University Circle	160	Section 236	$3.25	1974
Antioch Apartments	Hough Development Corp.	170	Section 221d3	$3.5	(proposed 1974)
Community Circle II	Hough Development Corp.	120	Section 221d3	$3.25	Completed 1975
Center Post Village	Presbyterian/University of Pennsylvania Hospital	84	Section 236, Rent Supplement	$1.5	February 1973

Like the academic and cultural facilities of the College, housing would contribute to the revitalization of the area and be scattered and intermixed with existing construction. As much existing housing, often beautiful Victorian structures, as possible would be restored. In addition, it would provide a variety of new housing—fit into "holes" in the community—for university personnel and for the community. "This kind of challenge represented by housing is exactly what this new kind of planning process is all about."

"A College in the City," based on the ideas of William Birenbaum (1969), President of Staten Island Community College, was dedicated to the late Senator Robert Kennedy, who was closely involved in the Bedford-Stuyvesant restoration efforts. The report outlines an exciting way for the very process of physical development of a college to improve both housing and other community facilities, to strengthen community fiber, while providing leadership in total urban redevelopment. The educational institution projected by the report opened as a four-year branch of the City University of New York, Medgar Evers College, in September 1971. Unfortunately, Medgar Evers College did not include a physical expression of an urban educational program, as "A College in the City" advocated.

Some of the report's innovative ideas have been picked up elsewhere. Public institutions like Minnesota Metropolitan State College in St. Paul and Evergreen College in Washington State have incorporated some of the report's thrust. The Committee for a Real Community College in Uptown Chicago pushed to implement the spirit of "A College in the City."[11]

JOINT PLANNING ORGANIZATIONS (JPO)

Joint Community/University planning organizations can also contribute to cooperative housing development. Five such organizations were developed and often included not only community and university but also other institutional members and the city as well. They worked on joint planning efforts for housing and other fields (Rauch, 1968). The groups are:

1. Oakland Development, Inc. (Pittsburgh, Pennsylvania; University of Pittsburgh and Community).
2. University District Organization, Inc. (Columbus, Ohio; Ohio State and Community).
3. The Neighborhood Support Organization (Cincinnati, Ohio; University of Cincinnati and Community).
4. Greater Homewood Community Corporation (Baltimore, Maryland; Johns Hopkins University and Community).
5. City of Berkeley-University of California Community Affairs Committee (Berkeley, California).

A sixth Joint Planning Organization, the Mission Hill Planning Commission in Boston (including Harvard Medical School, local hospitals, and numerous community groups), did not develop because of institutional objections. The 1975 housing report by Edward Meyers and Ira Fink at the University of California, Berkeley, details the joint planning organizations (Educational Record, 1974).

A RANGE OF VARIATIONS

In short, current and planned Community/University and related housing projects provide models for how to approach this important innovation. The Cambridge and Boston area presents the highest concentration of examples, but other cities demonstrate variations on the Community/University housing themes. They extend from rehabilitation to new construction. They serve the elderly to families. Others are in the planning stage or postponed.

Besides the more familiar joint development of community/university housing, there have been a number of innovative projects involving hospitals and joint planning organizations. This review of other community/university housing projects highlights the beneficial approaches to pursue and the problematic ones to avoid. These and the Cambridge and Boston examples, as (table 7.1) Toomey-Abbott shows, can inspire future forays into Community/University housing and development. What broader lessons can we learn from previous joint projects?

NOTES

1. Section 112 of the 1954 Housing Act provided two or three federal dollars for the city redevelopment costs for each dollar a university spent on site acquisition, construction, and relocation.

2. One of the ironies and problems of trying to build adequate low-income units is pointed out by a TWO experience: the 1969 *Gautreaux* decision against discriminatory concentration of low-income people kept the amount of low-income units in Woodlawn Garden Apartment below the 50 percent TWO sought (*Gautreaux v. Chicago Housing Authority*, 296 F. Supp. 907, 1969; *Hill v. Gautreaux*, 425 U.S. 284, 1976). For updates on the TWO situation with the University of Chicago, see Peterson, 2008, Samuels 2009, and Woodlawn New Communities Program, 2009.

3. SUNY-Buffalo and SUNY-Brockport, Illinois Benedictine, University of Oklahoma, St. Benedictine (Minnesota), Fairhaven (Washington State), and the University of Wisconsin at Whitewater have also explored dorm conversion for elderly housing, some with educational programs involved. Besides also suggesting the use of dorms for the elderly, "In Pursuit of Shelter" indicates, "We have been in touch with representatives of farm workers' organizations who indicated that migrant workers that

come to Hadley and surrounding towns might be able to live in the dorms part of the
year and have the cost paid by employers" (Magid, 1975a, 13).

4. The 1,500 units was the portion attributable to the demand created by institutional and municipal employees (Landauer, 1974, 17). The University responsibility
was over 2,000 units, according to consultant figures of 2,400 to 3,300 university low-
moderate household-head employees living outside of Princeton (Landauer, 1974, 6
v. 79). These figures understate the number of employees living outside Princeton
by over 500 (Gershen, 1967, 17 estimates by 1,500; Landauer, 1970, 17 estimates
by over 1000). Also, 3,000 University people, including 750 students in private units
(Sternlieb, 1971, 9), but not the 1,200 Princeton alumni residents (*Princeton Alumni
Directory*, 1974) or employees of University-attracted firms, occupy over 35 percent
(1,350 university plus 1,350 private unit) (Landauer, 1974, 79) of the town's 7,400
housing units (Sternlieb, 1971, 43–44). Moreover, there were 1,300 sub-standard and
too expensive units (New Jersey Department of Community Affairs, 1975, 20; 100
overcrowded units (Sternlieb et al, 1971, 153); the vacancy rate was 1.1 percent vs.
four to five percent normally needed (300 units); about 400 households were forced
out of town by housing pressures (Sternlieb, 1971, 40–41). These figures provide the
magnitude of the responsibility the University has for correcting the low and moderate housing problems and the needs it helped create in substantiating the 2,000+
figure for additional affordable units needed. (Figures approximate. Sources: Census
data; Sternlieb, 1971; Landauer, 1970; Hedden, 1974; Moulton, 1969; Brown, 1970;
Princeton Alumni Directory, 1974; and calculations.)

5. A wealthy Princeton alumnus, Edgar Palmer, built the Square in the 1930s as
a complement to his alma mater. While pleasantly colonial, a good source of De-
pression jobs, and providing 100 market apartments, the $4.5 million private urban
renewal project removed about eighty dwelling units. Plans to expand the Palmer
Square and "redevelop" a nearby low-income section of town through federal urban
renewal in the late 1950s were defeated by local opposition and legal action (*Griggs
v. Borough of Princeton*, 33 NJ 207, 1960; Sobel, 1971) at the start of the 1960s,
though follow-up development removed another twenty housing units (*Princeton
Packet*, 1935–41, 1955–62).

6. Two interesting illustrations of the local housing crunch and housing politics occurred then. First, the Planning Board refused to let the University convert a residence
it bought to office use; then the Borough Council requested the University not demolish a double house for a building site, both based on the severe need for housing. The
University demolished the house anyway (*Princeton Packet*, August 27, 1975)—two
of perhaps twenty-five units removed from residential use by University-related action in the last fifteen years. Princeton reevaluated use of the other current housing
unit.

7. Nearby Rider College planned to make 48 acres available to a developer land
for 480 market units, 25 percent for college personnel. The rest of the project, which
reverted to college ownership in thirty years, and was meant to provide housing and
income to the 4,000-student school, would be open to the public. A developer was
ready to proceed if the Town of Lawrenceville provided zoning.

8. Another state-related school, Temple University in Philadelphia, provided some seed money, technical assistance, and political support for two low- and moderate-income projects north of campus. Nearby Glassboro State College (renamed Rowan University) in southern New Jersey developed plans for a large commercial development to include low-income and college housing. The nearby Triad and Mansion Park Apartments already mixed college and community.

Across from Philadelphia, Rutgers, the State University of New Jersey in Camden, trying to expand its campus into the adjacent Cooper-Grant Community, was asked by the People of Cooper-Grant to work cooperatively on a Fulton Plan-like joint development (see p. 107). While Camden city and New Jersey state officials were more supportive, and Rutgers 1973 Master Plan mentions contributing to the needs of area low-income families, the university's actions continued to deteriorate the Cooper-Grant Community. In response, the city and community began a renewal progress on their own (see Barrett, 1974, 1975, and the epilogue here).

9. Just north of Columbia in the Bronx, Hostos Community College of CUNY, planned its new fourteen-acre campus next to 2,000 units of low-income housing. A predominantly Spanish-speaking, minority-oriented college, with a health care orientation and strong educational leadership, Hostos originally wanted to build student housing. This was meant to expand access to its health care programs and provide supportive and stimulating environments for its students, but City University of New York rules against having community college housing stood in the way. The new campus and housing are adjacent to San Juan Plaza, the first Puerto Rican developed and owned shopping center in the continental United States.

10. In an earlier era in housing development, predominantly the 1930s when the public housing program started, a number of philanthropic housing projects were created: (1) Charles Bank Homes in Boston, by Edward Ginn, 1911; (2) Franklin and Maple Terrace in Princeton, New Jersey, by Gerard Lambert of Listerine Company; (3) Mullanply Apartments in St. Louis; 4) Mariemont Homes in Cincinnati; (5) Lavanborg Homes in New York City; (6) Phipps Houses, by Henry Phipps ($1 million) in New York City; (7) Paul Lawrence Dunbar Apartments in Harlem, by John D. Rockefeller; (8) Marshall Field Garden Homes and Michigan Boulevard Apartments in Chicago; (9) Chatham Village in Pittsburgh, by Buhl Foundation (see Abrams, 1945).

11. There may be other projects whose identification is welcomed. Hastings College of Law in San Francisco, Portland Community College, and Cleveland State or the University of Pittsburgh have been involved in or are planning Community/University housing. Williams College in Massachusetts and the University of Louisville explored but dropped the plans.

Part IV

NEW SAWS FOR
BUILDING COMMUNITY/
UNIVERSITY HOUSING

Chapter Eight

Conclusions, Suggestions, and Lessons

Community/University housing around the country provides lessons about the benefits and challenges surrounding these campus-related projects. For example, MIT and Harvard began by building community housing for the elderly through the Cambridge Corporation. With university assistance, The Woodlawn Organization and The Riverside-Cambridgeport Community Corporation built family housing. The University of Massachusetts/Boston and the Fulton College also planned joint Community/University developments. Variations on these themes have been and can be created elsewhere.

Looking back on the Cambridge, Boston, and examples beyond, what insights are there for future development? Lessons and suggestions fall in several areas: Both university and community alike have to remember that community housing is both a political and technical process. In emulating successful approaches, it is essential to realize the full meaning of "Community" housing. It is important to recognize the difficulties in pursuing successful housing developments in order to avoid related problems.

REALITIES I: POLITICAL FACTORS

Universities generally become involved in community housing because they encounter pressures to do so. This is a fact community groups wanting university participation in community housing have typically recognized. By attempting to expand physically or by attracting an influx of school-related residents, universities help create the very pressures they must then respond to through involvement in community housing. Typically, however, a school will try to avoid assuming responsibility for housing problems.

Strong and effective organization, political sophistication, and persistent, undiscouragable pressures are the working tools of community groups. Organized pressure with critical publicity can point out disparities between a university's image as a progressive, liberal, and humanistic institution and the realities violating this image, like unprincipled expansion, provide especially effective leverage. Getting the city government, powerful figures, and groups on the community's side is also helpful.

Both universities and communities recognize that types of pressures differ and they elicit different responses. Direct, intense, confrontational pressures, as at Harvard and Columbia, appear most prominently in the headlines and often gain the strongest response. Sometimes pressures are applied through political channels, through the media, or involve powerful militancy. Sometimes pressures are sporadic. Occasionally protests are directed at issues like the Inner Belt that spill over onto the university and threaten the stability of its environment, if not the institution itself. MIT perceived and acted on tangential and potential problems before a crisis reached its doors.

Sometimes, on the other hand, universities like Wesleyan act without direct pressure because they want to stabilize their surroundings, avoid neighborhood deterioration, follow opportunities, or avoid potential problems. Often a more diplomatic approach can supplant a more confrontational one. Yet universities never act entirely out of selflessness, but instead they try to solve, avoid, or deal with problems and needs of their own when involved in community housing.

Because communities can appeal to a university's self-interest, it sometimes helps community groups to structure or phrase their demands in terms of how Community/University housing can help solve university problems. Showing the educational nature of university participation in community housing can also be helpful. Some community groups resist stressing the fulfillment of university interests, however, if that lessens the emphasis on community autonomy. Getting a university to admit that it has helped cause the housing problems it is asked to help solve can also facilitate community successes.

When Universities become Involved

While universities and colleges will normally resist movement in community housing, once convinced or pressured into action, the schools often try to structure participation to their advantage. The schools then also attempt to gain goodwill or public relations "points" to help fend off future pressures on the university, or to further university goals. Involvement also often increases a university's awareness of the educational benefits and values of participation in community housing. It may also increase a school's willingness to proclaim publicly a responsibility in the housing area. However, university statements of responsibility are poor guides to whether a university will willingly participate in community housing.

MIT projects director, Antony Herrey, advised universities that while they ignore the community at their own peril, they need not act in the housing area only because pressures reach a crisis (Herrey, 1969, 29). When no one else is able or willing to act, it is appropriate, even necessary, for a university to lead the way. To determine this point, schools should keep alert to community, especially housing problems, their possible solutions, and the ability or inability of existing agencies to handle the problems. Herrey also points out the importance of effective leadership for successful university involvement. Lack of or a decline in high-level university commitment, which continuing community pressure can help maintain, may slow the momentum of a project.

COMMUNITY INVOLVEMENT

There is a broad significance to the meaning of "Community Housing" for institutional leaders to keep in mind. Community participation is not just an appendage, but needs to be an integral part of the development process. To be legitimately "community" housing, a project's development must involve community members in all phases, unless the community chooses a lesser role. Community groups, of course, need to choose their role and its level carefully. Taking on a more difficult role than is manageable, or becoming inextricably entangled in problems, like tenant selection, can destroy legitimacy and ruin projects. To be sure of maintaining community integrity, groups must also have able leadership and wider community backing in developing housing.

In whatever role they take, community groups should have the opportunity to be involved from the very initiation to the completion of the development process. Maximum political sophistication and development skills come from full partnership in any project. Some groups may choose to co-sponsor projects; some may find community control results, as the Riverside Community Corporation once defined it, from the right to choose a developer and select tenants (Donham, 1972, 137).

As only the community can define its wants and needs, community members must also fully participate in project design, both outside and inside. As the MIT process showed, for instance, that community participation in design can often suggest, create, and approve imaginative solutions and lead to greater understanding and innovation by the initiating institution.[1] To be self-sufficient, and present their best case, moreover, community groups need their own fully competent and accountable professional planning and design help. Good architecture, planning, and legal assistance permit the community to negotiate on a more equal footing with the institutions. A community has a right to decide on site, types of units, size, and style of the housing projects.

The Roxbury Tenants of Harvard and Riverside Community Corporation examples clearly show the benefits to community and project of the community having its own competent professionals. It is best if community groups can pay professionals with community funds and grants, or can find able volunteers. Sometimes universities can provide the funds, as Harvard did, for the community to hire their own professionals. Communities will often want to have neighborhood residents working or being trained on the projects in which they are involved. While nonprofit development has been typical of low-income housing, for-profit development might suit some community needs (Urban Planning Aid, 1973). This is especially so in raising money for development costs or community activities. Some communities have chosen to "sell" tax shelter to raise capital.

WAYS A UNIVERSITY CAN HELP

Once a university becomes committed to participate in community housing, it can provide help in a number of ways. Without direct participation, a school can be a motivating force behind a project (Donham, 1972, 23–31). It can catalyze others by articulating a housing need and providing leadership to get others to move. For instance, a university, as a responsible public citizen, can call on local government or corporations to act in the housing area. It can also encourage or assist community-based housing corporations in housing activity.

The very fact of a university's direct participation in a project can vastly increase a housing development's chances of success. With the influence, resources, long-term nature, staying power, and prestige of a University involved, a project has better prospects of completion.

More specifically, a university can be helpful in successfully setting the process in motion, in the sponsorship and in the development of housing. A university can be a nonprofit or limited dividend sponsor, co-sponsor with community groups. It can assist the development of a community-based housing development corporation, through which the university and community can work. It can give the corporation, and housing projects envisioned, definite direction and momentum toward success. Because its staff knows how to find resources and competent people, a university can help assemble a development team, of architects, lawyers, contractors, and packagers, for a project. Universities with sophisticated technical capabilities can develop housing themselves, but joint development is a better way to ensure valid community involvement.

Additionally, a university can use its prestige, political power, contacts, and influence in following through on a program. Because of its long-term nature, continuity, and staying power, a university or college can also help move a housing venture beyond the initial organizational stages. Relationships with banks and other financial institutions can help secure loans or bonds. University influence and backing can help obtain housing subsidies, tax abatement, or zoning changes in some cases; of course, universities need community support for their own zoning changes. Because of their resources and contacts, a university can also absorb or encourage others to absorb tax costs and overhead, like office space. Providing supplies, discounts, absorbing or subsidizing carrying costs, which might overburden a small organization experiencing the uncertainties and delays of housing development, are also helpful. Of course, a university can contribute money directly or indirectly to a housing venture through direct gifts or subsidies. A certain amount of a school's funds are normally unrestricted enough for this.

Because obtaining land for low-cost housing, particularly in urban areas, is a severe problem, universities can sometimes legitimately acquire land on better conditions than a community group can. A school might obtain and write down land costs to aid housing development. Some schools already own land that they can contribute, lease, or sell at reduced costs for low-income housing. Sites should, of course, be accessible to amenities and transportation to serve and attract residents.

CAVEATS FOR COLLEGES

Buying land on its own, however, as opposed to obtaining a community-chosen site like Inman Square, is an activity universities should avoid. Unilaterally and secretly obtaining land is to be especially avoided since secret acquisition is a technique identified with University expansion. Also, while secrecy may affect possible cost savings, it is just as likely that, unfamiliar with buying land for low- cost housing, a university may pay too much. Overpaying for a site, or choosing a bad location, as Harvard did at River-Howard and Blair Pond, respectively, reduces the chances for successful low-income housing. Working jointly with a community group, and consulting with real estate advisors familiar with subsidiary housing needs, to seek land is a better approach. Secrecy and deception, in fact, should be avoided in all aspects of

Community/University joint development, while openness and straightfor-
wardness need to be stressed.

Universities are well advised to avoid managing community housing. They
should, however, make sure the management is effective and tenant-oriented,
as unhappy tenants, like unhappy dormitory students, can lead to the failure
of the project. When a traditional housing authority tries to operate an innovative Community project with traditional housing authority methods, problems can be expected. Tenants may find it beneficial to have participatory
management for their projects, but community groups should be wary of the
problems of becoming landlords.

Funding the Progress

In building community/university housing, Section 236, usually with rent
supplements, and public housing programs provided most of the funding.
Turnkey I and III, and Section 8 leasing have financed successful low-income
housing. The Turnkey Apartments avoided a problem of Section 236 projects,
which provide only middle-income units and require further subsidy, leasing, or rent supplement to reach low-income levels. The future of these other
housing subsidies programs, and numerous housing projects were in limbo
after the Nixon freeze began in January 1973 when, except for Section 8
leases, they virtually went out of existence.

Implementation of the Housing and Community Development Act of 1974
cleared up some of the uncertainty following the freeze. The act provided for
both rehabilitation and new construction for low and moderate units. Programs in the act included public housing, interesting leasing provisions (Section 8), elderly housing, Section 236 (with deeper subsidies), experimental
financing, and urban homesteading. There now need to be more federal and
state subsidized housing programs.

Obtaining funds under either Title I of the Community Development of
the 1974 Act or Assisted Housing remained a difficult political and technical
task. Universities could assist communities both in preparing applications and
pushing for their acceptances. This included letter writing, attending meetings
with officials, and visiting City Hall and Washington. "New Community"
civic associations were eligible to receive funds under Title I.

There are other possibilities for funding housing. Some states have housing
finance agencies, which can fund mortgage loans at below-market rates, and
can sometimes provide subsidies. University and community groups might
lobby for using the College Housing program for joint housing. *The Chronicle of Higher Education* of August 19, 1974, promoted the "return to campus"
initiative for community/university housing. Schools might invest or put part

of their often burgeoning endowments at lower interest rates in community housing. Schools might investigate internal subsidies like including luxury housing or commercial parking facilities to subsidize lower-income units.[2] With their varied research capabilities, universities can learn about existing housing programs and develop and propose new ones. Some schools and communities might investigate using pension funds, insurance company proceeds, and foundation endowments as sources of investments at low-interest rates to aid low- cost units.

Unusual times call forth innovative solutions. All these ideas are within the realm of the possible and some have been suggested or tried by established, though innovative, institutions. In 1968 Wesleyan University set up a $1 million revolving low- and moderate-income mortgage fund. In February 1969, the trustees of the University of Pennsylvania proposed a $10 million fund. At least part of a school's endowment can be used for unusual purposes. For instance, Harvard helped build a $3.5 million underpass in Cambridge in 1968. In early 1975, the head of the New Jersey Homebuilders Association proposed investing pension funds for housing mortgages at below-market rates, and soon after the mayor of New York sought no-interest federal loans for housing.

REALITIES II: POSSIBLE OPPOSITION

In starting community housing, university and community groups should recognize there will be opposition to low-income housing. Sometimes the opposition may voice valid concerns about the quality of architecture or impact on municipal services and the environment, and these criticisms should be considered in rethinking a project. Some opposition to low-income housing may reflect racial or class biases. Opposition on environmental grounds may be valid or mask other more unpleasantly motivated attitudes. If a university is working closely with a valid community group and responding to community articulated needs, such opposition can often be avoided or overcome. Sometimes this type of controversy has to be endured at length to avoid defeating or weakening a project. This is not to suggest that a university should impose its will or views on a community. It should work with the community. The point is that even community-supported projects may involve unavoidable controversy, despite a school's desire to avoid bad publicity. Still they need to follow through. While "participation only where wanted" is good advice, some people will want and need housing others oppose. Yet a progressive university will sometimes have to take a position in support of controversial housing projects (University Circle Letter, November 7, 1974).

Building elderly housing can provide for needs of low-income groups without fatal opposition. Although building elderly housing may free some apartments for families, it does not solve the family housing problem. Despite controversy more family housing needs to be constructed as part of building and sustaining viable communities.

FUTURE DIRECTIONS

Joint Community/University housing may be the direction of the future. Students and the community have lived together "organically" for years in city apartments. They have continued to live together in the same project as do the Roxbury Tenants with Harvard affiliates in the Mission Park project. Joint development is even more effective when it is part of a total community development process, including shops, services, and schools to complement the housing. The plans at the University of Massachusetts in Boston follow this concept. Joint Planning Organizations, where school and community plan total needs together, certainly point in this direction.

Community/university housing may have increasing relevance in the future. If energy expenses and rising travel costs create an in-town residential trend, community/university housing may be a solution for more people seeking to live near the cultural and educational resources of attractive university neighborhoods. As private college costs rise, some inner-city public institutions may experience rising housing pressures as their enrollments increase. Suburban schools may find community/university housing necessary if faculty members are to retain a sense of campus community where rising housing costs threaten to drive lower-income residents and university affiliates away. It is not fair or reasonable to expect local residents to suffer quietly or to move because of university impact; so joint community/university development may become an increasingly popular solution. And finally, future housing and community development propsects may provide possibilities for different variations on Community/University themes.

REINFORCING THE BASIC POINTS

Though the conflicts of the urban past have receded from memory as university/community affairs left the headlines, an urban crisis continues. The need to pursue better community/university relations remains pertinent today. In encouraging cooperation between communities and universities, this book explains social opportunities and political difficulties in fostering joint development of housing. As housing remains an issue for the political, institutional, and community groups of most cities, this book can interest and encourage others beyond university/community groups to enter the community development process.

Since the numerous details of developing housing require full attention, those interested in moving forward need to remember not to move too fast. Leadership, for both university and community, and knowledge and respect for the capabilities of the people working together are also essential. Projects must be reasonable in size to fit community needs and promote viable family life. Developing housing can be a long-term, technical, abrasive, and tiring process for all involved. Especially at the start, problems are inevitable, while at least setbacks are possible for the best-intentioned and planned projects. This should not discourage action. It only suggests perspective and diligence.

With commitment and skills, community/university housing can reach its technical and political potentials. Learning from and extending on the lessons of Cambridge, Boston, and beyond can create imaginative solutions. As noted architect and planner Daniel Burnham articulated exactly a century ago in his vision for a greater Chicago: "Make no little plans, for they have not the power to stir men's [and women's] souls."

NOTES

1. User participation in design and results in the MIT projects and in River-Howard were more complete and effective than at Putnam Square and Inman Square Apartments. The participation process needs to be evaluated at each completion to see the quality of results and identity required improvements. Developing a checklist of common problems, such as inadequate closet space, kitchen cabinets, possible leaks, and improperly located common space can improve future planning and implementation.

2. Real Estate Research Corporation reported to the Princeton Regional Planning Board that, in mixed developments, proper internal subsidization could produce perhaps 30 percent lower cost units. See the Princeton Regional Planning Board report on plans for 5,700 mixed units (*Princeton Packet,* 1955–62).

Epilogue and Reflections
How This Book Developed

THE SIGNIFICANCE OF STUDYING JOINT COMMUNITY/UNIVERSITY HOUSING

Coming into the Cooper-Grant Community in Camden, New Jersey, as a college intern initially and later as a community organizer, I needed to find out how other communities had persuaded universities—that were gobbling up local homes and destroying the urban fabric nearby—instead to cooperate with their neighbors. The original goal, then, in writing this study was to educate myself, and indirectly the urban community where I was working, about the politics and dynamics of housing and community development. After learning of examples where Cambridge and Boston communities persuaded powerful Harvard and MIT to build housing for their neighbors, I decided to investigate and learn from these successful experiences.[1]

This work, in essence, became a text for my course of study to explore the politics and processes of development of university/community housing. It focuses on Cambridge and Boston, but touches on many other areas. It deals with issues in higher education, community development, housing and planning, politics, and architecture. It aims to assist members and aides of urban communities facing similar housing problems. It also seeks to inform architects, planners, university administrators, city officials, academics, alumni, and students of expanding schools on what others have done successfully. While the pace of the earlier era of university expansion slowed from the recession in the 1970s to the Great Recession, the pertinence of this report continues in its anticipation of future trends like gentrification, homelessness, or the next wave of university expansions these may well generate similar controversies and concerns around housing and community development.

135

Another motivation for writing a book about Cambridge and Boston came from respect for the desire of members of the People of the Cooper-Grant Community not to be studied by local researchers. Except for the dedication, acknowledgments, and a footnote in the original version, the report hardly mentioned the Cooper-Grant community and its members (Sobel, 1975, 108). Yet, Cooper-Grant's story remains a fascinating one that deserves to be told more fully (see People of the Cooper-Grant Community, December 1973 for a summary). The invitation by a press editor to introduce this book with the history of the study provides the opportunity to extend both the provided background and the Cooper-Grant story, too.

HOW I LEARNED ABOUT THE COOPER-GRANT STORY

The Camden and Cambridge sojourns were outgrowths of my long-standing interest in urban affairs. As an undergraduate at Princeton, I took two early African-American Studies courses, "Black History" and "Third World Literature," just as urban and Afro-American Studies were becoming programs at the University. During the summer after my sophomore year, I interned at the Department of Housing and Urban Development (HUD) in Washington, D.C. There I learned about subsidized housing programs and Washington politics by reading congressional reports and *The Congressional Record* daily cover-to-cover and attending events for interns organized by "Princeton in DC." That fall on returning to school, I became an upper-class "University Scholar," able thereby to construct an independent study program that combined interests in political sociology and urban studies. That fall of junior year, I also helped initiate a seminar on "Princeton and the Community." In the spring, I pioneered in an "urban field study" placement by student teaching at two city "high schools without walls," the Metro School in Chicago and Parkway Program in Philadelphia (Sobel, 1970; 1973). Writing a participant-observer paper about student decision making at the two schools deepened my concern for where community involvement in housing development fell on the "ladder" of citizen participation in planning (Arnstein, 1969) between "manipulation" (1) and "citizen control" (8).

Then as a college senior, at the geographically-near, but economically-distant Princeton, I partook in an "urban work assignment" placement at a Community Legal Services office in Camden through the Woodrow Wilson School of Public and International Affairs. At the same time, I was researching and writing a thesis about *Urban Renewal in Princeton, 1955–62.* My trips to Camden Regional Legal Services (CRLS) with Princeton classmates, Mark Moorstein and another future academic, John Padgett, alternated with thesis writing, participating in campus politics, and high jumping on the Princeton track team (see Sobel, forthcoming).

THE CAMDEN PERSPECTIVE

The Cooper-Grant Community in North Central Camden was a fascinating, multi-ethnic neighborhood nestled between the Benjamin Franklin Bridge to Philadelphia and the once-professional Cooper Street offices and stores.[2] Once Cooper-Grant had been a fashionable upper middle class neighborhood like Ocean Hill Brownsville in the Bronx, where my soon to be graduate school advisor, Rhody McCoy, had been a notable unit administrator for Ocean Hill Brownsville school system (see Berube, Gittel, and Magat, 1970). The children's novel, *Catchpenny Street* (Cavanna, 1951, 1975) had memorialized the beautiful Cooper-Grant neighborhood and Camden resident Walt Whitman had praised the Cooper-Grant elementary school in a 1900 poem, "An Old Man's Thoughts of School." Whitman himself first recited it himself at the school's dedication in 1874, and Allen Ginsberg repeated it in his inimitable voice (recorded on tape for posterity) during the school's centennial on April 3, 1974, as "not just a lot of boys and girls/not just a public school." By the early 1970s, Cooper-Grant was a mix of working class and poor black, Hispanic, and elderly white residents. As in many urban areas facing daunting problems, indigenous community leaders rose to positions of influence once the opportunity and necessity developed.

The Neighborhood Betterment Survey in 1974 described Cooper-Grant's promise well: It was a "unified community with an intense desire to plan the rehabilitation of the neighborhood." It was located in "one of the most historic districts of Camden," with a "stock of historic residential units of different classifications and architectural styles." Its "geographic location near the center of Camden" had "low enough density to give the neighborhood a green, open feeling." Finally, to connect to nearby Philadelphia, it had "good regional transportation linkages," with the Benjamin Franklin Bridge overlooking Cooper-Grant, and a High-Speed Rail station nearby (Lang and Murray, 1974, 2).

For my Princeton internship at Camden Regional Legal Services in spring 1971, I was asked to research what a group of state agencies and private organizations were planning for the land of Cooper-Grant, without the knowledge or participation of community members. My first assignment was to figure out what various organizations were devising for (more accurately, against) Cooper-Grant, and report back to my legal services attorney supervisor who would ultimately notify the community.[3] The internship produced a paper called "In Ben Franklin's View: Planning in North Central Camden" (Sobel, 1971, 1973). The title derived from the famous span that overlooks Cooper-Grant, and connects the two cities across the Delaware River, from then impoverished Camden to Franklin's more prosperous hometown of Philadelphia.

What I learned was that in late 1969, the Cooper-Grant community had been put through what seemed an exciting educational facilities planning "Charette" to develop a scheme for a local "Rutgers Elementary School." Energized by the process, community members devoted a great deal of time and energy to the planning process. Toward the end of the Charette, community representatives inadvertently discovered they need not have gotten excited about their ideas because there were outside plans to turn the area into an industrial park, including the schoolyard into a parking lot! The Camden Economic Development Advisory Board (CEDAC) planned an industrial park, in conjunction with the nearby RCA (Victor Talking Machines) and Campbell's Soup headquarters, and a related highway (Route 51) to remove the entire neighborhood up to the waterfront. (This would parallel the controversy over the "Inner Belt" in Cambridge; see chapter 1 here.) Though there might have been some spillover benefits to Camden from the 1976 Bicentennial Plans for Philadelphia and the housing developed in the local Northgate II Urban Renewal Projects, these would be peripheral to Cooper-Grant.

All the outside organizations were planning for the Cooper-Grant area without any community representation or involvement. "For the people living in North Central Camden in 1971 the past had been disappointing and the future was uncertain" (Sobel, 1971, revised 1973, 11). The most prominent entity planning for the Cooper-Grant area was a branch of Rutgers University, whose main campus was 60 miles north in New Brunswick. Only about ten years after becoming "the state university of New Jersey," Rutgers had recently begun a branch campus in Camden, on land previously occupied until the early 1960s by 150 families. As the state university, Rutgers' status as a state "instrumentality" (*Rutgers v. Piluso. 60 NJ 142, 1972*), partly private, partly public, would have seemed to enmesh the university in constitutional and procedural constraints. But the Rutgers administration maintained that the University as an "instrumentality" was not a state agency obliged to provide relocation housing for people it displaced. And, in any case, Rutgers claimed it was only buying from a willing seller.

Instead, the special status reinforced university leaders with arrogant ivory tower conceptions of being incapable of doing harm. Rutgers was undertaking the same kind of "block busting" and land banking activities that profit-making businesses used to undermine neighborhood integrity and destroy the housing market in other urban communities. By the time of the issuance of

Rutgers' Master Plan for Camden in late 1973, the University owned 22 more houses and 20 lots in the Cooper-Grant neighborhood (People of Cooper, December 1973, 3). In the process, it was destroying the beautiful neighborhood and neglecting the elementary school.

The details of Rutgers plans also emerged in my frequent trips to the New Brunswick administration building to read the notes of the Board of Trustees meetings. These included proposals for at most housing for graduate or law students, but not for community members. Later pressure brought Rutgers to a temporarily more-cooperative stance (Bauer, 1973), but the University did not follow through on its promises to assist and work together with the community or city government.

A position paper by the People of the Cooper-Grant Community (PCGC) demanded that Rutgers cooperate in community redevelopment. Learning from my research on the example of the Roxbury Tenants of Harvard's plan for community/university development in Boston near Harvard Medical School, Cooper-Grant leaders stated, "the poor and powerless are not un-imaginative or uningenious. They have just been denied rights to plan their own lives and the power to carry through their plans" (3). Community leaders indicated "The Rutgers 1973 Master Plan as proposed is unacceptable to the People of the Cooper-Grant Community. To be exact: it does not meet with our approval" (6). Recognizing that the Rutgers Camden campus was also a stepchild of the state system, People of the Cooper-Grant Community proposed an alliance with campus officials for future joint development. Though the City of Camden ultimately included the Cooper-Grant plan in its urban renewal submissions, the prospects dimmed for actual redevelopment of Cooper-Grant.

In making many personal and professional friends in Cooper-Grant, I extended my 1971 internship into working and eventually living there from late 1971 to summer 1975. Beginning with the internship, I worked at but not directly for Camden Regional Legal Services (CRLS), a community legal services program under the Office of Economic Opportunity (OEO). CRLS became famous for challenging insensitive housing policy. In fact, CRLS was the agency that brought the landmark low-income housing *Mt. Laurel* case.[4] That notable decision required suburban communities to build a fair share of low-income units. For background research for the suit on the housing problems in the suburban areas outside of Camden, I helped survey people living in chicken coops practically within view of the Philadelphia skyline and located within the affluent southern New Jersey suburbs.

CRLS was also famed for its aggressive class action strategy in defense of the poor. In response in 1972, then Vice President Spiro Agnew attacked CRLS, which galvanized support for the program. Agnew's comments appeared on the front page of *New York Times*, when local newspapers, including the *Times'* New Jersey edition only occasionally covered the Cooper-Grant controversy (Barrett, 1974).[5] The conservative political backlash against the Great Society anti-poverty programs, including Legal Services, ultimately produced restrictions on the kinds of class-action suits community legal services programs could previously provide.

So to help my Camden community work by writing this study, I set out to learn as much about Cambridge, Boston, and the Harvard and MIT housing projects in those communities as I could in a relatively short time. Researching and writing the report largely in the Boston area became the vehicles for my and Camden community leaders' education.

After graduating from Princeton, I continued to live in South Jersey, teaching in a "College Discovery" Program at Ft. Dix for servicemen and women getting out of the Vietnam-era Army and heading to college. This was located near enough to follow the events in Camden during the hot summer of three days of rioting in late August 1971, just after the "Camden 28" draft board raid (Narvaez, 1971, Montgomery, 1971). When the riots broke out, I contacted one of the Legal Services attorneys, Peter O'Connor, to offer help with his legal support. This led to my return to Camden.

After our internship ended, Princeton classmate John Padgett and I put together a "Proposal for North Central Camden NJ Development Project" (October 1971). It stated boldly "our goal, in the long run, is to make ourselves unneeded" (5) by helping the community develop self-sufficiency. In any case, soon afterwards, John began graduate school at the University of Michigan (PhD, 1978), and I returned part time to Camden, delayed full-time graduate schools, and continued learning about community development in Camden and Cambridge.

In late 1971 and early 1972, I wrote a proposal and received a small grant from Educational Facilities Laboratories (EFL), an offshoot of the Ford Foundation. This covered part of the cost of conducting the study and subsidized my work as a typically underpaid community organizer. But the report was no easy task to complete, and even with a team, it took almost three years to finish.

By fall 1972, I had begun part-time graduate study for a master's degree at the School of Education at the University of Massachusetts in Amherst, though most of my work was done from afar as independent studies. In July 1973, then dean and innovator, Dwight Allen, made me a "wild-card" doctoral student to permit more flexibility in my work.

Living mainly in Camden from 1972 to 1975, I researched and drafted the community housing report, and finished it as the predecessor to this book, in late 1975. During the middle of summer 1975, I left Cooper-Grant and in the fall headed to my graduate school "residency" year at the University of Massachusetts in Amherst. That New England college town is located in rural (except for the UMass high-rise dorms) Western Massachusetts, 100 miles across the Commonwealth from the eastern urban areas and the joint housing developments in Boston and Cambridge.

On almost a weekly basis, I commuted from Camden—where I was living, working, and teaching part time—to do research in Cambridge and Boston. My Camden law student housemate, Eric Olson, would occasionally fill in on a "Family Finance" (basic math) course I was teaching at Camden County Community College.[6] I made eleven trips in 1973, and five in 1974 in the pre-frequent flyer, no air ID, era.[7] Often traveling through Metuchen by New Jersey Transit or north of New York by Amtrak to see friends, I stayed in the East Cambridge apartment of a Princeton contemporary, Murray Lamp.

Some tired mornings, I would wake up not knowing where I was. I remember sitting at the kitchen table in Cambridge staring out the window late one night when I had finally gotten far enough up the literary mountain that I could finally see that the climb would be successful; I was overwhelmed with emotions mixing joy and relief that the draft would soon be finished, and it would be done well. The first draft was completed in February 1974, another at the end of the year, and two more in April and November 1975.

The report was both an individual and group effort. Many able research associates, including a high school and Princeton classmate, Bob Kuenzel, destined for law school, helped research and draft parts of this study. But, in my first experience in hiring a research team, the Homestead Research Group, I discovered that some of the researchers could not or would not complete their assignments and left me to do more than I had bargained for. Similarly, when some Cambridge and Boston community members refused interviews, we had to rely on others or often incomplete written sources to fill out the stories. This is partly why I donated my source materials to the Cambridge Library Local History Collection to fill out the historical record. The complications of understanding and explaining the details of housing and politics underscored the need to persevere in completing complex tasks.

GRADUATE EDUCATION

During the early years I was working in Camden, I had also became a part-time, largely off-campus, graduate student in higher education and social sciences at the University of Massachusetts Education School in Amherst. The nature of the school and flexibility of my program facilitated getting academic credit for independent study of community/university politics and presenting preliminary findings at the school's semi-annual "Marathons" academic fairs.[8] This was during the heyday of UMass Education School, when innovative and controversial dean Dwight Allen[9] (1968–1975) admitted Bill Cosby (EdD, 1976) and others like me to the doctoral program as "wild cards." Like the "University Scholar" designation at Princeton, becoming a "wild card" admission in 1973 provided more flexibility to structure my own program than remaining in the Master of Arts in Teaching (MAT) program to which I had been admitted in 1972.[10] Somewhat later, Allen's successor from 1976 to 1987, well-known urbanist, Mario Fantini, fostered a different approach to alternative[11] and urban education (Fantini, Gittel, and Magat, 1970).[12] In the same spirit in spring 1974, I attended the opening of the new "urban" campus of the University of Massachusetts in Boston at Columbia Point near Dorchester and wrote an Alice in Wonderland-based story that *Change Magazine* proposed to publish, but the revisions were never completed (Sobel, 1974).

While serving my UMass residency, I used some of the same skills and knowledge about community housing problems developed for Camden to help write reports for the Student Center for Educational Research (SCER) on the similar housing problems in Amherst. There the largest UMass campus dwarfed the small New England town (Magid, 1975; SCER, 1975). The title of one of the reports, "Rural Amherst Has an Urban Problem" summed up the nature of the housing situation a hundred miles west of Boston.

Just before that report appeared in 1975, the Cooper-Grant community was on the cusp of success and in line for a sizable outside foundation grant for community development. The City of Camden was also about to co-opt and incorporate the Cooper-Grant development plan into its Model Cities program. The People of the Cooper-Grant Community and its professional aides had put together a "Revival Plan of the People of the Cooper-Grant Community" in June 1974, emphasizing housing renewal, commercial revival, and educational and health development. The Cooper-Grant School got a playground on a Rutgers parking lot and was in line for $170,000 for school repairs (February 1975, 3). The People of Cooper Grant developed with my help a proposal to the Fund for New Jersey for $80,000, including funds for my job as a coordinator and research director (People of the Cooper-Grant Community, February 1975).[13]

But in anticipating success, the community leaders were apparently unwilling to share the rewards. The leadership seemed not to recognize the importance of my hard work and strategizing in bringing them to the point of success. They did not acknowledge that my outside research for this report helped to position them to avoid the pitfalls many other community groups there and elsewhere fell into in community development and political conflicts, and that my work helped the community leaders to take advantage of opportunities to move Cooper-Grant forward.

What the community did not see, and perhaps I could not make adequately clear without seeming to take more credit than some thought was due, was that I was able to use researching and writing the predecessor report as a means to develop housing and political strategy to advance the community goals and protect the group from debilitating political and legal pressures. This I accomplished by studying and learning from the literature of community organizing cited here, most famously by Saul Alinsky (1969, 1971) and William and Louride Biddle (1965, 1968), to develop a viable strategy and program though writing this book.

From discussions with and reading the dissertation of a PhD student in politics at Princeton, Robert Curvin, later a Ford Foundation grants officer, I had also learned about the levels and dynamics of repression in Newark and Camden and how to avoid or buffer them (Curvin, 1974). This protection could be accomplished by working for and with a powerful institution like Camden Regional Legal Services and keeping open communications and dialogue with potential civil and professional adversaries. These strategies reduced the likelihood that the city administration or police could derail or crush the community efforts. (A much more famous former community organizer would institutionalize the community development approaches in his electoral victories in 2008 and 2012; see Obama [1995], 2012.) Yet, as an organizer trying to foster neighborhood participation across class and racial lines, I could often not ask or get the community to recognize and reward the value of what I was doing with and for its members. So, owed never to be collected back pay, I went off at midsummer 1975 to full time graduate school at the UMass in rural Amherst.

BACKGROUND TO THE HOUSING
CRISIS IN CAMBRIDGE

What the pages of the original report and this book portray are the problems that Harvard, Massachusetts Institute of Technology, and their spin-off research and development firms were creating for the housing market and community members in Cambridge and Boston. A "class substitution process" was replacing working class families with professional singles (Harvard Strikers, 1969). The sustained and intense political pushback from the community, including the takeover of the Harvard commencement in 1970, led both Harvard and MIT, and their jointly sponsored Cambridge Corporation, to build housing for the community members, not just for their students.

This book portrays the fascinating political and technical processes of the Cambridge and Boston projects. It updates the details of the projects not yet completed when the earlier report appeared in 1975.[14]

To represent the differing perspectives and jointness in the original community/university housing report, I solicited dual forewords. A community architect and a university official each wrote one: Brett Donham, a Harvard alumnus and the architect for a community housing project in Cambridge provided a community perspective. Antony Herrey, former head of MIT's Housing Program in Cambridge, by then at the Ford Foundation[15] (coincidentally the sponsor of Educational Facilities Laboratory), provided an institutional view.[16]

The report originally had a rather prosaic title, *Community/University Housing and Relations: Cases in Cambridge and Other Places*. It focused on the Cambridge examples and the housing program around the Harvard Medical School, in the Mission Hill neighborhood of Boston. In addition, it summarized shorter examples, among others, in New York, Philadelphia, Princeton, Middletown, and Stanford.

It also briefly chronicled the issues I helped advocate with the Princeton Housing Group in the mid-1970s when we were trying to get our alma mater, Princeton University, to build community housing to address the housing problems the school was creating. This PHG attempted to prevent the University from tearing down badly needed housing near campus (Sobel and Hosford, 1974).[17] I had returned to Princeton after my UMass residency (1975–1976) to take a job researching the economics of education with conservative economist Fritz Machlup (1980–1984). And I stayed the next year (1977–1978) to be able to work with my UMass dissertation adviser, radical economist Herbert Gintis,[18] who was on sabbatical at the nearby Institute for Advanced Study. It was quite unusual to be working with distinguished economists at opposite ends of the ideological spectrum.

During the same period, I also used some of the housing and community development skills and knowledge developed in Camden and Cambridge to serve as an occasional consultant on urban issues to my father's architectural firm, Walter H. Sobel, FAIA & Associates in Chicago.[19] For instance, in early 1975, I helped in planning for a day-care facility at the Abraham Lincoln Center, one of the city's oldest social services programs in the South Side Black community.[20] In 1977, the Council of Planning Librarians issued bibliographies on community/university housing drawn largely from the report. And in late 1978 *Practicing Planner* (now *Planning*) published "Joint Development of Housing," summarizing the report's findings (Sobel and Sobel, 1977a, b; Sobel, 1978b).

Also during this period, I wrote about the end of "big box" modernist architecture in the *New Art Examiner* (Sobel, 1978a; see Blau, 1984). I also spoke and wrote about Frank Lloyd Wright's prairie architecture (Dodge, 1974, Sobel, 1978, 1980)[21] and low-cost architecture.[22]

From 1976 through the early 1980s, I stayed in Princeton as a researcher and began as a teacher while finishing my UMass dissertation (Sobel, 1982). In 1982, a graduate student, Emmett Carson and I led a group of Woodrow Wilson School urban affairs undergraduates in Jennifer Hochschild's policy conference to Chicago to study school desegregation. This included meeting with Judge Milton Shadur, author of a famous housing decision ("U.S. Finds," 1982). Toward the end of this period, I researched and taught as a lecturer in the Department of Politics (1981–1983) at Princeton.

Then I headed for six residentially well-situated but academically grueling years in New England, four at Smith College in the Five College area near rural Amherst. Afterwards, I spent two more enjoyable years at the University of Connecticut in very rural "store-less" Storrs, where I taught in Public Administration and Political Science. While also serving there as a Research Associate in the Roper Center for Public Opinion Research at the behest of its renowned director, Everett Ladd, I made occasional side trips to Amherst, Cambridge, and Princeton. During that period, too, a University of Chicago (and later Harvard) colleague, John Coatsworth, invited me to speak in 1988 for the first time at that august Hyde Park campus which spawned community development controversies and ultimately a joint housing development.

PLUS CA CHANGE CAMBRIDGE

Princeton again became my home from 1989 to 1996, when I first returned to develop a foreign affairs conference on the contra funding controversy and edited a subsequent book (Sobel, 1993) before writing another on public opinion and foreign policy (Sobel, 2001). Then I taught part time in African-American Studies and Sociology, before becoming a full time lecturer on American political history in the History Department. At the start of March 1991, I led a group of Woodrow Wilson School students on a tour of Camden, a decade after and a world apart from a previous Wilson School educational outing to Chicago. During that Princeton sojourn, I "precepted" (taught in discussion sections) and occasionally guest lectured for eminent Civil War historian, James McPherson, including serving as his "lieutenant" for a trip to Gettysburg in fall 1995, and historian of the South, Nell Irvin Painter.

After leaving this third stint at Princeton in fall 1996, I returned to Cambridge for a Fellowship at the Shorenstein Center for Politics, Press and Public Policy at Harvard's Kennedy School of Government. While living in Cambridge on and off for a decade, I occasionally walked or drove by the same community housing projects there and in Boston I had studied over a quarter century before. Their stories were vaguely in my mind on catching the inter-campus bus in front of the Putnam Square Apartments on Mt. Auburn Street or in noticing the high rise North Cambridge housing from Mass Ave. When I became a "lay" member of the Program in Psychiatry and the Law (PIPATL) at Harvard Medical School, I would see from afar the Mission Hill project near Harvard Med, even closer to my office when I became a post-doctoral fellow in the Division of Medical Ethics in 2005–2006. Perhaps the issues of university/community politics began to rise again in my perspective when I became a senior fellow in a fledgling civic engagement program in the Lincoln Filene Center at Tufts in 1999. But community housing developments were more in the background than prominent features of my Harvard academic endeavors or weekly travels.[23]

My sense today from living in Cambridge and reading the local newspapers is that, in the major upward movements in rents and homeownership costs, the housing issues there remain similar now. There is still a housing crisis in Cambridge because there are far from enough affordable housing units, even if the economic downturn marginally held down rents and housing prices. Only now, housing is not in acute crisis but forms part of a chronic problem: The economic and political forces play themselves out in less pressure to build affordable housing and more homelessness.

My impression of how the country has changed over a generation is reflected in the extent to which the Great Society housing programs, whose 1968 national housing goal promised 26 million new and rehabilitated units, with 6 million for low and moderate incomes, in the next decade, was long ago unfulfilled and then abandoned.[24] The civil rights constituency, which produced the Great Society, pressed for Department of Housing and Urban Development (HUD) programs, and supported community housing, fragmented during the long conservative era. Cities and suburbs are still supposed to create "affordable" housing but that phrasing belies the reality, that when housing is built at all, it is more likely units that relatively affluent people can just afford,[25] but remains out of range for the poor and the growing homeless population.

The ongoing problems for increasing the housing supply is that the unit costs of building housing, both in materials and money, make it impossible for new construction to be affordable for even middle class renters, let alone for low-income tenants, without some sort of subsidy. With federal and state programs cut or destroyed (only a limited Section 8 program for rent subsidies remains of the 1960s housing support programs), affordability can only come from internal or external subsidies or investments. For instance, universities like Harvard, MIT, and Princeton could use their endowments to provide housing capital. The subprime mortgage crisis and Great Recession have undermined some of these prospects while reinforcing the need for affordable housing and heightening the threat of homelessness even for middle class people.

Yet, gentrification has continued apace in Cambridge and Boston, driving many old-timer families and their newer generations from their hometown. Downtown Harvard Square is awash with banks, ATMs, chain stores, and upscale boutiques. The older stores and restaurants have largely disappeared. The character of the Square has been economically transformed, though the proliferation of homeless panhandlers for spare change reminds affluent shoppers that others have largely been left behind. With rents escalating, how can anyone afford to live or run a small business there?[26]

STILL CURRENT COMMUNITY/ UNIVERSITY CONCERNS

University/community issues remain significant factors in Cambridge, Boston, and other urban settings. But today they typically manifest more subtly than in the old confrontations. The Cambridge community can still prevent Harvard and MIT from building projects, but they rarely pressure the universities to build housing. The development of a recent Harvard social science complex, the Center for Government and International Studies (CGIS), is a prime example of the dynamics and differences. Harvard wanted to build a pedestrian bridge over the traffic between the north and south parts of the buildings across Cambridge Street. The community refused, in an act that represents a flexing of its political muscle against the university, but worsens congestion, raises the delays to drivers, and increases the dangers to pedestrians.

More extensively, Harvard began building an entirely new campus, just across the Charles River in the Allston section of Boston, after years of secretly buying up most of the land before announcing a virtual *fait accompli*. Severely criticized by Boston Mayor Thomas Menino when the major project became public, Harvard's community relations director had to acknowledge that the university had broken its pledges of openness to the community (Cassidy and Alguin, 1997; Stone, 1997). The process initiated under Harvard President Lawrence Summers was hardly community-friendly, though it has been more open under his successor, Drew Gilpin Faust. For instance, Harvard created a Holyoke Center arcade office to publicize the development, but it was only open at odd hours and was not particularly informative. Though there has been the prospect of moving residential units to new sites, Harvard did not initially propose to build community housing for the neighbors or to integrate mixed units into the academic plans. Whether community concerns about the housing issues would lead to a renewal of interest in community university housing has yet to be realized.[27] The economic downturn delayed progress on the Allston development until recently, when part of the proposed development was begun.[28] The proposed 325 Barry's Corner units of mixed housing appear more in line with current trends to integrate income levels rather than developing groupings of subsidized units. But even affordable units may be initially or ultimately too expensive for lower income residents.

HOW THE RESEARCH BECAME A REPORT FIRST

When Educational Facilities Laboratories published the community housing report in 1975, I had not yet decided to become an academic. In fact, I had entered graduate school in a Masters of Art in Teaching program, and moved under Dean Dwight Allen's initiative to a doctoral program partly for the added flexibility for independent study, mostly on community issues.[29] So, facing the choice of EFL's publishing the manuscript shortly as a report or after many unsuccessful inquiries, continuing to seek a publisher for a book, I was not sure what factors to consider. At that point, I did not recognize the difference between a report and a book since the contents were the same. EFL offered to print 500 copies of the report and promised to include a synopsis in a publication of the Society of College and University Planners (but it apparently never appeared).

When Westview Press offered in late 1977 to issue the report as a book in their Replica series, foremost among my concerns was that the editor wanted me to pay the extra amount for copyediting and retyping the entire manuscript. The retyping alone would have cost of $400, about two months of a community organizer's sporadic salary (vanity presses asked up to $8,000 for the privilege). Little did I know the value of a book for my future academic career, which would have been better launched by the investment in getting a scholarly publication out earlier and reviewed in journals.

Moreover, rather than requesting that EFL send most copies of the report to journals for review, which might have raised the visibility of the study and generated request for other articles or consulting, I asked the able EFL assistant, Margaret Nyhus, to send the reports at no cost to 150 community members and colleagues that helped with its research. The reports also went *gratis* to libraries like Princeton, Harvard, and Northwestern,[30] which I had used for researching the project.[31] I did ask EFL to send copies to *Change Magazine* and the architectural critic of the *Boston Globe*, but I had no clear rationale or strategy for getting the study and its findings better known.

HOW THIS REPORT BECAME A BOOK

Yet, turning the report into a book remained a hoped-for prospect. For a sense of closure, over the past five years, interns and I have researched updates, such as the completion dates of the projects unfinished when the study came out in 1975,[32] replaced the sketches for those projects with photographs, and added projects initiated more recently. These now completed developments, in particular, the Mission Park Apartments became available for occupancy in 1978, and the 32 units at River-Howard Apartments opened in 1981. I have also reviewed in full, revised, and rewritten substantial parts of the report to create instead a book.

Over many years, I came close to opportunities to republish the report as a book. Besides the Westview offer in 1977, in 1997 University Press of America offered to republish it if my classes purchased enough copies to make it economically feasible, but I was not offering a course that might use the book. At the 2006 meeting at the American Political Science Association in near-to-Camden, Philadelphia, Editor-in-Chief of Edwin Mellen Press, Herbert Richardson, liked the idea of making this report into a book and offered the opportunity to republish it. Meeting one of the authors whose works informed the original report, John Mollenkopf, at the fortieth anniversary celebration of the Institute for Policy Research at Northwestern in spring 2009 and asking him for suggestions about who might write a new foreword led to the idea that the study was scholarly enough to explore publication by a more academic press. A couple of inquiries to academic presses produced less promising responses, and the new prospect of self-publishing in print on demand form seemed less appealing than achieving the goal of making the book available from an established press. Beginning to work with an agent in 2013 finally produced the offer from Rowman & Littlefield, which had published two of my earlier political science books.[33]

Turning a generation old, pre-computer, typed, atypically cited manuscript into a book was not an easy task. It took months of inquiries to find an available scanner to translate the previous contents into text files. But fortunately Boston intern, Cathy Richards, and Northwestern intern, Anna Crane, almost simultaneously figured out how to do so in 2007 (see acknowledgments). The report and figures needed to be reformatted and some updated, and an unexpected request to supervise an architectural intern, Han Gyeol Kim, from Korea provided the opportunity to return to my architectural and housing roots to update the manuscript. As the Acknowledgement notes, Agnes Gyoffi, Andrew Nho, and Olympia Banerjee helped with the text, while Hangyell assiduously completed revising the maps and tables from Korea and Singapore. Olympia finished the table of contents and explored the prospects for indexing, which Barbara Leary extended. Before heading off to South Africa, my former Northwestern intern, Zack Nolan, took photographs of River Howard Homes and Mission Park Apartments to substitute for drawings of the uncompleted projects. In finalizing the book, however, architects Brett Donham and John Sharratt offered photos that show the larger scales of the River Howard and Mission Park projects.

For practical reasons and learning from the advice of colleagues in a seminar[34] headed up by Graham Allison and Theodore Marmor at the Kennedy School at Harvard not to revise completely a classic beyond what was most appropriately needed,[35] I have rewritten major parts of the text but not altered major substantive insights from the report. I have generally updated completion dates for projects finishing after the study appeared in 1975, revised updates on Harvard projects, completely edited phrasings, added introductory and concluding comments to chapters, and wrote this epilogue. I have also incorporated information from footnotes into the text. For ease of use, the text had to be consolidated and reformatted into more of a book-like form; the unique categorization of the original bibliography had to be completely reorganized, and the citations updated, particularly for conclusions.

Finally, in responding to an editor's request to write a lengthy new introduction to explain how the report initially developed and its history since then, I began putting together these remarks. This provided an opportunity to reflect on the housing and political issues the report explores as well as my scholarly and career opportunities and frustrations over a generation.[36] In considering adding introductory material, I began to explore the possibilities with a Northwestern colleague who works on the community issues both as an urban sociologist and a planning board member in Evanston, home of Northwestern, drafting a new foreword. More recently, I asked my former urban work assignment intern partner in Camden, now University of Chicago sociologist and political scientist, John Padgett, Columbia architecture professor Mary McLeod, who had interned and written a housing report in Cambridge, and John Mollenkopf of CUNY Graduate Center, to add a few words. But ultimately, the original forewords by Brett Donham from a community perspective and Antony Herrey from a university view remained timely and insightful enough to stand alone.

THE IMPACT OF THE STUDY

One of the most valuable parts of the original report was the section in part IV on "new saws" for building community housing meant to share the insights developed there with others who might explore similar projects. The importance of authentic involvement by a unified community, which has its own professional assistance from architects and attorneys, remains an essential theme. Rereading these suggestions today heightens their ongoing pertinence for future development. This epilogue with reflections seeks to complement and highlight their utility for the future.

How much influence this study has had so far is hard to say. The checkout records on the old library cards in copies of the report in the Guttmann Library (long closed to the public) at Harvard's Graduate School of Education and at Loeb Library at the Graduate School of Design (GSD) (unfortunately more recently closed to the public) show a fair number of people have taken the study out and presumably read it. Some have cited or written about it (see Echelman, 2013).[37] A reference librarian's search of the citation indexes for the 1975 report or 1978 *Practicing Planner* article (Sobel, 1978) found a few citations elsewhere.[38] I do not recall speaking to or hearing from anyone who read the report (though a Princeton student contacted me in Camden about my urban renewal thesis). Yet, it served its original purposes of helping to educate the Cooper-Grant community and me about housing and community development. Perhaps it will generate future interest.

Another goal of turning the report into a book is to increase the study's impact. The more attractive and substantial book format would encourage more thoughtful reading at least in the university communities whose libraries are likely to purchase a book. The possibilities of wider reviews and Internet publicity may also attract a bigger audience. The greater focus on solutions to urban problems anticipated from a more urban-oriented national administration may also increase the impact of the timely republishing of the study.

CAMDEN AND COOPER-GRANT TODAY

The fate of Camden and the Cooper-Grant community remain telling benchmarks for the ongoing relevance of community development studies. Occasionally even today, I notice articles in the press about Camden and picked up with interest several years ago at the 2006 APSA meetings in Philadelphia a new book on the topic (Gillette, 2005), *Camden After the Fall, Decline and Renewal in a Post-Industrial City*. But I only loosely keep up with community development issues.[39] I have visited Camden two of three times in the ensuing years, most prominently on the tour in March 1991 for a group of Woodrow Wilson School policy students. That Camden visit was discouraging for the further physical deterioration of the city, especially in Cooper-Grant. But it was uplifting to recognize that the spirit of the people and city boosters remains upbeat and optimistic in the face of adversity. In June 2011 around a Princeton reunion, I spoke with current Camden residents about an update tour but the plans did not work out.

Camden today is a study in contrast to vibrant Cambridge and Boston. Perhaps with East St. Louis, which I once visited in fall 1977, Camden remains one of the most distressed cities in the nation. On occasional trips on the Interstate 95 at the Delaware River's edge of Philadelphia, I watch out for familiar landmarks like City Hall visible across the water, whose tower famously and sadly reminds all of the Biblical injunction that "where there is no vision, the people perish." Nonetheless, Camden now has both a popular natatorium and minor league baseball park for the Camden Riversharks on the banks of the Delaware.

Camden returned to national news as I began writing this introduction when at the start of 2011 the mayor had to lay off half the police force and a third of firefighters for financial reasons, which was a telling testimony to its continually distressing situation ("Deep Layoffs," 2011).

Digging a bit deeper into reports and recent articles, however, revealed the startling news of an exciting new housing development in the heart of Cooper-Grant! The Cooper-Grant Homes have already brought 18 new market rate townhouses to the neighborhood (City of Camden, 2005; Ung, 2005). Ten more single-family homes are beginning construction (Pennrose Properties, 2010). These are, in a sense, community/university housing, because Rutgers donated eight vacant properties (the city 14) to make the project economically feasible. The project is a joint venture of the Cooper-Grant Neighborhood Association and Pennrose Properties. Construction on the $10.2 million project began in February 2007 for the first 18 units; the other ten began in early 2011. (They are also near the 341-apartment Victor Loft Building [formerly RCA Victor headquarters].) These may begin the revitalization of Cooper-Grant and perhaps serve as a sign that the long-desired renewal of Camden is in the offing.

This good news reinforces the optimism I have shared that someday group efforts, economic forces, and new investment strategies of a well-situated urban location across from the stunning Philadelphia skyline will revitalize the distressed smaller city to its former glory. The City of Brotherly Love, which underwent a remarkable revitalization and liberalization from the repressive days of Mayor Frank Rizzo in the 1970s, remains a model for what its disadvantaged sister city could accomplish with vision and fortune.[40] Cooper-Grant Homes may begin the process.

IN CONCLUSION

So, this study saw the light of day as a report to learn and teach about community development. And it got published as a book because it turned out to chronicle a fascinating and instructive saga. For professional reasons, I wanted this proudly amidst other publications on my resume and bookshelf. The book still constitutes a compelling story and helpful background for new ventures capitalizing on its lesson. Responding to the editorial request for an epilogue provided the opportunity to reflect historically and autobiographically on the era that produced the original study and its aftermath.

Beyond providing hints here to inspire curious readers to plunge into the prose, the book is left to speak for itself about the innovative community/university housing projects in its pages. When a new round of university expansion and its community challengers emerge,[41] here will be insights for others to draw upon in addressing ensuing housing problems and opportunities. I commend these "old saws" to those who might create new ones.

Richard Sobel
Evanston, Illinois
November 28, 2013
Cambridge, Massachusetts
January 30, 2014

NOTES

1. There are many sources of the idea for a community/university housing study. These include a Princeton intern paper "Rutgers in Camden" (Comfort, 1972), a memo by Princeton architecture student (now professor), Mary C. McLeod ' 72, *75, *85, "Housing for Law Students" (in Cambridge) (August 4, 1969); a report from the Southern Connecticut Housing Corporation, "When Students and Community Share the Same Housing Needs: Housing Report to the Yale and New Haven Communities," 1972, and a Princeton University report, "Princeton University Land Planning and Housing Development: A Preliminary Assessment," October 1970. Related studies include the Syracuse University, "Preserving the Urban Fabric," 1966, Committee of Concerned Alumni, "Harvard and Housing in Cambridge," May 1972, EFL's, *Student Housing*, Fall 1972.

2. In 1974, Cooper Grant had a population of about 790 people, average income there was about $5,600 for families and $4,100 for individuals (Lang and Murray, 1974, p. 70, see also p. 39). The neighborhood was evenly divided between men and women, with about one-third black (and similar proportions Hispanic and non-Hispanic white). See also "Goals," 1973 for community concerns.

3. When my supervisor asked me to do the interviews under the cover of a student writing a class paper, without revealing my community ties or the destination of the information, somewhat nervously I let him know I would be informing my interviewees that the information might be shared more widely. He somewhat reluctantly accepted my decision, which apparently made little difference in the information the officials provided. Interestingly, years later when I interviewed former Defense Secretary Richard Cheney for a book (Sobel, 2001), even answering affirmatively to his

question about whether it was on the record did not seem to affect the completeness of his explanations.

4. *Southern Burlington County N.A.A.C.P. v. Township of Mount Laurel*, 67 N.J. 151 (1975).

5. The lead attorneys on the *Mount Laurel* suit were Peter O'Connor, Carl Bisgaier, and Ken Meiser. Working as a non-lawyer at a Legal Services office led to occasional tensions when legal prerogatives seemed to conflict with community interests. Moreover, when I was struggling financially and the community's lawyer was backing away from his initial indications of a basis for a suit, the director offered him an extra $500 that happened to be found in the budget. (Lacking health insurance, I waited to treat an eye infection until it worsened and went on the recommendation of a former Princeton teacher, Marvin Bressler, to the Will's Eye Clinic at the University of Pennsylvania. The swelling had become so bad, the doctors wanted to take a picture, but someone had stolen the camera!) In mid-July 1975, Don Griesmann, who, with his wife Carolyn, was continually supportive, wrote to commend my extraordinary efforts. Also helpful was Dennis Rockway who accompanied me when a traffic mishap briefly marred my departure in July 1975 and tried to get my back salary paid after I left the community. Unfortunately, despite precautions, this would not be the last time colleagues in Princeton, Boston, or Chicago areas would take adverse advantage of my professional contributions as faculty, fellow, adviser, visitor, or visionary.

6. I also taught at the urban campus of Glassboro State College's (now Rowan University) in downtown Camden on Cooper Street. I don't recall the course topic but do remember the director asking for a social security card after I was hired, and my refusing out of privacy principles, and that he should trust the number was correct. This was about 15 years before the Immigration Reform and Control Act of 1986 (IRCA) began requiring the awful I-9 form that assumes everyone is an "illegal immigrant" until otherwise proven. I was also stopped by Camden's finest one night for a missing headlight only to discover that my driver's license (without a photo) had expired. In 2008, I discovered in an obscure part of my family home, the renewal application for 1975!

7. During that period, air travelers could board, for instance, People's Express flights until 1987 and Eastern Shuttle flights until 1991, and pay cash on board anonymously without providing any ID (see Steve Chapman, 2013).

8. Two of my "Marathon" presentations were on "Community/University Conflict (Ala the Columbia Strike)," January 25, 1974, and "Perspectives for the Future I: Communities & University: 6 Years After Columbia," November 13, 1974.

9. In January 1974, Dean Dwight Allen (1968–75) invited me to travel with him to Chelmsford High School for a speech on educational innovation. Though later that year he turned down the Higher Education search committee's candidate for director as too radical, he thereby created a rare opportunity for us during his last year as dean, 1974–75, by permitting the use of the vacant directorship salary to bring in a group of distinguished visiting professors. These included political scientist Alan Wolfe, Wesleyan provost Sheila Tobias, Staten Island Community College president William Birenbaum, and Hostos Community College president Candido de Leon, to discuss issues in higher education and politics. We also visited SICC and Hostos in

spring 1975. During that year the Higher Education program developed an inspiring proposal (Program in Higher Education, 1974), which, in Birenbaum's words, "raised high the banner of social justice." During the next year, in which I fulfilled my residency requirement and took my comprehensive exams on March 29, 1976, when a new director, political scientist David Schuman, came in and reversed all the plans; to my great surprise, virtually everyone acquiesced to the coup.

10. Originally admitted to a Master's of Arts in Education program in 1972, when a year later I explained to Dean Allen my goals, he recognized that the doctoral program provided more flexibility needed for the Camden project and transferred me as a "wild-card" status. That track to a doctoral degree made sense for my professional goals, although an education doctorate proved to be an anomaly. Though I pursued a social sciences-oriented program, undertook sophisticated comprehensive exams, and wrote a more scholarly dissertation than most members of the education school in anticipation of an academic career (Sobel, 1982), getting this doctoral degree turned out to be a problematic academic career decision.

11. On January 9, 1977, and again on February 9 and 16, 1984, I attended seminars at UMass with Brazilian education, Paulo Freire. He also spoke at Princeton on February 19 and 25, 1985 (for which I have audio tapes) and gave a seminar there on February 28, 1985 (see Freire, 1970). Much to our surprise, we discovered that the inspiring writer Freire was a diffident teacher.

12. After Dean Allen was ousted in an alleged scandal tied to his innovative style's conflict with traditional fiscal stringency (see coverage in the *Hampshire Gazette* in 1974), the next Dean, Mario Fantini, visited Princeton on May 4, 1978, to speak to "Issue in Education," a group I informally advised at the University. My mother Betty Debs Sobel framed a letter from Dean Fantini (February 10, 1982) and picture of us recognizing my attaining the doctoral degree "with all the intellectual energy and acumen characteristic" of the accomplishments and as "a foundation of still further achievement." In making a last minute decision to attend the graduation, I didn't invite my family, much to our chagrin.

13. The director of the Fund for New Jersey (originally, the Wallace Eljabar Fund), Gordon MacInnes, later a New Jersey state senator, visited Cooper-Grant during summer 1974 to evaluate the proposal, when he noted the community was much better off than some of the places he had visited. At that point, the premise in community organizing and foundation funding was often that the places with the most severe problems (as opposed to promise) deserved the most funds. We also discussed the idea of creating a "University of New Jersey," perhaps as part of Rutgers as the State University of New Jersey. Princeton was originally called the College of New Jersey, now the successor name to Trenton State College.

14. In December 1972, EFL president Alan Green provided a grant for $4,635 to cover part of the cost for a study of community/university housing. The funds were exhausted by the time of the first draft in March 1974, hand-delivered in May 1974. The revisions were done by May 1975, and the copyediting and retyping finished by the middle of the year. The study was finally typed and ready for EFL to print in November 1975, at a total cost of $5,550. This included $400 for final typing, less than a thousand dollars over budget. It was published in December 1975, three years after

it began, a year late but still timely and a bargain as it only covered part of expenses and a fraction of my research time (see Marks, 2009).

15. From Antony Herrey's secretary's assiduously proofing his draft foreword on a day of a spring 1975 meeting at the Ford Foundation just before one at EFL, I learned the spelling was not "forward!" (I proofed the manuscript for spelling his name correctly, only to learn on receiving his permission to reprint the foreword in 2014 that I had added an "h" to the copy sent to him! [personal communication, January 27, 2014].) In that same e-mail (preferring to leave the foreword as is) he noted that the "study of the important subject of how universities interact with their surrounding communities . . . as housing is concerned . . . is a matter of enormous significance for many urban universities and continues to challenge these institutions and their neighbors in complex and demanding ways that are often difficult to resolve or even to control. You are providing an important service in studying this vital subject and bringing your insights to the attention of the interested parties."

16. My architect father, Walter H. Sobel, FAIA, provided two of the maps in the report. The beautiful opening on "The Communities and the Universities" is retained at the front here.

17. Ironically and reluctantly, I ended up living for part of a noisy year in 1979–80 in a Forrestal Village apartment, which the Princeton Housing Group encouraged the University to build as part of the community housing solution (Princeton Housing Group, 1974). It appears that the Forrestal Village is now luxury housing.

18. At the same time as two of my UMass graduate advisers were the famed radical economists, Samuel Bowles and Herbert Gintis (Bowles and Gintis, 1976; Sobel, 1996), I was working as an education consultant on a multi-volume series about the "knowledge industry" for a well-known conservative economist of international trade and higher education, Fritz Machlup (1962; 1980–84). Out of this research came a paper, "How Much Education Is Necessary for Jobs" (Sobel, 1983) which contributed to my dissertation in 1982 on educated labor and my first book, on *The White Collar Working Class: From Structure to Politics,* in 1989. (See Sobel, 1982 on the new working class theory, and Sobel, 1989, chapter 6; Sobel, 1993, 1994 on the impact of work participation on political participation; see also Arnstein, 1969 on the "ladder" of eight levels of participatory involvement). Before his untimely death at eighty-one in January 1983, Machlup expected to get the Nobel prize for his research and innovation on international trade and the knowledge industry, some of which Paul Krugman's work extended in receiving the prize in 2008.

19. During the 1970s, I helped my father's office, Walter H. Sobel FAIA & Associates, on various urban projects, including planning a day care facility for the Abraham Lincoln Center social services program on the South Side of Chicago (January 9, 1975). Earlier, I helped research possible building sites for a government facility on the east coast in Dover, Delaware (March 25, 1974; July 18, 1974), as a consultant to my father's judicial architectural practice. The office supported some of my urban and educational research, including the original report and its current revisions. In 2003–2004, I talked with a Boston contact about consulting on university/community issues around the rebuilding of Mass Mental Health Center, which might have made

this study come full circle. He offered to raise my name in the discussions but nothing came of it. That housing is about to start construction.

20. My long hope has been to join both the Board of the Abraham Lincoln Center when Dad goes off and I get a permanent position in Chicago, and the Board of the University of Chicago Baby Alumni Program for Lying-In Hospital where I was born. A great story emerged about this when I met University of Chicago President Hannah Gray at Smith College in February 1984, for the Smith Medalist ceremonies. Because I knew so much about the University, President Gray asked if I were an alumnus, and I replied, "Only baby alum!" Sadly, ALC recently closed.

21. My draft article, "Six Wright Houses in the Late Prairie Period" (1978, 1980, 2011), has the signal distinction of being accepted by at least two prominent journals (*Prairie School Review* in 1979 and *Inland Architecture* in 1983), right before they went out of business (no cause and effect) and I also submitted it to *Frank Lloyd Wright Building Conservancy Newsletter* on December 16, 1997. During the year of the Shorenstein fellowship bringing me to the Kennedy School, on sitting in on Neil Levine's Harvard course on "Frank Lloyd Wright and Modern Architecture (Lit and Arts B-33)" in spring 1997 (class notes March 19, 1997), I began revising the article and discussed possible revisions with Professor Levine. After a conversation following Anthony Alofsin's lecture at Unity Temple in February 2010, I finished the revisions and submitted the revised piece unsuccessfully to *The Journal of the Society of Architectural Historians*. I also began considering a book on Wright's Frank J. Baker House (1909). Like this book, I have long hoped to see the "Six Wright Houses" article in print. In May 1980, I co-organized a symposium on Wright's lectures on *Modern Architecture* (1930) at the Princeton School of Architecture ("Wright Remembered," 1980), for which I was initially scheduled to give a talk. My interest in Wright developed from growing up in and researching the Baker-Sobel House near Chicago.

22. For the Wright symposium at Princeton I was briefly scheduled to give a talk on "Frank Lloyd Wright and Low Cost Housing" on May 16, 1980. In the mid-1980s, I also gave two lectures on "Frank Lloyd Wright as Social Architect" at Princeton (March 23, 1982) and at Smith College (April 9, 1985) about Wright's multiple and low cost ("Usonian") housing. The first was well regarded, and the second poorly received, partly for including slides of my father's Midwestern architecture. More recently we have explored using Wright's low cost approach for preservation and sustainability. Recently I spoke on Dad's religious architecture in Springfield, IL.

23. After returning to Cambridge in fall 1996 for a fellowship at the Shorenstein Center for Press, Politics and Public Policy at the Kennedy School at Harvard and corresponding with Harvard, MIT, and local libraries, in September 1997, I gave most of the research materials from this study to the Local History Room of the Cambridge Public Library. A recent attempt to locate the materials there has proven unsuccessful. I plan to donate the files around the current publication, and my Camden notebooks from 1970 to 1975, to the Northwestern archive where most of the research materials for my work participation and foreign policy books reside (Sobel, 1989; 2001, 2003, 2005). The UMass Social Change collection has expressed interest in acquiring my

extensive collection of books and pamphlets about the politics and culture of the 1960s and university and community protests.

24. For national housing goal of 26 million units, see www.presidency.ucsb.edu/ws/index.php?pid=2930. For how far from the goal the numbers of new housing units fell, see www.jessejacksonjr.org/query/creadpr.cgi?id=%22000256%22.

25. Sadly, while completing this book, a controversy arose in my home community where the village government cut off government support for an affordable housing program (Routliffe, 2013). As in the Mount Laurel decision, every community needs to contribute and provide low income housing. See note 4 above.

26. Housing rents that seemed extreme at $250 per month decades ago, now top $2,500. While once a quarter of monthly income was the standard, half of Cambridge and Boston tenants now pay a third of their incomes or more for rent and utilities.

27. On May 7, 2009, an aide in the Allston room indicated neighbors had raised the issue of community housing. Harvard proposed housing at Barry's Corner but its initial plan limited the potential benefits for community members, particularly families. Community concerns included, "Hopefully it will be possible to balance Harvard's goals for a money-making development of Barry's Corner with the type of housing that will also advance the housing and social goals of Allston" (Allston blog, 2012). The plan announced at the groundbreaking on December 13, 2013, included 325 studio through three-bedroom housing units at 219 Western Way, but no details on the mix (see Harvard University, *Institutional Master Plan*, October 2013). Plans include 80 studies, 121 one bedrooms, 111 two-bedrooms, and 13 three-bedroom units (462 bedrooms), with an affordability proposal for 15 percent being developed. While none was reserved for Harvard-affiliates, tenants are likely to include a mix community and Harvard members (Cohen, personal communications, January and April 2014). There are also plans for other graduate student housing projects in the Allston Harvard area.

28. Harvard has also been involved in the 20/20/2000 Affordable Housing Initiative. Based on 1999 concerns for affordable housing and the need for low cost capital to increase affordable housing, Harvard developed a program with community input to provide 20 year loans at 2 percent interest to area nonprofits. The funding is managed by three Cambridge and Boston area housing organizations, Boston Community Capital, Cambridge Affordable Housing Trust, and Local Initiatives Support Corporations. Harvard provided half the $20 million in loans to the Cambridge nonprofits and half to the Boston nonprofits which create or preserve housing for local residents (Bluestone, et al., 2003, 5). So far the program has contributed to 50 units of affordable housing in nine buildings at Brian J. Hanan Apartments. The Hano Homes are 20 renovated rental units, 15 affordable. Harvard helped fund it working with the Allston Brighton Community Development Corporation (Harvard, October 2013, 274).

29. In applying during senior year at Princeton for a Sachs Scholarship, I articulated my hope to become more than an academic as someone studying and helping to implement policy but not just in government. At that time such hybrid positions did not seem to exist. On entering Princeton I was also hoping to pursue another hybrid study of international affairs and molecular biology, similarly then an unseen possibility. Both are now possible, for instance, in public policy think tanks and in environmental studies.

30. Holdings and citation searches on the report found it owned by five schools, Amherst Harvard (2 copies), Smith, University of Massachusetts/Amherst, and Princeton (listed in 2011 in the catalog, but unfound in the collection). The Texas A&M website archives of Educational Facilities Laboratories provided a copy (crs.arch. tamu.edu/archives/efl/) that is not currently accessible online.

31. I also published two bibliographies on community/university and housing issues for the Council on Planning Librarians (Sobel, 1977a, 1977b). These are held by 73 libraries. In addition, in the late 1970s, I proposed an anthology of cases gathered from articles I collected about community/university conflicts, for instance around Columbia, Vanderbilt, and the University of Chicago, but did not find a publisher.

32. My Camden interns included Princeton students, Hal Candee '75, Robert Comfort '73, Tony Murry '76, and at least one Penn student, Allison Feldman. Hal and I had many discussions of why community members sometimes did not follow through on their commitments. Co-authors of a funded grant proposal (Sobel and Comfort, 1972), Bob and I discussed whether Harvard Law School was more diverse than Yale. Tony Murry was a Camden native, now living in Oakland, California, whose son also went to Princeton.

33. *Public Opinion in U.S. Foreign Policy: The Controversy over Contra Aid* (1993); *International Public Opinion and the Bosnia Crisis*, with Eric Shiraev (2005).

34. Graham Allison and Theodore Marmor, "Analytic Framework for Explaining and Predicting Actions in Domestic and Foreign Affairs," Kennedy School, Fall 1996.

35. Marmor (1973) revised his classic with a new introduction (2001). Allison (1971) with the assistance of Philip Zelikow (2007) integrated new material into the original model, which somewhat expanded on the classic original edition.

36. Unless a biographer decides to study my work as Steven Harper (2007) did for fellow Princeton alumnus and Northwestern faculty, Richard Leopold in *Straddling Two Worlds*, this epilogue provides the best overview of my work, especially in the early to middle 1970s (see also Sobel memoir, 2014). I have donated parts of my papers to the Seeley Mudd Library at Princeton and the University Archives at Northwestern. Most of my father's architectural papers are at the University of Minnesota, Midwest Architectural Archives, Art Institute of Chicago, and the Spertus Institute in Chicago. As mentioned above (note 23), most source material for the original community housing report is in the Cambridge Public Library and my Camden notebooks (1971–75) and correspondence files will likely go to Northwestern.

37. As I was completing the revisions for this book, Antony Herrey provided a copy of Matthew Echelman's paper, "Navigating Identities in an Urban Environment," about how MIT's housing development policies in the 1960s and 1970s "constructed its relationship" to working class, low-and-middle income Cambridge residents. It draws upon the 1975 EFL report in critiquing the MIT Housing Program in Cambridge. It also provides helpful citations for other community-university development projects to update the references here (see Urban Planning Aid, 1974, et al.). Similarly, Brett Donham alerted me to Davenport Commons, a joint project between Northeastern University and the Lower Roxbury Community (see Bluestone, et al, 2003, which provide information on other community/university projects and updated citations, not including the EFL report).

38. A reference librarian at Northwestern found copies of the 1975 report at Harvard, Smith, University of Massachusetts, and Princeton, though the Princeton catalogue did not have the physical report. The report was cited in *Index to Current Urban Documents,* Greenwood Press, Vol. 5, 1976–77, p. 18. The 1978 article has been occasionally cited (e.g. *Urban Affairs Abstract,* Vol. 8, 1978; and *Recent Publications on Governmental Problems Chicago,* Joint Reference Library, 1932–1991, Vol. 48: no. 3, 1979). The community/university bibliographies were more widely held and cited (see Geo Abstracts F, Regional and Community Planning, Norwich, Eng., 1978; *National Civic Review,* NYC: National Municipal League, Vol. 66: p. 586, December 1977). The Texas A&M Architecture School archive for Educational Facilities Laboratories previously included the 1975 report on its website at www.tamu.edu.

39. *Camden after the Fall* (2005) mentions two of the community activists from my era, Gualberto Medina and Barbara Broadwater. It does not mention the leaders of the People of the Cooper Grant Community, Carthina Davis, Naomi Holtz, Tony Vasquez, or Roy Jones. As far as I know, no history of Cooper-Grant has ever been written, though perhaps a Rutgers graduate student wrote a paper or thesis on the topic (see Lang, 1974). The community's preference mentioned above to keep Rutgers students and professors from studying Cooper-Grant may have contributed to the lack of information and insights from the Cooper-Grant experience. I went back to Philadelphia occasionally, for instance, for the Nation's Bicentennial in 1976 when I passed out the Declaration of Independence and Bill of Rights at Independence Hall and was briefly stopped by a Park Ranger asking what I was doing (Towarnicky and Caparella, 1976).

40. The Cooper Grant Historic District, between Point, North Front, Linden, Penn and North Second Streets in Camden (250 acres, 93 buildings), was added to the National Register of Historic Places for Camden County in 1989 (#87002229). It was included for its historical significance of the architecture and engineering, including Italianate, Second Empire, and Gothic Style buildings from 1850 to 1949. See Lang and Murray, 1974; Cooper Grant Community Association, 1977. See also City of Camden, 2005, for indications of progress.

41. As this epilogue was being revised, new university expansion and a town-gown conflicts emerged around Chicago. First, the University of Chicago quietly planned to tear down (and ultimately did) the childhood home of Ronald Reagan in Chicago. On the hundredth anniversary of Reagan's birth, his boyhood home on the South Side of Chicago faced demolition as part of the University's expansion plans, and those who want to preserve the site were vocally unhappy (Janssen, 2011). Second, the City of Evanston, where Northwestern University's undergraduate campus is located, planned to enforce an ordinance limiting occupancy of rental units to 3 unrelated individuals. This set off a widespread protest by undergraduates (Cohen, 2011, p. 16). Third, Northwestern decided to demolish the landmark Prentice and Women's Hospital designed by architect Bertrand Goldberg, famed for Marina City Towers, at the Medical School campus despite preservationist efforts to save it (Kamin, 2013).

Acknowledgments

I appreciate the opportunity to study Cambridge and Boston for more than two years and thank the many members of the communities who helped. Because Cambridge and Boston are complicated, politically conscious, and zealous cities, I expect no review of the issues and processes of Community housing will please everyone. I have tried to treat the Cambridge and Boston situations accurately and sympathetically, and provide insights for future developments.

I would like to thank those who assisted me during this study. Antony Herrey and Brett Donham have my great appreciation for reviewing and providing commentary on the manuscript and for contributing insightful forewords to the study. Robert Parks of Roxbury Tenants of Harvard was especially kind in answering questions and providing information. Frank Duehey, then a dean at Harvard Education School, made available several helpful background studies (1970a-f, A-55). Oliver Brooks of the Cambridge Corporation and Dexter Kamilewicz of MIT provided varied and continuous help.

Ginny Strawn has more than my thanks for expert typing and editing of the manuscript and continual support. I appreciate the help of June Traube for the final typing. Also, I would like to thank Educational Facilities Laboratories, especially Alan Green, Margaret Nyhus, and Peter O'Connor and Camden Regional Legal Services for partial funding and support of this project. I appreciate the first printing of the report by Educational Facilities Laboratories in December 1975. I welcome the interest of Jon Sisk, Justin Race, Brian Hill, and Meaghan White at Lexington Books in publishing this as a book, my third with the firm. Thanks, too, to David Loutzenheiser, Jennifer Raitt, and Chris Porter for timely assistance on journals and finding the previous report, and to Margaret Ormes for her thoughtful reading and suggestions on the epilogue. I appreciate the interest of other presses offering to publish the book. I also appreciate the updates from Brett Donham, John Sharratt, Will Donham, and Leslie Cohen. I thank my agent Nancy Rosenfeld of AAA Press Unlimited for her interest in finding a publisher for the book and Jerry Jenkins for his guidance on publication questions.

I would also like to thank Gloria Adlerman, Bob Comfort, Bob Kuenzel, and Guy Sikorra for their research assistance. Murray Lamp, Donna Macrini, Ken Meiser, and Eric Olson helped at crucial times. David McNally, Mary McLeod, Mark Winkeller, Margot Slade, Neil Peterson, Leo Wilkins, John Sharratt, Bob Egan, Badi Foster, Robert Simha, Doug Levinson, Steve Kaiser, Andy Sullivan, Marvin Gerstein, Ed Meyers, Betty Hepner, Arthur Krim, Mike Timchula, Frances Shaw, and Ben Graves also provided timely aid. I also appreciate tours of 2 Mount Auburn Street/Putnam Square Apartments by Becky Livengood, of Lyndon Johnson Apartments by Alfreda Simpson, and of Inman Square by Alexa Daley.

The chairperson, Carthina Davis, and the People of the Cooper-Grant Community, had to do without my services at times when I struggled with this study, but they benefited from my increased knowledge of Community/ University relations and housing development. The pleasure at the completion, and usefulness, of the original report Peter J. O'Connor, Dennis Rockway, and Don Griesmann at Camden Regional Legal Services expressed was also important, as was the support of CRLS directors, Carl Bisgaier, Barney Hamlin, and David Dugan. My advisors in the Higher Education Program at the University of Massachusetts Education School, Robert Wuerthner and Rhody McCoy, helped clarify important points verbally and visually.

Cathy Richards and Anne Crane scanned the text of the original report into an editable Word file. Hangyell Kim revised the maps, drawings, charts, and format. Olympia Banerjee, Agnes Gyorfi, Barbara Leary, Andrew Nho, and Zack Nolan helped with the final book revisions. Thanks also to Geoff Morse at Northwestern Library for citation searches, Michelle Pearse and Special Collections at Harvard Law Library, the Widener reference and resource sharing staff, Alyssa Pacy at Cambridge Public Library, and Barbara Leary and Jim Fuhr on indexing.

This book is dedicated to my father, Walter H. Sobel, FAIA, who created maps, particularly the one of "Communities and Universities," just at the right time, and provided other support through his office and Home and Studio. It is also dedicated to others concerned with finding and preserving housing. Those who were unhelpful during the study were also a part of the process. If I have not acknowledged or thanked anyone properly, I take responsibility among any other failings in this work.

SOURCES AND REFERENCE MATERIALS

The MIT Institute Information (MIT) Office supplied pictures of the MIT projects. The Cambridge Corporation (CC) provided photographs of Harvard-related Cambridge projects. Brett Donham Associates shared the River-Howard photo, and John Sharratt Associates provided the photo of the Mission Park. Zack Nolan also provided photos of River-Howard Homes and Mission Park.

To encourage future use by community members and researchers, I donated much of the research materials for the original report to the Cambridge Room of the Cambridge Public Library and the Archives of Northwestern University in Evanston, Illinois. Acknowledgment of the use of the research materials or this book in future publications would be welcome.

Interviews and Communications

Oliver Brooks, President, The Cambridge Corporation, Cambridge, Massachusetts, by telephone, February 14, 1973; March 7, 1973; July 8, 1974 (reader of the 1975 manuscript).

Leslie Cohen, Vice President, Samuel, Personal Communications, January 15, 21, 2014.

John Corcoran, Cambridge City Manager, Cambridge, March 29, 1973.

Brett Donham, Architect and Editor of *Harvard and Housing in Cambridge*, by phone Boston April 4, 1973 et al., October 23, 1973 (manuscript reader), e-mail correspondence, December 30, 2013.

Willard Donham, Senior Manager, Harvard Planning, personal communication, January 5, 6, 2014.

John Donovan, Executive Director, Cambridge Housing Authority, Cambridge, March 22, 1973.

Francis Duehey, Cambridge City Councillor and Assistant Dean, Harvard Graduate School of Education, Cambridge, March 5, 1973.

Roger Evans, Ely, Bartlett, Brown and Proctor, Harvard Attorney, Boston, March 29, 1973.

Harold Goyette, Director of Planning, Harvard University, Cambridge, February 3, 1973; February 26, 1973.

Saundra Graham, President, Riverside Community Corporation (RCC), Cambridge City Councillor, Cambridge, March 21, 1973.

Antony Herrey, Director of Real Estate and Negotiated Investments, the Ford Foundation; Former Director, MIT Institute Real Estate Office (IREO), New York City, March 9, 1973; Cambridge, March 31, 1973; New York City, July 23, 1974; July 30, 1974; August 5, 1974; March 26, 1975 (reader); personal communications, February 11, 1975, Cambridge, January 6, 2014, January 27, 2014.

Stephen Kaiser, Member, university negotiations committee of the Cambridge Housing Convention, by telephone, November 13, 1973.

Dexter Kamilewicz, Project Manager (IREO), MIT Cambridge, February 25, 1973; by telephone March 1, 1973; March 8, 1974 (reader).

Langley Keyes, Professor, MIT, and Advocate Planner to RCC from Greater Boston Community Development, Inc., Cambridge, March 22, 1973.

James Killian, former President, MIT, by letter, May 2, 1973.

Doug Levinson, former aide to Roxbury Tenants of Harvard, Philadelphia, Pennsylvania, April 11, 1973 (reader).

Mary McLeod, Intern to Riverside Community Corporation, Princeton, New Jersey, March 1973.

David McNally, Director, Undergraduate Urban Studies Program, Princeton University; Co-author, *Effective Government for Cambridge*, Princeton, January 1973.

Walter Milne, Special Assistant to President for Urban Relations, MIT, Cambridge, February 22, 1973; March 7, 1973.

Charles Moore, Chairman, Council on Aging, Cambridge, February 25, 1973.

Donald Moulton, Assistant Vice President for Community Affairs, Harvard University, Cambridge, February 6, 1973; February 13, 1973.

Robert Parks, President Roxbury Tenants of Harvard, Somerville, Mass., March 6, 1973; March 30, 1973.

Howard Neil Peterson, Cambridge City Manager candidate and Vice President, Edna McConnell Clark Foundation, Princeton, New Jersey, February 14, 1973.

Jon Pynoos, Fellow, Joint Center for Urban Studies, Cambridge, February 28, 1973, by phone April 23, 1973.

John Sharratt, Architect to Roxbury Tenants of Harvard, Boston, March 30, 1975.

O. Robert Simha, Director of Planning, MIT, Cambridge, February 27, 1973.

Dan Sullivan, Attorney, Boston Legal Assistance Project, Boston, April 4, 1973.

Kenneth Wadleigh, Vice-President, MIT; Officer Northgate Community Corporation, Cambridge, March 29, 1973.

James Q. Wilson, Professor of Government and Chairman of the Committee on the University and the City (*The Wilson Report*), Harvard University, February 26, 1973; March 5, 1973; and by letter. (The Wilson interview has been transcribed.)

Mark Winkeller, Author, *University Expansion in Urban Neighborhoods,* Cambridge, by telephone February 27, 1973; February 28, 1973.

Leigh Woodward, Associate Director, Institute Real Estate Office, MIT, Cambridge, March 6, 1973.

Students at Harvard and MIT, February/March, 1973.

PEOPLE WITH KNOWLEDGE OF
THE PROJECTS (NOT INTERVIEWED)

Barbara Ackerman, Mayor, Cambridge, Massachusetts

Henry Cutler, Director, Housing Office, Harvard University

Charles Daly, Vice President for Community Affairs, Harvard University

Robert Ebert, MD, Dean of Harvard Medical School

Justin Gray, Architect, Boston, Former Director at Cambridge City Community Development Section.

Chester Hartman, Former Director, Urban Field Science, Harvard University; later in San Francisco.

John Mollenkopf, Department of Political Science, Stanford University; Co-author, *Property, Politics and Local Housing Policy.*

Vincent Panico, Attorney, Cambridge (MIT).

H. Ralph Taylor, Boston developer.

Benjamin Thompson, Architect, MIT Housing Program.

References

Abrams, Charles, *The Future of Housing*, Harper & Brothers, 1945.

Abrams, Charles, *The City Is the Frontier*, Harper & Row, 1965.

Ad Hoc Housing Development Task Force, *Homes for People, Progress Report No. 1*, Ad Hoc Housing Development Task Force, September 1969.

Adams, Frederick J., "Cambridge Fifty Years from Now," reprinted from *Magazine of Cambridge*, January 1947.

Agle, Charles, "New Life for the Center of Princeton," Princeton Regional Planning Board, March 1972.

Alinsky, Saul, *Reveille for Radicals* (1946), Second Edition, Vintage Books, 1969.

Alinsky, Saul, *Rules for Radicals, A Pragmatic Primer for Realistic Radicals*, Random House, 1971.

Al–Khazraj, Majid G., *Beyond the Campus: Views on Higher Education and Community Services*, Inter–Institutional Cooperation; Jacob Padgug, *Organizing Colleges and Universities*, Massachusetts Board of Higher Education, 1971.

Allen, Robert and Edward Goldsmith, *Blueprint for Survival*, The Ecologist Vol. 2, No. 1, January 1972; *New York Times*, February 5, 1972.

Allison, Graham, *Essence of Decision; Explaining the Cuban Missile Crisis*, Little Brown, 1971.

Allison, Graham and Philip Zelikow, *Essence of Decision; Explaining the Cuban missile crisis*, Revised Edition, Longman, 2007.

Allston Brighton Community Blog, "What Kind of Housing Would Improve North Austin?" February 15, 2012, allston02134.blogspot.com/2012/02/what–type–of–housing–would–improve.html.

American Association of State Colleges and Universities, Office of Urban Programs, *Guide to Federal Funds for Urban Programs at Colleges and Universities*, Office of Urban Programs, American Association of State Colleges, 1971.

"Appendix A—RTH History," in Epsilon Associates, MMHC Redevelopment, 2009.

"Architecture Talk," *Hampshire Gazette*, April 8, 1985.

Arnstein, Sherry, "A Ladder of Citizens Participation," *Journal of the American Institute of Planners*, Vol. 35, No. 4, July 1969, pp. 216–224.

Atkins, Thomas and Louise Day Hicks, "Request for Information about Land Acquisition by Harvard in Mission Hill Section," City Council Resolution, Boston, August 3, 1970.

"Author Predicts Regeneration of Inner Cities by Energy Crisis," *Philadelphia Bulletin*, 1974, 37.

Baker, Larry, *The University and the City*, senior thesis, Harvard College, Spring 1972.

Barber, Robert C., *Influence, Interlock and Development Trends: An Analysis of Power Distribution in Cambridge, Massachusetts*, senior thesis. Harvard College, March 31, 1972.

Barrett, William P., "Camden vs. Rutgers: Expansion Fought," *New York Times*, New Jersey Edition, March 24, 1974.

Barrett, William P., "Expansion by Rutgers in Camden Is Assailed," *New York Times*, March 16, 1975.

Bauer, Dolores, "Rutgers under Fire by Camden Community," New Brunswick: *Rutgers Targum*, December 5, 1973, p. 1.

Bazell, Robert, "Boston Hospital Disputes: Harvard Rectifies 'Expansionist' Policies," *Science*, January 29, 1971.

Bellush, Jewel and Murray Hausknecht, *Urban Renewal: People, Politics and Planning*, Anchor Books, 1967.

Bertrand Goldberg Associates, *Master Plan Report*, Affiliated Hospitals Center, Inc., 1965 (revised 1972).

Berube, Maurice R. and Marilyn Gittell, *Confrontation at Ocean Hill–Brownsville; The New York School Strikes of 1968*, Praeger, 1969.

Biddle, William and Loureide J. Biddle, *The Community Development Process. The Rediscovery of Local Initiative*, Holt Rinehart and Winston, 1965.

Biddle, William W. Biddle, with the collaboration of Loureide J. Biddle. *Encouraging Community Development, A Training Guide for Local Workers*, Holt, Rinehart and Winston, 1968.

Bitman, Terry, "Community Fights to Block Rutgers' Expansion Projects," *Philadelphia Inquirer*, June 30, 1975.

Birenbaum, William, *Overlive: Power, Poverty and the University*, Delacorte Press, 1969.

Birenbaum, William, *Something for Everybody Is Not Enough*, Random House, 1968.

Blau, Judith R., *Architects and Firms: A Sociological Perspective on Architectural Practice*, MIT Press, 1984.

Bluestone, Barry, Richard Maloney and Eleanor White, "A Primer on University–Community Housing Partnerships," Center for Urban and Regional Policy, Northeastern University, May 2003.

Bookchin, Murray, *The Limits of the City*, Harper & Row, 1973.

Bookchin, Murray, "The Myth of City Planning," *Liberation, The Boston Globe*, September 1973.

Boston Globe, "House Reviews Mental Health Expansion Law," *Boston Globe*, April 24, 1963, p. 8.

The Boston Phoenix

Boston Redevelopment Authority, *Proposed Policies for Development of Educational Institutions in Boston*, Boston Redevelopment Authority, July 1970.

Boston Redevelopment Authority, Planning Department, *Educational Institutions Study*, Boston Redevelopment Authority Planning Department, October 1970.

Boston University Metrocenter, *Boston University Is the Community: A Report on Some Aspects of the Current Relations of the University to its Community and to the Problems of an Urban–Metropolitan Environment*, Boston University Metrocenter, May 1967.

Boston University Metrocenter, *Education for Metropolitan Living, in The Urban University and the Urban Community* (Self–Study), Boston University Metrocenter, March–May 1966.

Boston University Metrocenter, *Problems of Town and Gown, in The Urban University and the Urban Community* (Self–Study), Boston University Metrocenter, March–May 1966.

Boston University Metrocenter, *The Future, in The Urban University and the Urban Community*, (Self–Study), Boston University Metrocenter, March–May 1966.

Boston University Metrocenter, *The University and Its Environment, in The Urban University and the Urban Community* (Self–Study Metro–Seminars), Boston University Metrocenter, March–May 1966.

Boston University Metrocenter, *The Urban University and Community Action, in The Urban University and the Urban Community* (Self–Study Metro–Seminars), Boston University Metrocenter, March–May 1966.

Bowles, Samuel and Herbert Gintis, *Schooling in Capitalist America, Educational Reform and the Contradictions of Economic Life*, Basic Books, 1976.

Bowles, Samuel and Herbert Gintis, "Power and Wealth in a Competitive Capitalist Economy," *Philosophy and Public Affairs*, August 1992.

Brown, Lance, et al., *Princeton University Land Planning and Its Potential: A Preliminary Assessment*, School of Architecture, Princeton University, October 1970.

Burnham, Daniel and Edward Bennett, *Plan of Chicago*, ed. Charles Moore, Chicago: Commercial Club, 1909.

Cabot, Cabot, and Forbes, "Technology Square," Cabot, Cabot and Forbes, Cambridge, Mass., June 1965.

Caldwell, Earl, "Stanford Scans Low–Income Housing," *New York Times*, June 2, 1970, p. 18.

Cambridge Advisory Committee, *Another Housing Department?* Cambridge, Mass., July 29, 1969.

The Cambridge Chronicle, especially 1969–1973.

Cambridge Community Development Program, *1960 Census Summary Statistics for Cambridge*, Mass., Social Economic and Housing, 1962b.

Cambridge Community Development Program, *1970 Census Summary Statistics for Cambridge*, Mass., Social Economic and Housing, August 1972a.

Cambridge Community Development Program, *City–wide Sample Household Survey*, Office of Community Development, City of Cambridge, May 1969.

Cambridge Community Development Program, *Directory of Cambridge Establishments*, Community Development Program, 1972f.

Cambridge Community Development Program, *Ethnic Minorities in Cambridge: The Portuguese*, Office of Community Development, City of Cambridge, March 1972d.

Cambridge Community Development Program, *Housing Needs in Cambridge: No. 1, The Elderly,* June 1971.

Cambridge Community Development Program, *Housing Needs in Cambridge: No. 2, The Family, Low and Moderate Income,* March 1972b.

Cambridge Community Development Program, *Housing Needs in Cambridge: No. 3, Market Rate Housing,* January 1973.

Cambridge Community Development Program, *Housing Needs in Cambridge: No. 4, Housing Supply: A Profile,* December 1972c.

Cambridge Community Development Program, *Social Characteristics of Cambridge,* Office of Community Development, City of Cambridge, 1972e.

The Cambridge Corporation, *Changes in the Cambridge Housing Stock since 1960 Census*, The Cambridge Corporation, June 1969.

The Cambridge Corporation, *Prospectus for a City: An Outline of the Philosophy and Purposes of the Cambridge Corporation*, The Cambridge Corporation, 1965.

Cambridge Department of Planning and Development, *Comprehensive Planning for Cambridge,* No.1: *The City's People: Who Were They? Who Are They? Who Will They Be?* School of Education, Harvard University, December 1973.

Cambridge Economic Opportunity Committee, *Survey of Cambridge Elderly and Families*, July 1, 1968.

Cambridge Historical Commission, *Survey of Cambridge Architecture*, Cambridge Historical Commission, 1965.

Cambridge Housing Authority, *A Proposal from Cambridge, Mass.: Modernization of Locally Owned, Federally Assisted, Low–rent, Public Housing Projects*, Cambridge Housing Authority, December 20, 1968.

Cambridge Housing Authority, "River Howard Homes: Construction Begins at Last." *CHA Bulletin,* Winter 2006, Vol. 2:2.

Cambridge Housing Authority "Development Update: River Howard Homes Modernization Move Ahead," *CHA Bulletin,* Summer 2007, Vol. 3:2.

Cambridge Housing Convention, *Cambridge, Crisis in Housing*, Cambridge Housing Convention, December 1968.

Cambridge Planning Board, *A Suggested Housing Program for Cambridge*, Cambridge Planning Board, September 1965.

Cambridge Planning Board, *Suggested Goals for a Cambridge City Plan*, Cambridge Planning Board, November 1965.

Cambridge Planning Board, *Thirteen Neighborhoods in Cambridge*, Cambridge Planning Board, 1953.

Cambridge Planning Board, *Zoning, Housing, Density, Tax Base*, Cambridge Planning Board, June 23, 1969.

Cambridge Tenants Organizing Committee, Background Material on the Transformation of Cambridge, Cambridge Tenants Organizing Committee, April 1972 (mimeo).

Cambridge Tenants Organizing Committee, Background of the Current Tenants' Movement, Cambridge Tenants Organizing Committee, 1971 (mimeo).

Cambridge Tenants Organizing Committee, *CTOC Fact Sheet No. 1 on Cabot, Cabot and Forbes*, Cambridge Tenants Organizing Committee, January 3, 1974.

Cambridge Tenants Organizing Committee, *MIT's Real Estate Operation and MIT's Relation to Kendall Square*, Cambridge Tenants Organizing Committee, April 1969.

Cambridge Tenants Organizing Committee, *Stop Kendall Square Project!* Cambridge Tenants Organizing Committee and Hard Times, March 1973.

Cambridge Tenants Organizing Committee, *Tenants' Newsletter*, Cambridge Tenants Organizing Committee, June 1 and August 24, 1972.

Cambridge Tenants Organizing Committee, "The New University City," Cambridge Tenants Organizing Committee, 1973 (mimeo).

Carmichael, Stokely and Charles V. Hamilton, *Black Power, the Politics of Liberation in America*, Random House, 1967.

Carnegie Commission, *The Campus and the City, Maximizing Assets and Reducing Liabilities*, Carnegie Commission, December 1972.

Carroll, Robert, Hayden May and Stan Noe, *University–Community Tensions and Urban Campus Form*, University of Cincinnati, October 1972.

Cassidy, Tina and Don Aucoin. "Harvard Says Its Purchases Violated Trust," *Boston Globe*, June 11, 1997, p. 1.

Cavanna, Betty [Elizabeth Headley]. *Catchpenny Street,* Philadelphia, 1951, Macrae Smith; Philadelphia: Westminster Press, 1975.

Chapman, Herrick, *Campus and Community: Princeton and the Search for Boundaries,* senior thesis, Princeton University, May 1971.

Chapman, Steve, "Why the No–Fly List Doesn't Fly," *Chicago Tribune*, March 31, 2013.

Christian Science Monitor, "Cambridge/Harvard, MIT Add Up to Unique University," *The Christian Science Monitor*, April 24, 1973.

Christopher, Rand, *Cambridge USA: Hub of a New World*, 1964.

Citizens Advisory Committee for Cambridge, *How to Make Cambridge a Better City*, Citizens Advisory Committee for Cambridge May 1957.

Citizens Housing and Planning Association of Metropolitan Boston, *To Rebuild a City: A Report on the Organization of Housing Functions In Boston*, Citizens Housing and Planning Association of Metropolitan Boston, 1969.

City of Cambridge, *Capital Budget and Capital Improvements Program*, City of Cambridge, 1972–1977

City of Cambridge, *City and Town Monograph*, City of Cambridge, November 1967.

City of Camden, "Cooper Grant Neighborhood Homes: Proposed Section 108 Loan Guarantee Application," Camden Department of Development and Planning, 2005.

Clinchy, Evans and the Bedford–Stuyvesant Restoration Corporation, Education Affiliate, *A College in the City: An Alternative,* Educational Facilities Laboratories, 1971.

Cohen, Jodi S. "Evanston Gets Look at NU's 'Good kids.'" *Chicago Tribune*, February 20, 2011, p. 16.

Colcord, Frank C. Jr., *The University View*, Grass Roots Housing Council Newsletter, vol. V, no. 2, May 1965.

Coleman, John R., "Little Man on Campus," *New York Times*, December 15, 1975.

Comfort, Robert, "Rutgers in Camden," August 3, 1972.

Comfort, Robert, *University–Community Politics*, senior thesis, Princeton University, April 1973.

Committee for Economic Development, *Financing the Nation's Housing Need*, Committee for Economic Development, April 1973.

Committee on the University and the City, *Preliminary Report of the Committee on the University and the City (The Wilson Report)*, Harvard University, December 1968; Summary Report: "The University and the City," Office of the President, Fall 1969.

Community Development Section, City of Cambridge, *Study Design: Community Development Program, Fiscal Base*, City of Cambridge, September 29, 1968.

Community Involvement Council, *University–Community Relations: Proposal for Change*, University of Pennsylvania, April 1973.

Cooper, Robertson & Partners, et al. "The Plan for Harvard in Allston (Draft), Executive Summary," January 2007 http://isites.harvard.edu/fs/docs/icb.topic130901.files/IMP_Exec_Summary_010907.pdf

Cooper Grant Community Association, "A Comprehensive Cooper Grant Housing Assistance Proposal," Cooper Grant Community Association, Inc., 1977.

Coordinating Committee, *Cambridge Housing Convention*, Statement to MIT, President's Office, MIT, October 23, 1968.

"Council Communicator," Cambridge City Council, January 1973.

Cummings, e. e., *i:six–nonlectures*, Harvard University Press, 1953.

Cummins, John M., "Housing Project Is Part of Preventive Care Program." *Hospitals; Journal of American Hospital Association*, February 1, 1973, pp. 94–95.

Curvin, Robert. *The Persistent Minority: The Black Political Experience in Newark*, Ph.D. Dissertation, Department of Politics, Princeton University, 1975.

Curvin, Robert. "Black Power in City Hall," *Society*, September/October 1972.

"Deep Layoffs to Police, Firefighters Shake Camden, N.J.," *USAToday*, January 18, 2011.

Dennis, Robert, Harvey Baker, Alan Baumgardner, and Alex Markowski, "The Cambridge Housing Crisis," *The Tech*, MIT, November 5, 8, 12, 1968.

"Development Plan for Planned Development Area, RTH Residential Building, Former Massachusetts Mental Health Center Site, Mission Hill Neighborhood, Boston, 2010.

"The Disposition of Urban Renewal Land to Sectarian Institutions of Higher Education," *Notre Dame Law Review*, 1965, p. 251ff.

Dobbins, Charles, *The University, City and Urban Renewal*, American Council on Education, 1964.

Donham, Brett, *Harvard and Housing in Cambridge*, Committee of Concerned Alumni, May 1972.

Downie, Leonard, *Mortgage on America*, Praeger, 1974.

Downing, Margot. "Cooper Grant on the Move, But a Little Skeptical," *The Philadelphia Tribune*, January 17, 1975.

Duberstein, Gary. "Housing Questions Sparks Formation of Group Concerned with Forrestal," *Daily Princetonian*, March 11, 1974.

Duehey, Francis, *Cambridge Housing Crisis and Rent Control,* Graduate School of Education, Harvard University, Fall 1970a, A–55.

Duehey, Francis, *Citizen Participation, The Wellington–Harrington Urban Renewal Project,* School of Education, Harvard University, Fall 1970b, A–55.

Duehey, Francis, *Harvard and the Housing Crisis,* Graduate School of Education, A–55, Harvard University, Fall 1970c.

Duehey, Francis, *Redevelopment of Kendall Square: The Research Center,* Graduate School of Education, A–55, Harvard University, Fall 1970d.

Duehey, Francis, *The City Manager,* Graduate School of Education, Harvard University, A–55, Fall 1970e.

Duehey, Francis, *The Inner Belt,* Graduate School of Education, A–55, Harvard University, Fall 1970f.

Echelman, Matthew, "Navigating Identities in an Urban Environment, How MIT's Housing Development Policies in the Late 1960s and Early 70s Constructed Its Relationship to Cambridge's Working Class and Low–and–middle–income Residents" Papers for "Cities, Schools, and Spaces," University of Massachusetts, Amherst, May 12, 2013.

"The Ecology Action Bust," *Boston Phoenix,* September 3, 1971.

Educational Facilities Laboratories, *A Campus in the City,* Educational Facilities Laboratories, 1969.

Educational Facilities Laboratories, *Student Housing,* Educational Facilities Laboratories, 1972.

Eisenhuth, Dan, "Rutgers to Ask Neighbors Before Expanding," *Camden Courier–Post,* December 5, 1973, p. 10.

Engels, Friedrich, *The Housing Question,* International Publishers, 1970.

Epsilon Associates, "Massachusetts Mental Health Center Redevelopment, Project Notification Form, Institutional Master Plan," June 16, 2009. www.bostonredevelopmentauthority.org/getattachment/70ac7c68–7f05–4fd7–801b–7e6aa7acc6a5.

Exchange of Correspondence between Cambridge Redevelopment Authority Director Rowland [January 18, 1973] and Cambridge Tenants Organizing Committee [CTOC] [March 2, 1973] regarding Kendall Square.

Faculty Civil Rights Group, *The Community and the Expansion of Columbia University,* Faculty Civil Rights Group, December 1967.

Fantini, Mario, Marilyn Gittell, and Richard Magat, *Community Control and the Urban School,* Praeger, 1970.

Fellman, Gordon, "Neighborhood Protest of an Urban Highway," *Journal of the American Institute of Planners,* March 1969.

Fernandez, Manny, "Doors are Closing on U.S.–Subsidized Tenants, Advocates Say," *New York Times,* December 30, 2007.

Field, Robert, *Student–Initiated Housing,* Educational Facilities Laboratories, 1972.

Finberg, Irving William, *Economic Impact of MIT on Cambridge and Metropolitan Boston,* unpublished Master's Thesis, MIT, City Planning, 1964.

Fink, Ira and Joan Cook, *Campus/Community Relationships: Annotated Bibliographies I and II,* University of California Berkeley, April 1971 and April 1972.

Fish, John H., *Black Power/White Control: The Struggle of the Woodlawn Organization in Chicago,* Princeton University Press, 1973.

Foster, S. M., *Out of Small Beginnings . . . An Economic History of Harvard College in the Puritan Period* (1636–1712), Harvard University Press, 1962.

"Frank Lloyd Wright A 'No–Show'" at Thursday Session," *Dodge–Construction News*, Friday, June 7, 1974.

Fried, Joseph P., "Columbia Plans Limited Growth," *New York Times*, May 9, 1969, p. 27.

Fried, Marc, "Grieving for a Lost Home," *The Urban Condition*, 1963.

Gallant, Jonathan A. and John W. Prothero, "Weight Watching and the University, The Consequences of Growth," *Science*, January 1972.

Galeota, William R., "Harvard Reveals Program Of Housing for Cambridge," *Harvard Crimson*, September 25, 1969.

Gardner, John, "The University and the City," *Educational Record*, Winter 1969.

Gans, Herbert J., *The Failure of Urban Renewal*, League for Industrial Democracy, 1966.

The Gerontologist, Summer 1971.

Gershen, Alvin E., *An Examination of Moderate and Low Income Housing Accommodations, Princeton Borough and Township, N.J.*, Gershen Assoc. June 15, 1967.

Gillette, Howard, *Camden After the Fall, Decline and Renewal in a Post–Industrial City*, University of Pennsylvania Press, 2005.

"Goals for a Cooper Grant Rehabilitation Plan, Based on Neighborhood Betterment Survey," August 9, 1973 (references in Lang and Murray, 1974, 2).

Golino, Carlo "The Effort Must Be Sustained," *The Urban University in the 1970s, Symposium at the University of Massachusetts/ Boston*, April 27, 1974.

Gonzales, Gizela M, "500 Vie for Spots in Mission Park Housing Complex," December 11, 1976.

Greenhouse, Linda, "College Plans Stir Opposition, West Chester Residents Fight Against Apartments," *New York Times*, February 28, 1971, p. 32.

Griefen, John O., "A Research Park Does Not Live by Research Alone: The Success Story of Tech Square," *Urban Law*, March 1965.

Haar, Charles M., *Land Use Planning, A Casebook on the Use, Misuse and Reuse of Urban Land*, Brown, 1959.

Haar, Sharon, *The City as Campus: Urbanism and Higher Education in Chicago*, University of Minnesota Press, 2011.

Halberstam, David, *The Best and the Brightest,* Random House, 1972.

Hanify, Edward, Statement on MIT and the Inner Belt, February 22, 1966.

Hanron, Robert. "M.I.T. Fears Disaster If Belt Takes Grand Junction Route," *Boston Globe,* February 21, 1966; 8.

"Hard Times," May 1972 (newsletter).

Harrkavy, Ira, "School–Community–University Partnerships: Effectively Integrating Community Building and Education Reform," A Joint Forum of the U.S. Dept. of Education, U.S. Dept. of Housing and Urban Development, Washington DC, January 8, 1998.

Harper, Steven, *Straddling Worlds: The Jewish–American Journey of Professor Richard W. Leopold,* Northwestern University Press, 2008.

Hartman, Chester W. and Gregg Carr, "Housing Authorities Reconsidered," *Journal of the American Institute of Planners*, January 1969.

"Harvard and the City/News," *The Harvard Crimson*, January 29, 1969 (cited in Echelman, 2013).

"Harvard–HRI Preserve Affordability at Putnam Square," *Harvard Gazette*, March 22, 2013.

"Harvard to Establish Affordable Housing Partnerships," Harvard Gazette, November 11, 1999.

The Harvard Crimson, 1969–73.

The Harvard Gazette, 1969–73.

Harvard Gazette, "Harvard–HRI Preserve Affordability at Putnam Square Apartments," *Harvard Gazette,* March 22, 2013. news.harvard.edu/gazette/story/2013/03/harvard–hri–preserve–affordability–at–putnam–square–apartments/

Harvard Planning Office, *An Inventory of Planning*, Harvard Planning Office, 1960.

Harvard Planning Office, *Harvard University and the Cambridge Housing Supply: Impact During the Past Fifty Years*, Harvard Planning Office, December 1971.

Harvard Planning Office, *Long–Range Plan for Harvard University and Radcliffe College in Cambridge and Allston, Interim Report*, Harvard Planning Office, June 1974.

Harvard Planning Office, *Survey of Harvard Residential Patterns in Cambridge*, Harvard Planning Office, October 1969.

Harvard Strikers, "Cambridge: Transformation of a Working Class City; Harvard and MIT Create Imperial City," New England Free Press, Spring 1969.

Harvard Strikers, *The Affiliated Hospitals Complex: A Critique of Harvard's Expansion*, Harvard University, April/May 1969.

Harvard University, News Releases, 1969–73.

Harvard University, *Community Housing Developments Sponsored by and Developed in Conjunction with Harvard University*, March 1971.

Harvard University, "Harvard University's Campus in Allston, Institutional Master Plan," July 2013, Revised, October 2013.

Harvard University, Information Center, *Building Harvard: Architecture of Three Centuries*, Office of Public Information, Harvard University, 1968.

Harvard University, Office of Public Information, *Harvard and Radcliffe College in Cambridge*, Harvard University, 1972.

Harvard University President and Fellows, *Education, Bricks and Mortar*, Harvard University, 1949.

Harvard University, University Committee on Governance, *Harvard and Money: A Memorandum on Issues and Choices*, Committee on Governance, Harvard University, 1970.

Harvard University, Vice President for Government and Community Affairs, *Report to the Cambridge Community from the Office of Government and Community Affairs of Harvard University (Daly Report)*, Office of Government and Community Affairs, October 1972.

Hawley, Willis D., *Search for Community Power*, Prentice Hall, 1968.

"Hearings on Section 112 of the Housing Act before the Senate Committee on Banking and Currency," *86th Congress, 1st Session*, p. 500ff, 1959.

Hedden, Linda, "Intergenerational Living: University Dormitories," *The Gerontologist*, August 1974.

Henderson, Tom. "Undergrads Plan Diverse Seminars, Initiators Extend Curriculum Scope," *Daily Princetonian*, May 21, 1969.

"Here's a Switch for Urban Mix: Complex for Students and Elderly," *Apartment Construction News*, April 1972.

Herrey, Antony, "Housing in Cambridge: The Birth of an Action Program," *Harvard Alumni Magazine*, October 27, 1969, (1, 3).

Hough East: New Hopes Replace the Despair and Decay of the Past, Cleveland Press, January 5, 1974.

Herzog, Roger and Bill Brauner, "Cambridge Is a Model for Affordable Housing Initiatives, Putnam Square Apartment Plan Latest in Preserving Affordability," *Banker and Tradesman*, October 6, 2013.

"High Rents Seen Forcing Residents to Leave the City," *Cambridge Chronicle*, August 29, 1970.

"Housing," (Mission Park), *Architectural Record*, February 1978.

"Housing Crisis of Our Very Own," *Technology Review*, December 1968.

"Housing Supplement," *Society Magazine*, July/August, 1972.

"HUD Urban Renewal Handbook," (formerly HHFA Urban Renewal Manual), Department of Housing and Urban Development, 1965.

I. M. Pei and Partners, *Interim Study Report to the Harvard Medical Area Planning Commission*, March 1971.

Jackson and Moreland, Inc., *Impact on MIT of Alternate Inner Belt*, Inc., October 1962.

James Landauer Associates, *Development Feasibility Study of the Hulfish Street Site in the CBD*, Princeton, N.J., James Landauer Associates, October 8, 1971.

Janssen, Kim. "Razing a Ruckus: On the 100th Anniversary of Ronald Reagan's Birth, His Boyhood Home on the South Side Faces Demolition as Part of the University of Chicago's Expansion Plan—and Those who Want to Preserve the Site Are None Too Pleased," *Chicago Sun Times*, February 6, 2011, p. 10A.

Johnson, Howard W., "*MIT and Cambridge*," President's Office, MIT, October 27, 1966.

Joint Center for Inner City Change, *The Riverside Press Site: Alternate Uses*, Joint Center for Inner City Change, Roxbury, Mass., 1972.

Joint Report, Mayor of Boston, University of Massachusetts, et al., *The Columbia Point Peninsula, A Program for Revitalization*, University of Massachusetts, January 1974.

Joncas, Richard, et al., *Stanford University: Campus Guide*, 2nd Edition, 2006.

Kahn, Ely Jacques Jr., Harvard, *Through Change and Through Storm*, W. W. Norton 1969.

Kaiser, Stephen, *Citizens University Negotiations on Community Housing: The Cambridge Experience*, MIT, June 1969 (mimeo).

Kaiser, Stephen. "The Erie Street Development: Zoning Changes—Interaction Between MIT and the Cambridge Community," Cambridge Corporation, 1970 (unpublished paper).

Kamilewicz, Dexter, *Relevant Housing through the Use of Information Systems*, Real Estate Office, MIT, June 10, 1971.

Kamin, Blair, "As Prentice Comes Down, Stakes Rise on Its Replacement, Northwestern has a Chance to Replace Goldberg's Innovative Hospital with Something Better, But Will it," *Chicago Tribune*, October 12, 2013.

Keller, Suzanne, *Community: Pursuing the Dream, Living the Reality*, Princeton, 2003.

Kelman, Steven, *Push Comes to Shove: The Escalation of Student Protest*, Houghton Mifflin, 1970.

Kerr, Clark, "The Urban Grant University: A Model for the Future," *City College paper No. 8*, 1968.

Killian, James A. Jr., "An Interview with James Killian," *Boston Herald Traveler*. April 10, 1969.

Killian, James A. Jr., "MIT and the Inner Belt," A Statement by Chairman of the MIT Corporation, February 20, 1966.

Killian, James A. Jr., "Text Prepared for Coordinating Committee Meeting, CEOC Housing Convention," October 23, 1960.

Killian, James A. Jr., "The University and the Community," speech, October 29, 1957.

Kireker, Charles, *Humanism and Housing Policy: The Grass Roots Approach*, Senior thesis, Princeton University, 1972.

Klemesrud, Judy, "Campus with a Fading Generation Gap," *New York Times*, February 28, 1970, p. 46.

Klotche, Martin J., *The Urban University and the Future of Our Cities*, Harper & Brothers, 1966.

Korn, Sandray, "Forgetting Barry's Corner, Harvard Overlooks Its Neighbors in Expansion Plans, Again," November 26, 2012.

Kramer, Stephen, "Harvard—AHC—The Community," *Harvard Medical Area Newsletter*, May 1969.

Landauer, James D., *Local Housing Market Analysis, Landauer Land Use Study and Housing Policy Recommendations for Princeton University*, Associates, October 1970.

Lang, Michael H. and Tony Murray, *A Guide to the Housing Rehabilitation Process: With Special Emphasis on the Cooper–Grant Community*, Camden NJ, 1974.

Lederer, Tom. "Boro House Set to Fall... But it Didn't Have to Go," *Princeton Packet*, August 27, 1975, p. 1.

Lederer, Tom. "Two–unit House Doomed," *Princeton Packet*, June 25, 1975.

Lelchuk, Alan, *American Mischief*, Farrar, Straus and Giroux, 1973.

Levi, Julian H., *Municipal and Institutional Relations Within Boston: The Benefits of Section 112 of the Federal Housing Act of 1961*, University of Chicago Press, 1964.

Levin, Melvin, and Norman Albert, *University Impact on Housing Supply and Rental Level in the City of Boston*, Urban Institute Occasional Papers, Boston University, February 1970.

Louis, Mary and Louis Lusky, "Columbia 1968: Wound Unhealed," *Political Science Quarterly*, June 1969.

Machlup, Fritz, *The Production and Distribution of Knowledge in the United States*, Princeton University Press, 1962.

Machlup, Fritz, 1980–84. *Knowledge, Its Creation, Distribution and Economic Significance*, Princeton University Press, 1986.

Magid, Lawrence, *In Pursuit of Shelter—the Housing Crisis at University of Massachusetts*, Student Center for Educational Research, UMass–Amherst, March 19, 1975.

Magid, Lawrence. "Rural Amherst Has an Urban Problem," Student Center for Educational Research, January 8, 1975.

Malenfant, Geneva. "Student Populations in Cambridge," 1974.

"Many Student Residents," *Rutgers Gleaner*, May 4, 1972.

Marks, Judy, "A History of Educational Facilities Laboratories," National Clearinghouse for Educational Facilities, 2009.

Marland, Sidney, "Launching Pad for Thousands," *The Urban University in the 1970s, Symposium at the University of Massachusetts/ Boston*, April 27, 1974.

Marmor, Theodore R., with the assistance of Jan S. Marmor, *The Politics of Medicare*; Aldine, 1973.

Marmor, Theodore R., *The Politics of Medicare*, 2nd ed. A. de Gruyter, 2000.

"Mass Tries Mixing Income Groups in Subsidized Housing, Quality Buildings Attract Some with High Incomes; Salary Determines Rent; A Model for the Nation?" *Wall Street Journal*, May 25, 1974.

Massachusetts Housing Finance Agency, "All in Together, An Evaluation of Mixed–Income Multi–Family Housing," MHFA, January 24, 1974.

Mathiasen, Karen, *MIT's "A Housing Program in Cambridge: A Management Problem,"* unpublished MIT, June 1971, Sloan School dissertation.

McLeod, Mary Caroline, *Freedom and Planning. A Study of Radical Alternative Approaches to Environmental Design,* Woodrow Wilson School, 1972.

McLeod, Mary C., "Housing for Law Students" (in Cambridge?) August 4, 1969.

McLeod, Mary, "The River–Howard Project: An Examination of Advocacy Planning," Class Paper. Princeton University, Spring 1972.

McNally, David and Howard Mantell, *Effective Government for Cambridge,* Institute of Public Administration, The Ford Foundation, April 1970.

Meadows, Donella H., et al., *The Limits to Growth*, Universe Books, March 1972.

Metropolitan Area Planning Council, *Housing Metropolitan Boston: Housing Services and Supply, 1950–80*, Metropolitan Area Planning Council, 1969.

Meyers, Edward and Ira Fink, *Communities and Universities: Can They Plan Together?* University of California Berkeley, 1975 Draft Report, November 6, 1973.

Meyers, Edward and Ira Fink, *Universities and Communities: Together for a Change*, Educational Record, Summer 1974.

Meyerson, Martin, *The University and the Urban Community*, Gerstein Lecture, The City and the University, York University, 1968.

Miller, Delbert, "Town and Gown: The Power Structure of a University Town," *American Journal of Sociology*, January 1963.

Miller, Ronald, *Processes and Guides for Comprehensive Planning of the Urban University and the City*, Department of City and Regional Planning, Ohio State, March 10, 1971.

Minnesota Metropolitan State, Prospectus II, November 1, 1997.

Minter, John, *Colleges and Universities as Agents of Social Change*, Western Interstate Commission on Higher Education and East Campus, and Center for Research and Development in Higher Education, University of California, Berkeley, November 1968.

Miraval, Nathalie R. and Rebecca D. Robbins, "After Troubled Past, Barry's Corner in Allston Poised for Development," *Harvard Crimson*, October 5, 2011.

Mission Park http://www.missionpark.com/home.htm.

Massachusetts Institute of Technology, "Institute Housing Program," *Institute Report*, Office of Assistant to Chairmen for Urban Affairs, MIT, February 9, 1970.

Massachusetts Institute of Technology, Department of City and Regional Planning, *Institutional Expansion and the Urban Setting*, Special Summer Program, Department of City and Regional Planning, MIT, Proceedings, July 6–11, 1959.

Massachusetts Institute of Technology, "*Northwest Area Pilot Plan*," MIT, November 1970.

Massachusetts Institute of Technology, Institute Real Estate Office, *A Housing Program in Cambridge: Proposal for Turnkey Construction in the Cambridge Housing Authority*, MIT: Institute Real Estate Office, January 26, 1971.

"MIT Aims to Grow a New Route 128," (MIT Development Foundation), *Business Week*, July 22, 1972.

"M.I.T. as Cambridge Citizen: Arrogance or Beneficence?" *MIT Technology Review*, January 1970.

MIT, *Tech Talk*, 1969–75.

MIT Long–Range Planning Group, *1970 Housing Survey: Faculty and Technical Report, Planning Office*, MIT, March 1971.

MIT, "MIT BuildingProgram Update," June 2000, http://web.mit.edu/president/communications/Building.pdf

Mitchell, Dolores, *Rent Control: An Analysis*, Cambridge Tenants Organizing Committee, 1969.

Mollenkopf, John, "Rent Control: The Politics of Property," Cambridge, 1969 (mimeo).

Mollenkopf, John, *The Cambridge Housing Crisis*, Cambridge Tenants Organizing Committee, 1971.

Moncrieff, Robert P., *Harvard and the City: A Resident's View*, Harvard Alumni Bulletin, October 6, 1969.

Montgomery, Paul, "25 Draft Office Raiders Held in Jersey and Buffalo," *New York Times*, August 23, 1971, p. 1.

Moss, Hilary, Yinan Zhang, and Andy Anderson, "Assessing the Impact of the Inner Belt: MIT, Highways, and the Housing Market in Cambridge, Massachusetts," Unpublished, n.d. (cited in Echelman, 2013).

Moulton, Robert, "Moulton Report: Low Cost Housing Committee Report," Stanford University, April 17, 1969.

Moynihan, Daniel P., "The Urban University Symposium at UMass/Boston: Crisis in the City," *The Massachusetts Review*, Summer 1967.

Murphy, Martin. "Local Housing Group Opposes Proposed Biochemical Lab Site," *Daily Princetonian*, February 10, 1977.

Nash, George, *Leads Columbia Could Have Followed*, Columbia Bureau of Applied Research Reprint, A–549, June 1968.

Nash, George, "*The Role of Title I Programs in University Involvement in the Urban Crises*," Columbia Bureau of Applied Research, October 19, 1969.

Nash, George, "The Relation of Knowledge and Action: Proper Role of the Institution as Agent of Change," (speech), Columbia University, June 1967.

Nash, George, *The University and the City: Eight Cases of Involvement*, The Carnegie Commission, 1973.

"New England's Business Comeback," *U.S. News*, February 14, 1966.

New Jersey Department of Community Affairs, *An Analysis of Low and Moderate Income Housing Need in New Jersey*, New Jersey Department of Community Affairs, May 1975.

Nisbet, Robert, "Errand into the Wilderness," *The Urban University in the 1970s, Symposium at the University of Massachusetts/ Boston*, April 27, 1974.

Nitt, Thomas and Lawrence Suskind, *Residence and Rent: A Study of Cambridge, Mass.*, *Connection*, Fall 1968–Winter 1969.

Obama, Barack, *The Audacity of Hope, Thoughts on Realizing the American Dream*, Vintage, 2008.

Obama, Barack. *Dreams from My Father*, Three Rivers Press, 1995.

"Observing the First Anniversary," *Camden Courier Post*, August 23, 1972.

Old Mole, *How Harvard Rules*, New England Free Press, Spring 1969.

O'Mara, Margaret P., "Beyond Town and Gown: University Economic Engagement and the Legacy of the Urban Crisis," *Journal of Technology Transfer*, Vol. 3, No. 2, April 2012, pp. 234–50.

O'Mara, Margaret P., *Cities of Knowledge: Cold War Science and the Search for the Next Silicon Valley*, Princeton University Press, 2005.

Organization for Social and Technological Innovation, *Urban Universities: Rhetoric, Reality and Conflict*, U.S. Government Printing Office, 1970.

Padgett, John and Richard Sobel, "Proposal for a North Central Camden, NJ Development Project," Camden Regional Legal Services, October 1971.

Parsons, Kermit, "A Truce in the War between University and Cities," *Journal of Higher Education*, January 1963.

Parsons, Kermit, and Georgia Davis, *The University and Urban Change*, July 1971.

A Partnership in Ann Arbor: The City and the University, University of Michigan, 1967.

Paulus, Virginia, ed., *Housing: A Bibliography 1960–72*, Transaction Publishers, 1974.

Pendleton, William, "University/City Relations Revisited," *Colorado Urban Conference*, Ford Foundation, April 25, 1975.

Pennrose Properties, "Cooper Grant Homes, Camden, New Jersey," 2010 www.pennrose.com/portfolio/cooperGrant.shtml

People of the Cooper–Grant Community, "Community Position Paper," December 1973.

People of the Cooper–Grant Community, "Community Unites to Halt Rutgers Blockbusting Expansion," *Rutgers Reporter*, Rutgers Law School, Vol. 5: No. 3, December 1973.

People of the Cooper Grant Community, "Proposal of The People of the Cooper–Grant Community," February 1975.

People of the Cooper Grant Community, "Renewal Plan," June 1974.

People of the Cooper–Grant Community and Richard Sobel, "Proposal," February 1975.

Peterson, Robin, "Crossing the Line: After Forty Years Honoring 61st Street as Its Border with Woodlawn, the University of Chicago Is Positioning Itself to Move Farther South," *Chicago Weekly*, May 28, 2008.

Piven, Frances Fox, "Whom Does the Advocate Planner Serve?" *Social Policy*, July/August, 1970.

"Plea for State Aid Dropped by Manhattanville College," *New York Times*, April 14, 1971, p. 47.

"Princeton to Build 1,500 Housing Units," *Philadelphia Inquirer*, May 13, 1971, p. 42.

Princeton Housing Group, "Princeton University Forrestal Center, Another Homogenized Haven for the Rich?" Princeton, NJ, June 7, 1974.

Princeton Housing Group, "University Questioned," *Trenton Times*, February 19, 1976, p. 17.

The Princeton Packet, 1935–41, 1955–62, 1969–73.

"Princeton University Discloses Business–Housing Plans," *New York Times*, April 8, 1975.

Princeton University, "The Princeton Forestal Center," September 1974 (three volumes).

Princeton University Press Releases, May 12, 1971; October 15, 1973; April 1975.

"The Private Use of Public Power: The Private University and the Power of Eminent Domain," Special Project, *Vanderbilt Law Review*, May 1974.

Program in Higher Education, University of Massachusetts, "Rationale for the Development of the Program in Higher Education," School of Education, University of Massachusetts, Amherst, October 25, 1974.

Pusey, Nathan, *The University and Its Resources*, Office of Government and Community Affairs, Harvard University, 1968.

Pynoos, Jon and John Mollenkopf, "Property, Politics and Local Housing Policy," *Politics and Society*, Summer 1972, p. 407.

Pynoos, Jon. *Housing Urban America*, Aldine Publishing, 1973.

Rauch, Marc, et al., *Columbia and the Community: Past Policy and New Directions*, Columbia College Citizens Council, 1968.

Real Estate Research Corporation, *Future of Campus Housing Supplies—University of California—Problems and Prospects*, San Francisco: The Corp., January 1970.

The Real Paper (newsweekly, Chicago).

Reed, Bob, *The Urban Community College 1969: A Study of 25 Urban Community College Systems*, Houston, TX, Caudill Rowlett Scott, 1970.

Rein, Richard, "Princeton and Co., Realtors," *Princeton Alumni Weekly*, December 11, 1973.

Reisman, David, "Educating Individuals as Citizens," *The Urban University in the 1970s, Symposium at the University of Massachusetts/ Boston*, April 27, 1974.

Reisman, David, "The Urban University Symposium at UMass/Boston: The Urban University," December 10, 1966, *The Massachusetts Review*, Summer 1967.

Report of the U.S. President's Committee on Urban Housing: A Decent Home (Maiser Committee Report), Washington, D.C., 1969.

Ridgeway, James, *The Closed Corporation*, Random House, 1968.

Rocheleau, Matt, "Construction Begins on $400m Medical, Housing Project in Mission Hill," Boston.com, October 22, 2010.

Rodin, Judith, *The University & Urban Renewal: Out of the Ivory Tower and into the Streets,* University of Pennsylvannia Press, 2007.

Rom, Beth, editor, *Report on Town/University Relations*, Princeton University CE314, June 1972.

Romantowski, Peter J., *Problems of New Development of Public Housing in Cambridge*, senior thesis, Harvard College, March 1972.

Rosenthal, Jack, "Poverty Aide Hints Agnew Interferes in Suit in Jersey," *New York Times*, February 2, 1982, p. 1.

Rossi, Peter H. and Robert A. Dentler, *The Politics of Urban Renewal*, Free Press of Glencoe, 1961.

Roszak, Theodore, ed., *Blueprint for a Communal Environment*, Sources, 1972.

Routliffe, Kathy, "Wilmette Housing Group Looks to the Future, Invites Village Participation," *Wilmette Life,* December 1, 2013. http://glencoe.suntimes.com/news/housresp–WIL–10312013:article

Ryan, John W., "The Urban University Symposium at UMass/Boston: The University of Massachusetts in Boston, " *The Massachusetts Review*, Summer 1967.

Samuel, Leah, "Losing Confidence," *Chicago Reporter*, November 2009.

Samuelson, Robert, *The University and the City*, senior thesis, Harvard College, Spring 1967.

Samuelson, Robert, "Un–Fair Harvard," *Science Magazine*, March 1969.

Sanborn Maps, Princeton, New Jersey.

Sargent, Hon. Francis, "Accessibility for the Entire Public," *The Urban University in the 1970s, Symposium at the University of Massachusetts/ Boston*, April 27, 1974.

Sayre, Nora, "Strikes and Lulls at Harvard: School of Self–Distrust," *Village Voice*, February 15, 1973.

Schildlcraut, Susan, *Rent Control in Cambridge*, School of Education, Harvard University, Fall 1970, A–55.

Schlesinger, Arthur Jr., "The Urban University Symposium at UMass/Boston: The University in an Urban Society, December 10, 1966," *The Massachusetts Review*, Summer 1967.

SDL Systems Research Group, *The Impact at Boston–Area Colleges and Universities on the Local Economy*, SDL Systems Research Group, February 1974.

"Second Housing Development Started by Woodlawn Group," *Chicago Sunday Tribune*, January 6, 1974.

Shalom, Steve and Rob Shapiro, *Two, Three, Many Tech Squares: MIT's Role in the Transformation of Cambridge*, MIT–SDS, September 1969.

Sharratt, John, *Developing a Policy for Design Determinants Community Housing: Convent Site*, Boston, 1972.

Sharratt, John, *Mission Hill: Medical Center Area—Alternatives for a Community/ Institutional Area Plan, for Circle Federation*, Boston, August 1, 1972.

Sharratt, John Associates, "Project: Mission Park," (Fact sheet), April 1977.

Sharratt, John and Roxbury Tenant of Harvard, *Roxbury Tenant of Harvard: The Relationship of Harvard University Medical School and Affiliated Institutions to the Neighboring Residential Community: Its Problems and a Solution*, Boston, March 20, 1970.

Shipler, David K., "Columbia's Housing Will Include Poor," *New York Times*, November 27, 1968, p. 1.

Shiraev, Eric and Richard Sobel, *People and Their Opinions: Thinking Critically about Public Opinion*, Longman, 2006.

Silberman, Charles, *Up from Apathy: The Woodlawn Experiment*, Urban Planning and Social Policy, 1968.

Slaby, Steve M., ed., *Public Housing in the U.S: Analysis of Problems and Recommendations for Solutions (with Newark case study)*, Technology and Society Seminar, School of Engineering and Applied Science, Princeton University, June 1973.

Slaby, Steve and Beth Rom, "Town–University Relations in Princeton, New Jersey: Analysis of Problems and Recommendations for Possible Solutions," *Report of Town,* 1973.

Slade, Margot, *Out of the Ivory Tower: An Examination of the Interaction Between Harvard, MIT and the City of Cambridge*, Wellesley College, senior thesis, Department of Political Science, May 1974.

Smith, Larry and Co., *Kendall Square Urban Renewal Area, Land Utilization and Marketability Study*, Cambridge Redevelopment Authority, October 1965.

Sobel, Richard. "An Influential Intellectual Experience: Understanding the Correspondence Principle," in "Celebrating 40 Years, 1956–1996," *The School of Education Magazine*, University of Massachusetts, Amherst, Spring 1996.

Sobel, Richard, "At the Point, January 28, 1974: A New UMass in Boston: In a Midst," February 15, 1974 (accepted by *Change* Magazine but not published).

Sobel, Richard. "Community/University Conflict," Marathon Presentation, University of Massachusetts, Amherst, School of Education, January 25, 1974.

Sobel, Richard, "Communities and Universities," Marathon Presentation, University of Massachusetts, Amherst, School of Education, November 13, 1974.

Sobel, Richard, "Even Here," *Daily Princetonian*, December 10, 1970.

Sobel, Richard, "Frank Lloyd Wright and Low Cost Housing," undelivered paper for the Conference on the 50th Anniversary of the Kahn Lectures at Princeton, May 16, 1980.

Sobel, Richard. "Frank Lloyd Wright as Social Architect" (lectures, Princeton University, March 23, 1982 and Smith College, April 9, 1985).

Sobel, Richard. "From Occupational Involvement to Political Participation: An Exploratory Analysis," *Political Behavior*, Vol. 15, No. 4, 1993. pp. 339–353.

Sobel, Richard, "How Much Education Is Necessary for Jobs?" Presented at the meeting of the Eastern Sociological Society, Eastern Sociological Society, Baltimore, MD, March 1983.

Sobel, Richard, *The Impact of Public Opinion on U.S. Foreign Policy Since Vietnam*, Oxford University Press, 2001.

Sobel, Richard, "In Ben Franklin's View: Planning in North Central Camden," Woodrow Wilson School 411, June 3,1971; revised May 2, 1973.

Sobel, Richard, "Is the Big Box on its Way Out?" *The New Art Examiner*, November 1978.

Sobel, Richard, "Joint Development of Housing," *Practicing Planner*, December 1978.

Sobel, Richard. 'Participation in Planning at the Metro and Parkway Schools,' Junior Independent Work, Princeton University, Spring 1970; revised 1973.

Sobel, Richard, "A Planning Study of Educational Facilities Charettes," Camden Regional Legal Services, December 19, 1971.

Sobel, Richard, "A Proposal for a Project Study on University–Community Housing," to Educational Facilities Laboratories, New York City, December 19, 1971.

Sobel, Richard, "Proposal for Project on Community/University Housing and Relations," Camden, July 25, 1973.

Sobel, Richard, *Public Opinion in U.S. Foreign Policy: The Controversy over Contra Aid*. ed., Rowman & Littlefield, 1993.

Sobel, Richard, *Raising the Bar: An Upwards Memoir*, manuscript, 2014.

Sobel, Richard, "Six Wright Houses in the Late Prairie Period" (unpublished manuscript, 1978, 1980).

Sobel, Richard, "The New Working Class Theory: The New Left and the Search for Class," Presented to the American Sociological Association, San Francisco, 1982.

Sobel, Richard, "The Politics of the White Collar Working Class," *Research in Micropolitics*, Vol. 4, 1994.

Sobel, Richard, *Urban Renewal in Princeton, 1955–1962*, Senior Thesis, Princeton University, April 26, 1971.

Sobel, Richard, "What Is Unique about a Princeton Education," *Daily Princetonian*, February 24, 1996.

Sobel, Richard, *The White Collar Working Class: From Structure to Politics*, Praeger, 1989.

Sobel, Richard and Peggy Burchenal, "Protest the Injustice of Tenure," *Daily Princetonian*, February 21, 1972.

Sobel, Richard with Robert Comfort, "Proposal for a Study on University/Community Housing," August 1972.

Sobel, Richard, Peter Furia, and Bethany Baratt, ed., *Public Opinion and International Intervention: Lessons of the Iraq War*, Potomac Books, 2012.

Sobel, Richard and Robert Hosford, "Grieving for a Lost Home," *Daily Princetonian*, March 14, 1977, p. 6.

Sobel, Richard and Eric Shiraev, *People and Their Opinions: Thinking Critically about Public Opinion*, Longman, 2006.

Sobel, Richard and Walter H. Sobel, FAIA & Associates, "Community/University Study I: A Selected Bibliography on Housing and Planning Issues in Cambridge and Boston, Mass.," Council of Planning Librarians, Exchange Bibliography, No. 1395, November 1977.

Sobel, Richard and Walter H. Sobel FAIA & Associates, "Community/University Study II: A Selected Bibliography on Housing and Planning Issues," Council of Planning Librarians, Exchange Bibliography, No. 1396, November 1977.

"Sobel Spawns Colloquium," *Wilmette Life*, June 1980.

Source Collective, Source Catalog No. 2, Communities/Housing, 1972.

"Special Conference Summary," *Non–Profit Housing*, October/November, 1971.

Spiegel, Hans and Stephen D. Mittenthal, "Workable Program for Community Involvement: Answers on Citizens Participation," Citizens Participation in Urban Development, Columbia School of Architecture, 1968.

Spiegel, Hans and Stephen D. Mittenthal, *Neighborhood Power and Control: Implications for Urban Planning*, Columbia School of Architecture, 1968.

Stanford University, Press Releases, June 9, 1971, et al.

Starr, Roger, "The Case of the Columbia Gym," *Confrontation*, 1968.

Stein, Harold, ed., "The Cambridge City Manager," *Public Administration and Policy Development: A Case Book*, 1952.

Sternlieb, George, et al., *The Affluent Suburb: Princeton*, Transaction Books, 1971.

Stockard, L. "Crisis in University City," *Urbanaction*, December 1969.

Stone, Kaya. "And Room to Grow. Harvard Puts a Strain on Town–Gown Relations by Announcing its Secret Land Purchase across the River in Allston," *Harvard Independent*, September 18, 1997, p. 4.

Stone, Michael, "Housing, Mortgages and the State," *Upstart*, January 3, 1972.

Stone, Michael, *Reconstructing American Housing*, Urban Planning Aid, 1975.

Student Center for Educational Research, *Rural Amherst Has an Urban Problem, An Analysis of the Impact of UMass on the Surrounding Housing Market*," University of Massachusetts, Amherst, January 8, 1975 (draft).

Student Community Housing Corporation, *Housing: A Report to the Yale and New Haven Communities*, Educational Facilities Laboratories, February 1971.

Sullivan, Ronald, "Princeton Adopts Plans for Big Tract," *New York Times*, November 3, 1973, Real Estate section, p. 1.

Syracuse University, "Preserving the Urban Fabric," 1966.

Taber, David, "Tower Work to Start in 2013," Missionhillgazette.com, November 11, 2011.

The Tech (MIT), "Third Town Meeting Provides a Glimpse into Princeton's Future," *Trenton Times*, April 27, 1972, p. 1.

Tinder, Glenn, "The Urban University Symposium at UMass/Boston: Incipient Catastrophe, The University and The City," *The Massachusetts Review*, Summer 1967.

Todd, Richard, "The Ins and Outs of MIT," *New York Times Magazine*, May 18, 1969.

Tomasson, Robert E., "Puerto Rican–Run Shopping Center Is Due," *New York Times*, November 20, 1974, p. 45.

Towarnicky, Carol and Kitty Caparella, "Pageant and Protest—a Day to Remember," *Philadelphia Daily News*, July 6, 1976, p. 3.

Trumpbour, John, editor, *How Harvard Rules, Reason in Service of Empire*, South End Press, 1999.

Tryens, Jeff, *How a Community Attracts and Keeps Industry*, Urban Planning Aid, 1973.

Ung, Elisa, "Cooper–Grant Homes Are in Demand," *Philadelphia Inquirer*, October 24, 2005.

U.S. National Students Association, *Training Guide for Campus/Community Organizing*, U. S. National Students Association, May 1969.

United States, Education Office, *Casebook on Campus Planning and Institutional Development,* American Association of Universities, 1962.

University of Chicago, *Proposed Housing for Woodlawn, Joint Effort by TWO and the University of Chicago*, University of Chicago, September 4, 1969.

"University Reports on Plans for Palmer Square," *Trenton Times*, May 4, 1972.

Urban Design Associates, *The Fulton Plan*, Pittsburgh, Urban Design Associates, December 1972.

Urban Planning Aid, "The Empty Promise, Community Housing Development Corporations," Cambridge, Mass., 1973.

Urban Planning Aid, *Less Rent, More Control: A Tenants' Guide to Rent Control in Mass.*, Cambridge, Mass., 1975.

Urban Planning Aid, *People Before Property, A Real Estate Primer and Research Guide*, Urban Planning Aid, 1972.

Urban Planning Aid, *Tenants First! Research and Organizing Guide to FHA Housing*, Cambridge, Mass., 1974.

Urban Planning Aid, "The Transformation of Cambridge," Cambridge Mass, May 1974.

"The Urban University," Symposium at UMass/Boston, December 10, 1966.

"U.S. Finds Wide Segregation in Chicago's Suburban Areas," *New York Times*, January 11, 1982.

Van Til, Jon and Sally B. Van Til, "Citizens Participation: The End of a Cycle?" *Social Problems*, September 1970.

Waldo, Dwight, "The University as a Power Center," *Educational Record*, January 1967.

Walsh, Christine, "Davenport Commons: A Done Deal," *Northeastern News*, XXXII: 10, December 2, 1998.

Walshock, M. *Knowledge without Boundaries: What America's Universities Can Do for the Economy, the Workplace, and the Community*, Jossey–Bass, 1995.

Weaver, Robert, "The Urban University in the '70s," *The Urban University in the 1970s,* Symposium at the University of Massachusetts/ Boston, April 27, 1974.

Weidlein, Edward, "The University and the Town: New Answers to Princeton's Problems in Princeton," *Princeton Alumni Weekly*, November 4, 1969, p. 6.

Weiss, John, *The Role of the Urban University in Community Programs: A Case Study of Nineteen Selected Colleges and Universities in Greater Boston*, thesis, University of Rhode Island, May 1968.

White, Kevin, William Birenbaum, Colin Greer, and Warren Ravetch, "Confrontation: The Campus and the City," *Change Magazine*, January/February, 1969.

Whitman, Walt, "An Old Man's Thoughts of School," [1874] *Leaves of Grass*, 1900.

Wiewel, Wim, Frank Gaffikin, and Michael Morrissey, "Community–University Partnerships for Affordable Housing," *Cityscape: A Journal of Policy Development and Research*, Vol 5, No. 1, 2000.

Wilking, Leo, "The Prince and the Pauper: Harvard's Role in the City of Cambridge," *Harvard Crimson*, January 26, 1973.

Wilking, Leo, "The City Council's Summer of Discontent," *Harvard Crimson*, June, 1972.

Wilson, James Q. "The University and the City: The Wilson Report," *Harvard Alumni Bulletin*, February 3, 1969, Vol. 71:7, pp. 17–40.

Winkeller, Mark, *University Expansion in Urban Neighborhoods: An Exploratory Analysis*, Brandeis University dissertation, Heller School, May 1971.

Winling, LaDale, "Students and the Second Ghetto: Federal Legislation, Urban Politics, and Campus Planning at the University of Chicago," *Journal of Planning History*, Vol. 10, No. 1, 2011, pp. 59–86.

Wirth, Louis, "Urbanism as a Way of Life," *Community Life and Social Policy*, University of Chicago Press, 1956.

Withers, John, "The Institution and the City," *Liberal Education*, March 1970.

Wood, Robert, "A Singular Achievement," *The Urban University in the 1970s, Symposium at the University of Massachusetts/ Boston*, April 27, 1974.

Wood, Robert and Harriet Zukerman, "The Urban Crisis," in Robert Connery, ed., *The Corporation and the Campus*, 1970.

Woodlawn New Communities Program, "NCP Agency Partners: Woodlawn Preservation Investment Corporation, The Woodlawn Organization, and University of Chicago," 2009.

Wright, Gordon, *Final Report of the President's Ad Hoc Housing Advisory Committee (The Wright Report)*, Stanford University, May 12, 1970.

"Wright Remembered," *Princeton Alumni Weekly*, June 30, 1980, p. 7.

Zorza, Richard, *The Right to Say "We"; The Adventure of a Young Englishman at Harvard and in the Youth Movement*, Praeger, 1970.

Index

About the Author

Richard Sobel has researched and taught at Princeton, Smith, University of Connecticut, Harvard, and Northwestern, and been a fellow at the Kennedy School and Law School at Harvard. He is author and editor of six books and many articles, including *Community/University Housing and Relations* and "The Joint Development of Housing." As a consultant on urban issues, he has also researched and spoken on "Frank Lloyd Wright as Social Architect." A native of Chicago, he is a graduate of Princeton and the University of Massachusetts at Amherst.

Lightning Source UK Ltd.
Milton Keynes UK
UKOW05n1429280714

235908UK00001B/15/P